Marketing in the Emerging Markets of Islamic Countries

Also by Marin Marinov

MARKETING IN THE EMERGING MARKETS OF LATIN AMERICA

MARKETING IN THE EMERGING MARKETS OF CENTRAL AND EASTERN EUROPE: The Balkans

INTERNATIONALIZATION IN CENTRAL AND EASTERN EUROPE

FOREIGN DIRECT INVESTMENT IN CENTRAL AND EASTERN EUROPE (*with Svetla Marinova*)

Marketing in the Emerging Markets of Islamic Countries

Edited by

Marin Marinov

palgrave
macmillan

First published 2007 by
PALGRAVE MACMILLAN
Houndmills, Basingstoke, Hampshire RG21 6XS and
175 Fifth Avenue, New York, N. Y. 10010
Companies and representatives throughout the world

PALGRAVE MACMILLAN is the global academic imprint of the Palgrave Macmillan division of St. Martin's Press, LLC and of Palgrave Macmillan Ltd. Macmillan® is a registered trademark in the United States, United Kingdom and other countries. Palgrave is a registered trademark in the European Union and other countries.

ISBN-13: 978–1–4039–9173–7
ISBN-10: 1–4039–9173–1

This book is printed on paper suitable for recycling and made from fully managed and sustained forest sources.

A catalogue record for this book is available from the British Library.

Library of Congress Cataloging-in-Publication Data
Marinov, Marin, 1948–
Marketing in the emerging markets of Islamic countries / Marin Marinov.
p. cm.
Includes bibliographical references and index.
ISBN-13: 978–1–4039–9173–7 (cloth)
ISBN-10: 1–4039–9173–1 (cloth)
1. Islamic countries–Commerce. 2. Marketing–Islamic countries. I. Title.
HF3868.M37 2007
330.917'67–dc22 2006047187

10 9 8 7 6 5 4 3 2 1
16 15 14 13 12 11 10 09 08 07

Printed and bound in Great Britain by
Antony Rowe Ltd, Chippenham and Eastbourne

Contents

List of Figures

List of Maps

List of Tables

Notes on the Contributors

Adel A. Al-Wugayan is Vice Dean at the College of Business Administration and Director of the Center of Excellence in Management at Kuwait University. He has published articles in a number of international and local journals and has authored a textbook in Arabic. His research interests include consumer behavior, consumer ethics, cross-cultural marketing research, and marketing strategies. Dr Al-Wugayan has worked as a consultant on the marketing of healthcare services and underperforming organizations, and has trained marketers in the areas of marketing research, market strategy formulation and effective selling techniques. He has taught undergraduate and graduate classes in marketing management, marketing research, marketing ethics and integrated marketing communication.

Lyn S. Amine is Professor of Marketing and International Business at Saint Louis University in the United States. She is a Distinguished Fellow of the Academy of Marketing Science (AMS) and has received two Senior Fulbright Scholarships to teach and research in Bahrain and Morocco. She has served as President of the Faculty Senate of Saint Louis University and President of the Women of the Academy of International Business, has been a member of the board of governors of AMS and is currently serving on the editorial boards of the *Journal of International Marketing, Thunderbird International Business Review* and the *Journal of Asia-Pacific Business*. Dr Amine has published extensively in numerous highly rated journals. Her current research interests are cross-cultural consumer marketing and sustainable development.

Kenneth Gray is Professor of International Management at Florida A&M University and holds an Eminent Scholar Chair in Global Business. He also teaches in the Executive MBA program at Al Akhawayn University in Casablanca, Morocco, and with the Executive MBA Program at the City University of Los Angeles China Fellows Program in Beijing. He has published over 30 articles and five books on economic development, focusing on entrepreneurship and business management in various parts of the world. Dr Gray was twice a Senior Fulbright Scholar in Morocco and is an evaluator of Fulbright Scholar candidates for the Middle Eastern Program. He is a member of the editorial boards of the *Journal of Entrepreneurship & Management, The International Journal on World Peace* and the *Journal of African Business,* and is an active member of the board of trustees at the University of Bridgeport in the United States.

Marin Marinov is Professor of Marketing and International Business at the Business School of Gloucestershire. He has conducted extensive research on internationalization, marketing and foreign direct investment in emerging markets. He has published many books, contributions to books, conference papers and numerous articles in academic journals. He is on the editorial board of the *Journal of Euro-marketing* and the *Journal of East–West Business.* Dr Marinov has held professorial positions in Bulgaria, the United States, Denmark, Germany, France, Finland and Sweden. He has also acted as a consultant for companies, business institutions and agencies on both sides of the Atlantic.

C. P. Rao is Professor of Marketing and Director of the Case Research and Teaching Unit at the College of Business Administration, Kuwait University. He has held the position of Eminent Scholar at the Old Dominion University and of Professor and Walton Lecturer in Strategic Marketing at the University of Arkansas in Fayetteville. Dr Rao was elected Senior Fellow of the Academy of Marketing Science in 1991. He is a frequent contributor to various academic and professional journals in marketing and international business. He has also held leadership positions at the Academy of Marketing Science and the Academy of International Business. He has served as Visiting Professor at universities in Nigeria, India, Singapore, Norway, Malaysia, Taiwan, Australia, New Zealand, South Africa, Peru, the Netherlands, and the United Kingdom.

Ali Sanayei is Associate Professor at the Faculty of Administrative Sciences and Economics, University of Isfahan, Iran, and Advisor to the Isfahan Chamber of Commerce. He teaches marketing research, e-commerce, and e-business. In 2003 Dr Sanayei received the Best Researcher Award from the Governor of Isfahan. He has published in international journals and serves on the editorial boards of the *World Review of Science, Technology & Sustainable Development*, the *Journal of International Business and Entrepreneurship* and the *Journal of International Marketing & Marketing Research.*

1 Marketing Challenges in Islamic Countries

Marin Marinov

Introduction

Islam is nearly 14 centuries old and there are more than one billion followers of the Islamic faith all over the world (Ba-Yunus and Siddiqui, 1998), the majority in emerging markets. It is expected that in about 20 years a third of the world's population will be Muslim and Muslims will account for nearly two thirds of those under 18 years of age (Quelch, 2001). The followers of Islam believe in one supreme God, Allah. The Islamic faith has been spread in a variety of ways, including forceful conversion, proselytization, spiritual influences, and material inducement. Initially the followers of Islam were besieged by and involved in social unrest, wars and expansion through conquest and invasion. In European territories expansion was particularly marked between the eighth and fifteenth centuries AD. In some Islamic societies this period was notable for advancements in education, philosophy, law, scientific knowledge, art, and literature.

Most of the Islamic population and the other inhabitants of the conquered lands gradually came under the control of two highly centralized empires, the Ottoman and the Mogul. In these empires knowledge creation and scientific development declined during centuries of feudalism based on tribal structures and disincentives. The multiethnic, inefficiently ruled Mogul and Ottoman empires came to an end in the mid 1800s and 1920 respectively. During the twentieth century the political and economic development of the Islamic countries became strongly dependent upon the Western world (Forte, 2002).

The global distribution of the Muslim population in 1998 is shown in Table 1.1. In most of the Islamic countries in the Middle East, North Africa and Asia – such as Afghanistan, Algeria, Bahrain, Bangladesh,

Table 1.1 Global distribution of the Muslim population, 1998

	Population (number)	*Percentage of total Islamic population*
Africa	308,660,000	27.40
Asia	778,362,000	69.13
Europe	32,032,000	2.84
Latin America	1,356,000	0.11
North America	5,530,000	0.49
Oceania	385,000	0.03
World	1,126,325,000	100.00

Source: United Nations World Census, 2000.

Brunei, Indonesia, Iraq, Iran, Kuwait, Morocco, Pakistan, Senegal, Tajikistan, Turkmenistan, Turkey, and Uzbekistan – at least 80 per cent of the inhabitants are Muslim and together they number over 700 million. Two of these countries – Indonesia and Turkey – are among the 'ten big emerging markets', as defined by the US Department of Commerce. In Chad, Kyrgyzstan, Lebanon, Malaysia, Mali, Nigeria, Sudan, and Syria 50–80 per cent of the population are Muslim. Although in a minority the Muslim populations in France, Germany, India, the Philippines, South Africa, the United Kingdom, the United States are sizable.

There are varying degrees to which the Islamic religion affects the functioning of the economy and political life in Islamic countries. A growing number are applying *Shari'ah* ethics and law to their politics and the functioning of their economies, with the ideal of Islam determining all aspects of social life. The supporters of this doctrine are called fundamentalists. Among the states that base life on Islamic principles in a moderate, non-extremist way are the Islamic Republic of Pakistan and the Kingdom of Saudi Arabia.

Recently the impact of Islam on the conduct of international business operations has increased and banking and financial activities based on Islamic principles have spread. Followers of Islam see the religious and secular aspects of life in unity and aspire to adopt the Islamic religious laws as a basis for the functioning of the Islamic states (Lawrence, 1998). The pronouncements of Islam govern company operations, profits, business relationships and consumer behavior, and are associated with fairness and obedience to God (Bashir, 2002; Metwally, 1997; Sharif, 2003):

- Resources of all types are gifts from God and must be used in the most efficient and productive way to fulfill his plan for mankind and satisfy individual needs. Thus business conducted in accordance with Islamic principles is based on the impersonalized motive of fulfilling individual obligation and trust rather than self-interest.

- Economic activities must serve the interests of all in society, and to protect these interests the state does not allow private ownership of some productive assets, as reflected in the predominantly public ownership of utilities in the majority of Islamic countries and the significant size of the public sectors in the Arabian Gulf countries.
- Shari'ah law forbids the manufacture and sale of alcoholic drinks, pork and pork products, usury, gambling, gray market activities, deceitful transactions, hoarding and any other activities that can cause harm of any kind to other people. Any earnings or benefits derived from activities that do not follow the principles of Islamic teaching are illegal.
- Business transactions must be based on cooperation, not opposition and confrontation. This applies to institutional, group and individual market exchanges. Making exorbitant profits is not in line with Islamic principles.
- Under Shari'ah law, Muslim individuals who accumulate wealth above a fixed level (*nisab*) are obliged to redistribute a certain amount among the poor and needy. This is done through a tax called *zakat*.
- Shari'ah law forbids the charging of interest on all types of credit, which makes Islamic banking operations fundamentally different from those in the Western world.

The primary sources of Islamic law are the *Qur'an* – the book that Muslims believe was given by Allah to the Prophet Muhammad and the Sunna (*Sunnah*, a body of Islamic law based on the words and acts of Muhammad). Both promote fairness and socioeconomic justice and have governed economic practices since the thirteenth century, when it was recognized that free entry to the market was necessary but should be subject to strict Islamic principles. It was decided that the market should determine prices but that the government should control the level of market prices, thus protecting the interests of society.

Islamic business ethics and their impact on marketing

A number of books have been written on the importance of business ethics in Islamic countries, based on the teachings of the *Qur'an* (see for example Beekun, 1996; Saeed *et al.*, 2001). Islam governs all economic activities, including marketing. Here again, all individuals are accountable to God for all their activities throughout their working lives.

Islamic marketing ethics differ from their secular counterparts in two major respects (Saeed *et al.*, 2001):

- Based on the principles, of Qur'an marketing ethics are fixed and absolute and cannot depart from the officially accepted and proclaimed interpretations.
- Value maximization must be for the benefit of society, and not to maximize profits.

Thus Islamic marketing ethics are governed by two moral pillars; submission to the moral order of God, and empathy with and mercifulness to God's creations, which means abstaining from harmful actions and unethical practices (Niazi, 1996).

With regard to the production of goods and their sale in the market, this must be ethical from start to finish. The value of goods to society and their social impact are constantly scrutinized and evaluated. The primary objective of production is to ensure the supply of goods that satisfy the needs of individuals and benefit as a whole society.

In many countries of the world pricing practices are designed to exploit human psychology and retail prices are deliberately set high so that a discount can be offered. Thus purchasers are misled into thinking that they have secured a bargain. Islamic law prohibits this practices and disallows price changes that do not reflect a change in product quality and/or quantity, as well as intentionally deceiving purchasers for personal gain. Moreover merchandise must not be assigned qualities it does not possess. Producers and retailers are obliged to acquaint their customers with all the qualities of their products, both desirable and undesirable. Extra costs incurred by distribution problems must not be passed on to consumes.

With regard to promotional activities, appeal to the emotions, the use of female personalities, sexual images and exaggerated or false claims are forbidden. Honesty is encouraged and praised.

The ethical norms of Islam disallow burdening the final customer with higher prices or delays associated with distribution. Islamic marketing ethics stipulate that the major goal of distribution channels is to create value and improve the service provided to customers by delivering products ethically.

In recent years foreigners, many of them non-Muslim, have held a large proportion of managerial positions in some Islamic countries. For example the majority of managers in the Gulf region are from India, while in Indonesia and Malaysia most are of Chinese origin. This trend is slowly reversing as Western-educated young Islamic people are now taking up posts as managers in their native countries.

Western business operations in Islamic countries

The presence of Western companies in many Islamic countries is limited and in general foreign direct investment is lower than anywhere else in the world. However some Islamic countries, such as Egypt, Indonesia and Malaysia, have received sizable amounts of Western capital, and Nestlé has invested heavily in production facilities in Egypt, Saudi Arabia, Syria, Turkey, and the United Arab Emirates.

There are several reasons for the limited involvement of Western companies. First, there is a huge cultural gap between the Western and Muslim worlds, mostly based on religion. Second, some companies are deterred by the perceived threat of terrorist actions and hostility towards Westerners. Third, there is the legacy of colonial occupation and the subsequent resurgance of religious and cultural identity in countries such as Bangladesh, Pakistan, the Gulf states, the Maghreb countries and so on.

Intra-Islamic cooperation

There has been very limited economic cooperation between and integration of the Islamic countries (Zineldin, 2002), despite many efforts in that direction. However there has been some success with the Gulf Cooperation Council (GCC) and the Arab Maghreb Union (AMU) (Toye, 1987). There are many political, economic and religious reasons for the failure to create an Islamic or Arab common market, an idea that has been mooted for quite some time. One reason is that the significance accorded to and application of Islamic law varies substantially from country to country, and no country, not even Saudi Arabia, is held to be the model for center of the Islamic world.

One enduring example of inter-Islamic economic and trade cooperation is the Organization of the Islamic Conference (OIC), which was founded in 1969. It currently has 57 Middle Eastern, African and Asian member countries and four with observer status.[1] Although geographically dispersed they form a sizable market comprising about 15 per cent of the global population and occupying 20 per cent of the world's inhabited land. The participation of the member countries in world trade is significant. Since the mid 1990s their combined exports and imports have accounted for about 23 per cent of the total value of world trade. However this trade is predominantly with non-OIC member countries. The value of intra-OIC trade as a percentage of overall OIC trade has been in the range of 6–9 per cent since the early 1990s. The structure of foreign trade by Islamic countries differs. While some countries such as the Islamic Republic of Iran trade predominately with other Islamic countries, other countries, e.g. Saudi Arabia have their trade mostly with non-Islamic states. Oil, natural gas and their derivatives comprise more three thirds of the value of exports from Islamic countries.

In an attempt to increase the significance of the OIC the member countries held the First World Islamic Economic Forum in October 2005. There the groundwork was laid for an Islamic Common Market (ICM), which would start with the establishment of Islamic Free Trade Agreement (IFTA) comprising regional free trade agreements. This would make Islamic countries less dependent on trade with the rest of the world and provide more favorable conditions for improving the economic viability of Muslim countries (Beg, 1994). Future plans include an Islamic capital market with a common currency to facilitate inter-Islamic trade and counterbalance the dominance of the US dollar and the euro in international marketing exchanges. Only a few projects based on intra-Islamic foreign investment have been concluded to date.

Some believe that an ICM is essential because of globalization trends and the unfavorable attitude towards Islam that has arisen in various parts of the world as a result of terrorist attacks by extremists. However it is noteworthy that not even the Arab countries have managed to create a common market or any other form of economic integration that could be used as a stepping stone for the formation of an ICM.

Market segmentation

Güveli and Kılıçkaplan (2000) have evaluated the effects of 33 socioeconomic variables on Islamic states and divided the OIC countries into three major groups: those with a combined indicator of more than 1.00; those with a combined indicator of 0.01–0.99; and those whose combined indicator has a negative value (Table 1.2). The countries in each of the three groups have a high degree of socioeconomic homogeneity that can assist segmentation.

Table 1.2 Ranking of socioeconomic development, Islamic countries, 1998

Combined indicator of more than 1.00		*Combined indicator of 0.00–1.00*		*Combined indicator of less than 0.00*	
Kuwait	2.387	Libya	0.865	Yemen	–0.294
United Arab Emirates	2.219	Oman	0.759	Pakistan	–0.403
Bahrain	1.616	Jordan	0.687	Nigeria	–0.409
Qatar	1.500	Tunisia	0.656	Cameroon	–0.498
Lebanon	1.218	Algeria	0.624	Mauritania	–0.574
Malaysia	1.096	Turkey	0.604	Sudan	–0.717
Saudi Arabia	1.063	Iran	0.364	Senegal	–0.764
		Syria	0.249	Gambia	–0.874
		Egypt	0.236	Bangladesh	–0.894
		Iraq	0.226	Benin	–0.958
		Morocco	0.139	Sierra Leone	–0.959
		Indonesia	0.079	Guinea-Bissau	–0.996
		Gabon	0.034	Guinea	–1.021
		Albania	0.014	Mozambique	–1.117
				Uganda	–1.129
				Mali	–1.224
				Chad	–1.242
				Burkina Faso	–1.243
				Niger	–1.320

Source: Adapted from Güveli and Kılıçkaplan (2000).

The OIC countries also fall into three groups based on per capita income. The first group comprises the oil-rich states of Brunei, Kuwait, Qatar, and the United Arab Emirates, which have a high per capita annual income of more than US$9,000. All four countries are small and the total population consists of fewer than five million people. There are 21 middle-income countries with a per capita income of $800–9,000. These are Algeria, Bahrain, Djibouti, Gabon, Indonesia, Iran, Egypt, Jordan, Kazakhstan, Lebanon, Libya, Malaysia, the Maldives, Morocco, Oman, Saudi Arabia, Syria, Tunisia, Turkey, Turkmenistan, and Uzbekistan. The final group consists of 27 countries with a per capita income of less than $800: Afghanistan, Albania, Azerbaijan, Bangladesh, Benin, Burkina Faso, Cameroon, Chad, Comoros, Iraq, Gambia, Guinea, Guinea-Bissau, Kyrgyzstan, Mali, Mauritania, Mozambique, Niger, Nigeria, Pakistan, Senegal, Sierra Leone, Somalia, Sudan, Tajikistan, Uganda, and Yemen.

There have been few studies of market segmentation in Islamic countries, and those which have been published focus on Arab markets. These adopt one of two approaches. The first assumes that each national market is unique and there is no homogeneity among them

(Shilling, 1978; Elbashier and Nichollas, 1983). The second identifies commonalities among the countries in respect of general characteristics, macroeconomic specifics, socioeconomic factors, psychological features, and behavior (Kaynak 1985; Amine and Cavisgil, 1990; Souiden, 2002).

Amine and Cavusgil's (1990) approach focuses on macro-environmental, attitudinal and lifestyle dimensions. On the basis of the first dimension they identify four groups of Arab countries: those in the Arabian Gulf, North Africa, the Eastern Mediterranean and some 'unique' countries. In the second dimension there are modern societies, 'crossover' societies and slowly changing or resolutely traditional societies. The third dimension consists of the newly rich, the poor, and the young and modern in any particular society. This clustering can aid identification of 'cultural affinity zones' (Usunier, 2000) across national markets that can help international companies to develop a specific marketing mix strategies for each zone.

Souiden (2002) has studied Arab consumers' responses to a variety of marketing stimuli. He has found that commonalities exist and these allow for the implementation of standardized marketing strategies for particular segments at country and consumer level. Both macro and micro indicators can be used to define the profile of each segment. Thus a standardized marketing plan can be used for each identified market segment and differentiated marketing strategies applied to differing segments. However the choice of markets to be segmented and the marketing variables incorporated will have an impact on the validity of this approach.

Market characteristics of Islamic countries

The religious and cultural norms in Islamic countries must be addressed by any marketer operating there. In terms of culture there is considerable diversity among the countries. For example Kazakhstan, Tajikistan, Turkmenistan, and Uzbekistan were Soviet republics for 70 years and secularism rather than Islam held sway in the functioning of society. To a large degree this remains the case today. In Afghanistan, by contrast, Islamic fundamentalism under Taliban rule reached extreme proportions and resulted in almost total isolation of the country from the rest of the world.

Another factor that marketers need to take into account is the difference in wealth among the Islamic countries. For example most of Gulf states have a high per capita GDP, whereas in Bangladesh and Djibouti it is very low. In this regard the Islamic countries can be divided into those which are rich in natural resources and those which are not. However not all the countries in the former group have achieved high living standards. While living standards have improved markedly in Bahrain, Kuwait, Saudi Arabia and the United Arab Emirates, the same is not true in Algeria, Indonesia, Iran, Libya, and Nigeria. Islamic countries that have limited natural resources but a satisfactory level of economic development and stability are Egypt, Jordan, Lebanon, Tunisia, Turkey, Syria, and Pakistan. Recently Egypt has enjoyed economic growth of 5 per cent per annum on average. The most disadvantaged countries have limited natural endowments, weak economic growth and low or very low living standards. These include Afghanistan, Bangladesh, Chad, Gambia, Mali, and Niger. Thus the Islamic world is heterogeneous across the world and within particular regions. For instance in the Middle East the United Arab Emirates is one of the world's richest countries in terms of per capita income while the Republic of Yemen is one of the poorest.

Marketers should analyze this diversity in terms of financial and human resources, economic viability, income distribution, level of industrialization, policies towards foreign investment, and priorities for social and economic development. Countries with a well-educated population and a high proportion of affluent consumers, such as Bahrain, Kuwait, and the United Arab Emirates, are promising markets for both services and consumer goods, including foodstuffs, cleaning products, household appliances, consumer electronics, cars, and home entertainment products. Consumers' receptiveness to Western products and brands in the affluent societies of the Gulf region is facilitated by experiential learning and a balanced education that combines the religious with the secular. Highly educated young consumers are exhibiting purchasing patterns that are more typical of consumers in advanced market countries. For example the expectations of these 'cosmopolitan consumers' (Cannon and Yaprak, 2002) are more like those of North American and West European consumers than of consumers in other Arab countries (Raven and Welsh, 2004).

Regardless of the differences in their living standards all Islamic countries can be categorized as emerging markets because adherence to market principles is in its infancy or has yet to begin. In general Western products and brands are perceived to be of superior quality to their local equivalents, although in countries where there is strict adherence to Islam and a high degree of ethnocentrism, such as Iran, there is considerable animosity towards Western goods. Some consumers in Islamic countries are with high degree of price sensitivity, lack appreciation of high quality and have a limited understanding of the concept of value added. Thus drawing attention to core rather than augmented attributes of products is recommended when marketing in Islamic countries.

Financial services are governed by Islamic law. Therefore marketing campaigns for financial products, packages and services must fall within the requirements of Islam. For example it is forbidden to charge interest on credit and therefore invitations to purchase on credit would be considered inappropriate by the majority of Islamic consumers.

Promotion and distribution

Promotional activities in Islamic countries must take account of the role of religion and Islamic law in the functioning of society. In addition cultural differences between countries prevent a uniform approach to promotion. For example the Arab culture differs significantly from that in Indonesia and Malaysia, where the national culture has been strongly influenced by other religions and ethnic groups. However the cultural similarity of and unified business practices in Egypt, Kuwait, Lebanon, Saudi Arabia, and the United Arab Emirates mean that a uniform approach can produce positive results in their case (Melewar *et al.*, 2000).

Rice and Al-Mossawi (2002) offer several important guidelines for marketing in the Islamic world:

- Promotional messages should be gender specific, generally targeting male consumers and applying more subtle approaches to female consumers.
- Messages should not exaggerate, mislead or deceive; rather they should be mostly informative.
- The use of religious words and phrases in a promotional message generally has a reassuring effect. However, inappropriate use of religious terminology can repel rather than lure consumers.
- Promotion in general and advertising in particular should avoid negative publicity, both intentional and unintentional.
- Promotional messages should emphasize modesty, simplicity and the opportunity to save money when buying any particular goods or services. Coupling promotional messages with money-off offers can have negative consequences as consumers may question the fairness of the previous price and lose faith in the producer or retailer.

As a result of religious restrictions on private ownership and government restrictions on foreign ownership the distribution systems in Islamic countries tend to be underdeveloped. It is possible for foreign companies to set up their own distribution networks but in general this must be done through local partnerships or joint ventures. Most of the affluent Islamic countries, such as those in the Gulf region, have only small markets so a large investment in a distribution network is not justified. Franchising is a viable alternative because it overcomes the problem of foreign ownership and the financial risk is mostly borne by the franchisee.

Business-to-business and consumer markets

The world's Islamic population is mostly concentrated in the emerging markets in Asia and Africa, where as yet the possibilities for business-to-business marketing have been limited. However there are opportunities to do business with oil-rich countries and those wishing to purchase military equipment.

In most Arab states, and especially the Gulf countries, there is sizable proportion of affluent consumers and a high demand for imported goods and services. In the 1990s franchises grew at an average rate of 20 per cent per annum, and in most of the Gulf countries franchises now account for 70–80 per cent of the newly created businesses. Western fashion houses, car hire firms, and toy makers have entered the market on a massive scale by this means. Some of the best know franchisers are Benetton and Bhs in the garments market, and Dunkin Donuts, Kentucky Fried Chicken and Pizza Hut in the fast-food business.

Supermarkets and shopping malls are flourishing in the region. A unique shopping center called Deira City in Dubai provides locals and tourists with a huge choice of goods, services and entertainment all in one location.

As a rule the consumer base in the Gulf countries can be segmented according to ethnicity, religion and income; that is native and non-native residents, Muslim and non-Muslim, affluent and non-affluent. An additional segment consists of tourists (the United Arab Emirates) and pilgrims during the annual Hajj (Saudi Arabia).

Conclusion

The Islamic world offers a huge market with considerable potential and high growth. Despite the integrating effect of the Islamic religion there is great diversity among the countries. The political systems range from democracy to authoritarianism, the latter based on religious fundamentalism or dictatorship. The economic diversity is due to the presence or absence of natural resources, especially oil and gas, the possession of which facilitates economic development and improved living standards. Governmental control of the economy is the norm, although in some countries private ownership of productive asset has been encouraged. Foreign participation in the economy is generally allowed but it is still somewhat restricted and biased towards companies from certain countries. Ethnically the Islamic countries could not be more diverse, although there is some ethically homogeneity in the Arab world. The countries also differ in terms of overall development, stability, and degree of Westernization.

Because of all this tailored marketing strategies are required for each country. However because there are several commonalities within regions a regional marketing approach can sometimes be applied. This book addresses the particularties of the various regions of the Islamic world.

Note

1. The OIC member countries are Afghanistan, Albania, Algeria, Azerbaijan, Bahrain, Bangladesh, Benin, Brunei, Burkina Faso, Cameroon, Chad, Comoros, Côte d'Ivoire, Djibouti, Egypt, Gabon, Gambia, Guinea, Guinea-Bissau, Guyana, Indonesia, Iran, Iraq, Jordan, Kazakhstan, Kuwait, Kyrgyzstan, Lebanon, Libya, Malaysia, Maldives, Mali, Mauritania, Morocco, Mozambique, Niger, Nigeria, Oman, Pakistan, Palestine, Qatar, Saudi Arabia, Senegal, Sierra Leone, Somalia, Sudan, Suriname, Syria, Tajikistan, Togo, Tunisia, Turkey, Turkmenistan, Uganda, United Arab Emirates, Uzbekistan, and Yemen. The observer countries are Bosnia and Herzegovina, Central African Republic, Thailand, and Russia. Muslim communities associated with the OIC are the Turkish Muslim Community of Cyprus and the Moro National Liberation Front of the Philippines.

References

Amine, L. and S. T. Cavusgil (1990) 'Marketing environment in the Middle East and North Africa: The forces behind market homogenization', in H. Thorelli and S. T. Cavusgil (eds), *International Marketing Strategy* (Oxford: Pergamon Press), pp. 229–47.

Bashir, A. (2002) 'Property rights, institutions and economic development: an Islamic perspective', *Humanonics*, 18 (3/4), pp. 75–91.

Ba-Yunus, I. and M. Siddiqui (1998) *A Report on the Muslim Population of the United States of America* (New York: Center for American Muslim Research and Information).

Beekun, R. (1996) 'Islamic business ethics', discussion paper, International Institute of Islamic Thought, University of Nevada, November.

Beg, T. (1994) 'Islamic Common Market: Some conceptual and operational issues in the light of European Community experience', *Journal of Objective Studies*, January, pp. 23–35.

Cannon, H. and A. Yaprak (2002) 'Will the real world citizen please stand up! A critical review of cosmopolitanism as a consumer behavior construct', *Journal of International Marketing*, 10 (4), pp. 30–52.

Elbashier, A. and J. Nichollas (1983) 'Export marketing in the Middle East: the importance of cultural differences', *Journal of International Marketing*, 2 (1), pp. 68–81.

Forte, D. (2002) 'Islam, past and future', *Religion & Liberty*, 12 (1), pp. 1–5.

Güveli, A. and Kılıc[,]kaplan S. (2000) 'A ranking of Islamic countries in terms of their levels of socio-economic development', *Journal of Economic Cooperation*, 21 (1), pp. 97–114.

Kaynak, E. (1985) 'Comparative study of marketing and management systems in the Middle East', in E. Kaynak (ed.), *International Business in The Middle East.* (Hawthorne, NY: Walter de Gryter), pp. 19–42.

Lawrence, B. (1998) *Shattering the Myth: Islam beyond Violence* (Princeton, NJ: Princeton University Press).

Melewar, T., S. Turnbull and G. Balabanis (2000) 'International advertising strategies of multinational enterprises in the Middle East', *International Journal of Advertising*, 19 (4), pp. 529–47.

Metwally, M. (1997) 'Economic consequences of applying Islamic principles in Muslim societies', *International Journal of Social Economics*, 24 (7/8/9), pp. 941–57.

Niazi, L. (1996) *Islamic Law of Conduct* (Lahore: Dyal Sing Trust Liberty).

Quelch, J. (2001) *Cases in Strategic Marketing Management: Business Strategies in Muslim Countries* (Upper Saddle River, NJ: Prentice-Hall).

Raven, P. and D. Welsh (2004) 'An exploratory study of influences on retail service quality: a focus on Kuwait and Lebanon', *Journal of Services Marketing*, 18 (3), pp. 198–214.

Rice, G. and M. Al-Mossawi (2002) 'The implications of Islam for advertising messages: the Middle Eastern context', *Journal of Euro-Marketing*, 11 (3), pp. 12–35.

Saeed, M., Z. Ahmed and S.-M. Mukhtar (2001) 'International marketing ethics from an Islamic perspective: a value maximizing approach', *Journal of Business Ethics*, 32 (2), pp. 127–42.

Sharif, M. (2003) 'Application of Islamic economic system in a contemporary economy: an illustration with poverty and inequality in the USA', *Humanomics*, 19 (3/4), pp. 41–54.

Shilling, N. (1978) *Marketing in the Arab World* (Riyadh: Inter-Crescent).

Souiden, N. (2002) 'Segmenting the Arab markets on the basis of marketing stimuli', *International Marketing Review*, 19 (6), pp. 611–36.

Toye, J. (1987) *Dilemmas for Development* (London: Basil Blackwell Ltd).

Usunier, J.-C. (2000) *Marketing across Cultures* (London: Financial Times, Prentice Hall).

Zineldin M. (2002) 'Globalization, strategic co-operation and economic integration among Islamic/Arab countries', *Management Research News*, 25 (4), pp. 35–57.

2
Marketing in Central Asia

Marin Marinov

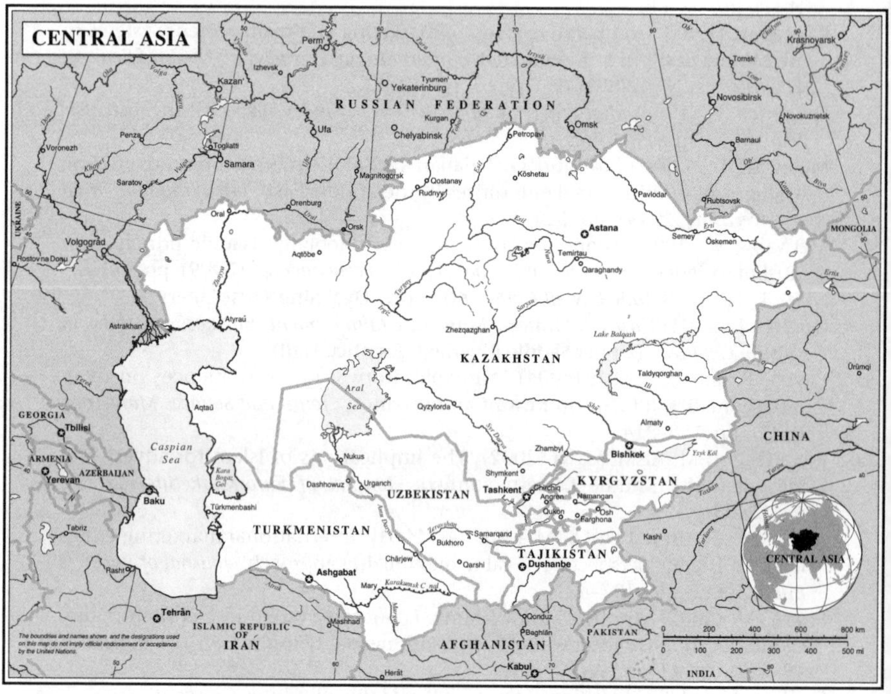

Source: www.un.org/Depts/Cartographic/map/profile/centrasia.

Map of Central Asia

Brief historical background

With the disintegration of the Soviet Union the five Central Asian countries became independent states: Kazakhstan, Kyrgyzstan (Kirgizstan), Tajikistan, Turkmenistan, and Uzbekistan. They cover a total area of

3,882,000 square kilometers, have a combined population of about 60 million and share borders with Russia, China, Afghanistan, and Iran. The main religion in neighboring Russia is Christian Orthodox; in China Confucianism, Buddhism and Taoism are the major religious doctrines; and the Central Asian countries are predominantly Muslim. In this respect they are similar to neighboring Afghanistan and Iran but they enjoy greater diversity, religious freedom, and secularism. Since independence internal and external forces have pushed for a greater role for Islam in social and political life, which would strongly affect the social fabric of the Central Asian countries if secularism were replaced by Muslim fundamentalism. Tajikistan has already experienced a devastating civil war that was triggered by extreme religious fundamentalists intent on increasing the role of Islam in the functioning of the state.

Situated between two of the world's most significant markets (China and Russia) the five Central Asian countries have been subject to the military, political, economic, social, and cultural influence of these great powers for many centuries. The Great Silk Road, which connected Asia with Europe, had a huge impact on the economic, trade and cultural development of the region. A mixture of ancient cultures and, more recently, ethnic and religious influences have determined the contextual specificity of Central Asia.

Historically the Central Asian region has been a melting pot of various ethnic groups and cultures. Persians and Turks exerted a strong influence on the Turkic nomads' identity. After the Arab conquest the Persian language and administrative system remained, but from the end of the tenth century AD the Turkish culture and language gradually became entrenched. Later the British and Russian empires vied for dominance of the region.

While there are cultural similarities among the countries due to their common history and the influence of invaders, there are also differences across the region. For example there are considerable cultural differences between the nomads who inhabit the steppes and mountains in Kazakhstan, Kyrgyzstan and Turkmenistan and the settled urban dwellers in Tajikistan and Uzbekistan.

From the 1920s until the early 1990s the development of the Central Asian countries was determined by the political and economic strategies of the Soviet Union. Under their divide and rule policy the Soviets moved people into and out of the area, mixing cultures, beliefs and ways of life. For the past 15 years these countries have been striving to re-establish their own national identity, despite the social and ethnic remnants of the Soviet past.

The economic environment

After gaining independence in 1991 the individual countries adopted different political, economic and social policies. Kazakhstan and Kyrgyzstan implemented ambitious economic reforms and their economies were strictly controlled by their governments. Turkmenistan introduced some reforms without causing internal disturbance, whereas Uzbekistan adopted Islamic principles and Tajikistan was scarred by the civil war between Islamic and secular forces that were strongly influenced by Afghanistan and Russia respectively.

Kyrgyzstan has found it difficult to restructure its economy as it has few natural resources, unlike Kazakhstan, which is rich in oil and natural gas. It is also by far the biggest country in the region – Kyrgyzstan and Tajikistan are only a fraction of its size. The most populous state is Uzbekistan, where there is a large concentration of people in the area around the capital, Tashkent. In all five countries there is a high proportion of rural dwellers and the urban–rural divide is reflected in differences in income and purchasing behavior. The main sociogeographic indicators for the region are shown in Table 2.1.

Table 2.1 Main sociogeographic indicators, Central Asia

	Kazakhstan	*Kyrgyzstan*	*Tajikistan*	*Turkmenistan*	*Uzbekistan*
Area (million sq. km)	2,724.9	199.9	141.1	491.2	447.4
Population (million, 2003)	15.7	4.6	5.9	4.7	25.6
Population growth rate (%, 2003)	–0.8	1.4	2.4	1.3	1.9
Population density (persons per sq. km)	5.9	23.1	41.8	9.3	52.5
Rural population (%, 2002)	45.1	67.2	72.5	56.3	62.8
Urban population (%, 2002)	53.9	32.8	27.5	43.7	37.2
Population of capital city (million, 2004)	0.6	0.8	0.6	0.9	2.3

Sources: National Statistics Institutions of Kazakhstan, Kyrgyzstan, Tajikistan, Turkmenistan, and Uzbekistan.

Despite democratization, authoritarian rule remains strong in Central Asia. The ex-communist elite have established political and economic dominance, limiting the activities of the opposition and restricting political rights, economic freedom and civil liberty (see for example Collins, 2002; McFaul, 2002; Åslund, 2003). All this has deterred business expansion.

Foreign direct investment

The flow of foreign direct investment (FDI) to the countries of Central Asia in 1992–2000 was rather small – less than 1 per cent of the total FDI flow to developing countries. Since then, however, FDI has increased by 25–30 per cent per annum, and when the inflows are measured as a percentage of GDP, foreign investment in the Central Asian countries seems sizable (Figure 2.1). FDI as a percentage of GDP is shown in Figure 2.2.

As will be discussed in Chapter 3, Kazakhstan has attracted considerable foreign investment in the oil extraction and refining industry. Similarly investment in Turkmenistan has gone mostly into oil and gas exploration and extraction. Uzbekistan has been unable to attract many foreign investors and lags markedly behind Kazakhstan, the leading economy in the region.

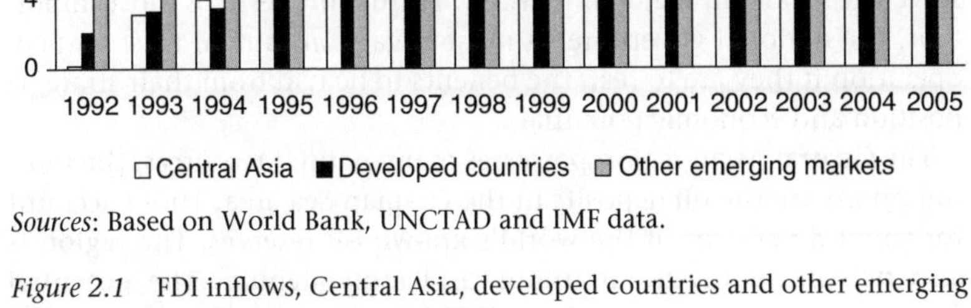

Sources: Based on World Bank, UNCTAD and IMF data.

Figure 2.1 FDI inflows, Central Asia, developed countries and other emerging markets, 1992–2005 (percentage of GDP)

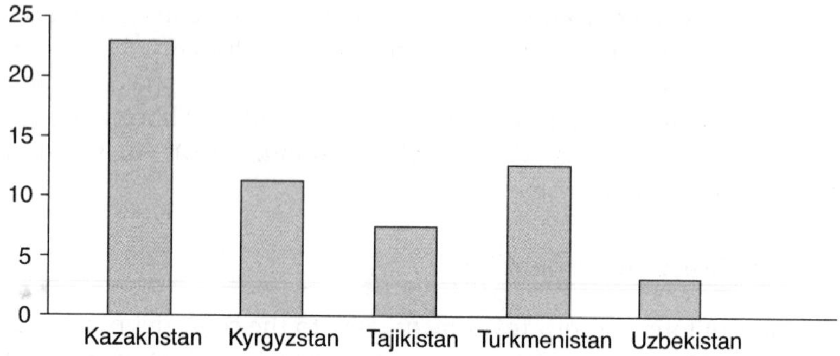

Sources: Calculations from national statistics.

Figure 2.2 Cumulative FDI, Kazakhstan, Kyrgyzstan, Turkmenistan and Uzbekistan, 1992–2003 (percentage of GDP)

Regional challenges

Central Asia is full of opportunities and challenges. The constituent countries are interdependent both economically and politically. They are all landlocked, have an integrated infrastructure and their markets are comparatively small. To stimulate international trade the governments have set low import tariffs, but the geographical distance from key exporting countries means high transportation costs and these have to be added to the selling price. In such circumstances regional cooperation offers a much better opportunity for economic development via specialization and mutually beneficial trade and investment arrangements.

Thus the Central Asian countries face three crucial challenges (Starr, 2004). First, they have to overcome the negative impact of their landlocked geographical position. Second, they need to devise a mutual economic policy based on their complementary strengths in order to serve the local and regional markets. Third, and perhaps most important, the national governments must engage in mutual trust and cooperation if they are to reap the benefits to be had from their strategic position and economic potential.

The Central Asian region possesses many natural resources, the most important are the oil deposits in the Caspian Sea area. Those account for about 5 per cent of the world's known oil reserves. The region is also rich in gold, zinc, uranium, and molybdenum. The potential for hydroelectric power generation is also significant. Agriculturally,

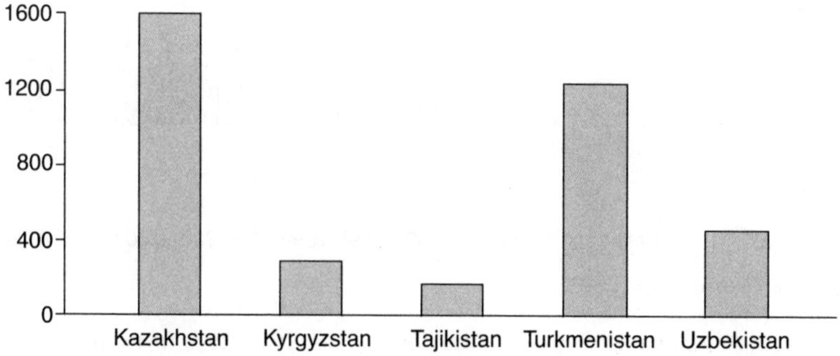

Sources: National statistics.

Figure 2.3 Per capita GDP, Central Asia, 2003 (US dollars)

Central Asia is the world's second largest cotton producer and grows high-quality organic fruit and vegetables.

Despite their developmental potential the average regional per capita GDP of US$726 in 2002 places these countries in the ranks of low-income developing countries. This already low figures conceals a huge disparity among the five states (Figure 2.3). The oil-rich countries – Kazakhstan and Turkmenistan – have a much higher per capita GDP than the other countries, although they are still classified as below the world average in terms of economic development. Tajikistan is one of the poorest countries in the world.

Economically, Kazakhstan focuses on the extraction industry, Uzbekistan on mechanical engineering, chemicals and light industry, Turkmenistan on gas production and cotton, Kyrgyzstan on power generation and gold mining, and Tajikistan on aluminium and light industry. Annual GDP growth was negative throughout the region during the early years of independence (1992–96) but since then growth has been positive (Figure 2.4). Kazakhstan has managed to achieve macroeconomic stability, but with the collapse of the military-industrial complex in Kyrgyzstan macroeconomic stability was weakened. Inflation has recently been brought under control in all countries but Uzbekistan.

Education is given high priority and is regarded by the population as a valuable asset. According to official statistics 98.6 per cent of children below the age of 14 attend school. In the academic year 2004–5 the school enrolment rate for high schools was 82.3 per cent of all children below the age of 18. Kazakhstan took the lead with 88.5 per cent. University attendance was also high – 36.8 per cent on average. Here

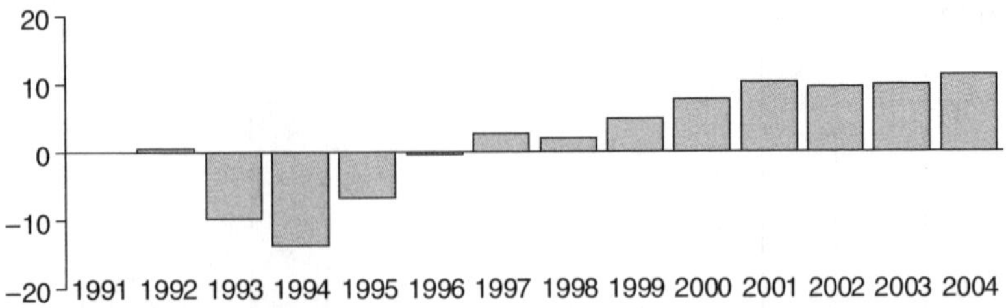

Source: World Bank (2005).

Figure 2.4 Annual GDP growth rate, Central Asia, 1991–2004 (per cent)

Kyrgyzstan took the lead with 42.1 per cent. A high proportion of students are female and in this regard the region is at the forefront of academic education worldwide. It also differentiates these predominantly Muslim states from other Islamic countries. The attention given to education is a valuable heritage of the communist past and unrestricted access to university education is offered to students from all income levels.

Unemployment, although not excessively high, is a cause for concern while poverty is severe and widespread. Hence there is a paradox between the creation of a knowledgeable population and the limited capacity of the economy to utilize this knowledge. The education systems in these countries are world class but their economies are among the poorest in the world. While many of the economic problems can be attributed to the Soviet period, the dismantling of the Council for Mutual Economic Assistance (CMEA) and the associated dissolution of the bloc markets has inflicted a harsh blow and led to regional instability and tension.

Thus Central Asia is a region with a myriad problems, including authoritarian rule, weak economic performance, stunted and strictly regulated private business activities, weak civil societies, a non-existent or miniscule middle class, poverty, inadequate law enforcement and severe environmental decline, to mention just a few. Nevertheless the countries in the region have highly educated populations and technically skilled workforces, abundant natural resources that lure investors, and a strong desire to develop a market economy by means of economic restructuring.

Central Asian integration can be facilitated by exploiting the complementarities between the regional economies. The greatest impediment to this is the poor technological development of the region as a whole, which render impossible the transfer of technologies between the constituent countries. The region's wealth of natural resources has attracted investors who wish to acquire those resources rather than investors who could aid economic diversification and development through up-to-date technology and managerial know-how. The immediate macroeconomic challenges are related to the construction of a modern transportation network within the region and between it and the rest of the world. There should also be a joint regional strategy to improve the international competitiveness of domestic companies and enable them to increase their presence in regional and world markets. All this will require trust, commitment and cooperation among the governments.

As noted earlier exports are dominated by oil, natural gas, a variety of ores and minerals, and some agricultural products, including cotton and wheat. Trade has been mostly dependent on the Commonwealth of Independent States (CIS), mainly Russia, but recently it has expanded to European Union member states such as Germany and the United Kingdom, Asian countries (mainly China and South Korea) and Turkey. A priority of the regional economies is to diversify their export markets and include more value-added products on their export lists.

The amount of private domestic and foreign capital invested in industry and commerce has increased but the central governments remain in overall control of all economic activities. Turkmenistan has the lowest level of private capital investment – in 2003 it accounted for only 25 per cent of all investment in the economy. Private investment is higher in Kazakhstan and Kyrgyzstan, where about two thirds of economic operations are privately owned. The region's financial sectors and banks have been restructured and now apply Western standards and accounting practices. Private capital plays a significant part in the financial sector of Kazakhstan but less so in the other countries. The privatization process in Kyrgyzstan is well advanced and it is the only country to allow private ownership of land. Private businesses in Turkmenistan are the result of individual entrepreneurship as the privatization of state-owned assets has been deferred.

Market structure and consumer behavior

The markets in Central Asia are very fragmented. There is a huge difference between cities and large urban towns, where purchasing power is relatively high, and small provincial towns and villages, where people have low incomes and often rely on their own produce. Consumer awareness of Western brands and products is low. The high price of Western imports and distribution difficulties limit their purchase. Moreover they have to compete against cheap regional, CIS and Chinese imports, which are generally perceived as good value for money and are therefore favored by the majority of consumers.

The markets in the region are dominated by bazaar traders and retailers, which coexist with some larger private and state-owned firms. The latter differ in size and extent from country to country, but small producers and bazaar-type business relations predominate in all the countries.

Purchasing behavior is mostly based on relationships and economic considerations are not paramount. The quality of buyer–seller relations and mutual help are key to any purchase. The majority of consumers shop in bazaars, where they have built up personal relationships with vendors and often spend time chatting about news, everyday issues and problems when buying goods from their stalls. For their part vendors do not necessarily seek to obtain the highest profit and are prepared to offer a good deal to customers they know. Friendly bartering is commonplace. Thus the buying process is not just a commercial exchange but also a mutually beneficial social interaction.

In contrast some sections of the national economies adhere to Western market principles and transactions are conducted according to economic rationality. Sellers are rivals and they segment the market into groups of homogeneous customers. They are mostly large private producers and traders and often have the backing of foreign capital. Exchanges are impersonal and based on set prices and conditions.

In the economic sectors that are still state-owned the centralization of production and distribution precludes competition. Here demand tends to exceeds supply because of insufficient production and government protection of state-owned industries against imports.

Conclusion

The Central Asian states face many challenges related to their geographic position, recent past and historical inheritance. The governments have recognized the need for economic reform and technological upgrading. However the spread of market principles is hampered by extensive state ownership and government control over the functioning of the economies. The low technological level and limited complementarities of the regional economies, coupled with restricted intraregional cooperation, are impeding regional integration.

Poverty remains a serious problem. Oil-rich Kazakhstan has managed to make significant changes to its economy and improve living standards, but in the rest of the region the people have little purchasing power, which limits marketing opportunities.

The influence of Islam was diminished by the secularization of society during the Soviet era. However the subsequent return of Islam brought with it radicalism in some parts of the region, and in Tajikistan it led to a three-year civil war (1992–94) after independence.

Economic internationalization is proceeding at a different pace from country to country. Foreign businesses that have entered the Central Asia markets have predominantly used franchises and joint ventures to set up production and trading facilities. These modes of market entry allow investment risks to be shared, investment resources to be kept relatively low and possible divestment costs to be minimized.

Foreign products and brands have a limited presence due to distance and transportation difficulties, the low purchasing power of consumers and their high degree of ethnocentrism. The majority prefer local or regional products and food stuffs, and when buying consumer durables, durability and performance are more important than brand. However economic recovery will certainly create more opportunities for the sale of foreign brands. Meanwhile the geographic proximity and shared history of the Central Asian states would be advantageous for developing a regional approach to market entry and expansion.

References

Åslund, A. (2003) 'Sizing up the Central Asian economies', *Journal of International Affairs*, 56 (2), pp. 75–88.

Collins, K. (2002) 'Class, pacts, and politics in Central Asia', *Journal of Democracy*, 13 (3), pp. 137–52.

McFaul, M. (2002) 'The fourth wave of democracy and dictatorship: Non-cooperative transitions in the post-communist world', *World Politics*, 54, pp. 212–44.

Starr, F. (2004) *Central Asia in the Global Economy* (Washington, DC: Carnegie Endowment for International Peace).

World Bank (2005) *Development Indicators* (Washington, DC: World Bank Publications).

3
Marketing in Kazakhstan

Marin Marinov

Source: www.lib.utexas.edu/ maps/kazakhstan.html.

Map of Kazakhstan

Brief historical background

Kazakhstan, which covers 2.7 million square kilometers, is the ninth largest country in the world and the biggest in Central Asia. The population of 15.2 million makes it comparatively small in world terms but it is the second most populous state in Central Asia after Uzbekistan.

According to archaeological evidence the southern part of Kazakhstan was inhabited in the Paleolithic era. Around 1500 BC the inhabitants raised cattle and produced bronzeware. By 1000 BC several tribes had settled in the territory of present-day Kazakhstan, including the

Saks, the Kangues, the Usuns, and the Savromats. Several hundred years later the Huns invaded the steppes. They introduced various crafts as well as military organization and discipline. During the first four hundred years AD the area was a meeting point for tribes in search of better living conditions and resources. It is believed that this period also marked the beginning of more stable types of state organization, such as the West Turkic khanate, which was founded in the sixth century and opened trading opportunities along the Silk Road.

At the end of the eighth and the beginning of the ninth century Kimak tribes settled in the Aral Mountains and along the banks of the River Syr-Daria. These tribes are believed to be the forefathers of today's Kazakhs. In the eighth and ninth centuries large parts of southern and eastern Kazakhstan were ruled by Arabs, who introduced Islam to the local tribes. The period between the seventh and eleventh centuries was rather turbulent in that tribes fought for domination, various state entities appeared and vanished, and rule frequently changed hands between local inhabitants and invaders.

When Islam became the state religion in the tenth century AD the country made considerable economic, social and cultural progress, but in the thirteenth century it succumbed to Genghis Khan and his mighty army. The Kazakh khanate was revived in the fifteenth century and the Kazakh nation differentiated itself from the various clan groups. The first Kazakh ruler was Khan Kasym, who united the Kazakh tribes into one nation. Gradually other tribes joined, attracted by the prospect of a more orderly, settled and secure life.

Russia turned its eyes to Kazakhstan at the beginning of the seventeenth century, lured by its strategic geographic position and trade links. The Cossacks built military fortresses to reinforce their position and help the Kazakhs to repel the Mongol raiders. In the first half of the nineteenth century, when the Mongol threat receded, Russia embarked on an expansion campaign that threatened the integrity of the Kazakh state. By the 1860s the Russians had more or less subdued Kazakh resistance and thousands of Russians and Ukrainians migrated to the country. Some Kazakhs continued to fight for independence, but in vain. Following the Bolshevik Revolution of 1917 a number of Kazakhs tried to form a state. They too were unsuccessful and in 1920 surrendered to the Bolshevik government.

Kazakhstan, then called the Kyrgyz Autonomous Soviet Socialist Republic (ASSR), was initially self-governing but in 1936 it became one of the fifteen constituent republics of the Soviet Union. Thereafter there was a continuous influx of immigrants, mostly Russians,

Germans and Tatars. Industrial and agricultural development suffered a setback due to forced collectivization and mass deportations, especially under the dictatorship of Joseph Stalin.

In the 1920s and 1930s many thousands of mosques were closed and the Arabic alphabet was replaced by Cyrillic. There was no resistance to this, but the collectivization of land was strongly opposed. Between 1928 and 1935 tens of millions of cattle, horses, goats, and sheep were slain by herdsmen rather than surrender them to collective farming. In the late 1940s the Soviet Politburo decided to turn Kazakhstan into a major grain producer, thus substantially reducing the land available for animal husbandry. A huge irrigation project in the 1960s caused the Aral Sea to shrink and the resulting salt pans had a negative impact on the fertility of the land.

The arms race in the Cold War years turned part of the country into a site for the location and testing of atomic weapons. In the 1950s Kazakhstan became home to the main Soviet rocket-launch center, which is still used by Russia and other countries for launching satellites into space.

In 1986 a proreformist government led by Dinmukhamed Kunayev came to power. Kunayev was succeeded by Gennady Kolbin, whose rule was ended by street demonstrations. His successor, Nursultan Nazarbayev, played a vital role in guiding Kazakhstan to independence, which was proclaimed on December 16, 1991. This process was spurred by the attempted coup against Mikhail Gorbachev. In the second half of the 1990s thousands of Kazakh families residing in neighboring countries decided to return to their homeland. Nazarbayev introduced various reforms and in 1997 it was decided to move the capital from Almaty to Astana (then called Akmola), an old Cossack fortress. Since independence Kazakhstan has been a constitutional republic with strong presidential power. It has made considerable progress in developing a market economy and there has been significant economic growth since 2000, mainly due to the country's large oil, gas and mineral reserves.

Ethnicity and culture

The ethnic structure of Kazakhstan is diverse and reflects the country's history. There are more than 20 ethnic groups, of which Kazakhs constitute the largest, followed by Russians, Ukrainians, Uzbeks, and Germans. There are also Jews, Koreans, and Tatars. The main religion, Sunni Muslim, coexists peacefully with Russian Orthodox, Protestant and several others. The secularism that was promoted during the Soviet era was embraced by the majority of people. Immediately after Kazakhstan became independent there was concern that the country might fall under the influence of Islamic fundamentalism because of the significant role that Islam had had in the past. This did not materialize and although all people are free to follow their religious beliefs, social development is secular and economic principles are market-led. There are two official languages: Kazakh and Russian. Two thirds of the population speak Kazakh, while Russian is used for business activities.

The early Kazakhs' culture was rooted in their nomadic way of life and this was slow to give way to the later influence of Islam. For a long time Islam coexisted with earlier shamanistic and animistic beliefs. Food, especially lamb had a special symbolic meaning. In contrast Russian rule had a strong impact on the Kazakhs' culture, value system and beliefs, especially during the Soviet era. The dismantling of the Soviet system brought confusion to the Kazakhs as their norms and beliefs were shattered. More recently American, Turkish and Chinese cultural traits have been passed on via television programs and the printed word. Nowadays young Kazakhs tend to be non-traditional and receptive to global cultures, and there is a small cluster of cosmopolitan consumers with high purchasing power and aspirations.

The business climate and practices in Kazakhstan are closer to European than to Asian. Handshaking and addressing people by their first names is customary at both formal and informal business meetings, although men do not shake hands with women. Business attire is a dark or black suit and tie for men and a dark suit or business dress for women. Gift giving is widespread, normally small tokens such as pens, books or paintings, which are exchanged at the end of first meetings. Exchanging business cards is commonplace – these are written in Kazakh and/or Russian and English. The center of international business is the former capital Almaty, which has a well-developed infrastructure, banking system, and business traditions.

Business people in Kazakhstan are less direct than their US and West European counterparts. Business dinners are used to establish contact and conduct negotiations. Formal attire is a must on such occasions. Toasts are made with strong alcoholic drinks such as vodka or cognac. Relationship and trust building via long informal gatherings, meals and hunting expeditions can be more important than official business meetings.

One of the legacies of communism is a high regard for education. Secondary education is compulsory and illiteracy does not exist.

Kazakhstan has one of the best education systems in the world, with very high standards in respect of curricula, course content and assessment (Dailey and Cardozier, 1989). At present educational institutions are government funded, but it is likely that this will change with the gradual introduction of market principles in the functioning of the economy.

Private educational institutions have already started to appear in Kazakhstan, offering US and West European education, including business courses. Business education, including marketing, is offered by state universities but expertise is limited and generally inadequate for marketizing economies. Some foreign educational and training institutions work together with local and Western business education providers. This form of business education is efficient but its impact is still limited (for further information on business education and providers see Rao and Rybina, 2004).

Kazakhs find the concepts of marketization and market orientation rather difficult to comprehend and deal with. Consumer preferences are often interpreted as impersonalized demand, which prevents a detailed understanding of consumer behavior. Consumer satisfaction is mostly viewed in terms of the quality of face-to-face relationships with traders and is associated more with social interaction than with market exchange. The mindset of Kazakh people is ruled by product availability and quality, and this is proving difficult to change.

Demographic and political profile

In 2005 there were almost 4.5 million households in Kazakhstan. Over the last 16 years the population has decreased by more than 7 per cent, but this is mainly due to the exodus of Russians, Germans and Ukrainians since independence and there is actually positive growth as the birth rate is higher than the mortality rate. More than 53 per cent of the population lives in urban areas. About 35 per cent of Kazakhs are younger than 19 and only 12 per cent are aged 60 and over. The workforce comprises 53 per cent of the total population. According to the Statistics Agency of Kazakhstan there has been a slight increase in the rural population in recent years – in 1991, when Kazakhstan gained independence, it was 41 per cent but by 2004 it had risen to 44 per cent. There are 26 cities with more than 50,000 inhabitants. The largest is the former capital, Almaty, which is home to about 10 per cent of the population. Astana and Karaganda follow with about half a million people each.

About 58 per cent of the population is concentrated in two geographic areas: south-east Kazakhstan, including Almaty, the Southern and Zhambyl Oblasts; and north-east Kazakhstan, including Astana, Karaganda, Kustanai, northern Kazakhstan, Pavlodar, and eastern Kazakhstan. The average income in these areas is somewhat higher than in other parts of the country. According to official figures at least a third of the population lives below the poverty line, which is defined as the minimum income required for subsistence. Two out of three poor Kazakhs live in the southern or eastern parts of the country. In southern Kazakhstan, where the levels of education, technical and vocational training are low, the poverty rate is more than twice the national average. Moreover the income gap between the urban and rural populations is widening.

In Soviet times Kazakhstan was one of the most affluent central Asian republics. However the sharp contraction in output since independence has caused an increase in poverty that cannot be countered by public transfer programs because the national revenues are insufficient and there is a need to maintain strict fiscal discipline. In 2000 consumers on average salaries could buy 30 per cent less than they could buy on the average salary in 1990, so purchases are now mainly related to satisfying everyday needs.

In 2000 the average monthly pretax income was below US$100 (*Crossborder Monitor*, 2001). People with a purchasing power of more than US$200 per month represent less than 10 per cent of the population. The highest earners are politicians and business people. Such consumers prefer branded imported products to locally produced goods.

Consumers in Kazakhstan are extremely price sensitive and expect value for money. More affluent consumers are willing to pay a premium for uniqueness and high quality. Higher than average prices have to be explained via customer education on the value of brand names or special features of the products offered. However in general Kazakhs have a negative attitude towards branded products (Reardon *et al.*, 2005). This may be related to the level of economic development of the country, a preference for proven quality rather than presentation and emotional appeal, limited exposure to foreign products and brands, and resentment about some advertising practices.

Unemployment has also become a problem. It stood at 5 per cent at the end of 1994, rose to 6 per cent in 1996 and peaked at almost 13 per cent in 2000. Currently it is about 8 per cent. Those who are most affected by unemployment are school graduates with no work experience, people with poor educational qualifications or low vocational and technical skills, and women.

While political environment is stable and the president enjoys full control, the success of the proreformist movements in Ukraine and Kyrgyzstan in unseating the political incumbents encouraged the revival of oppositional forces in Kazakhstan. Although there is little risk of armed conflict or domestic terrorism, business-related criminal activities are a significant problem. Nationalism has recently increased and foreign business people operating in Kazakhstan are now subject to pressures from domestic vested interests and regulations enforced by the authoritarian state. There are also problems with corruption, ineffective and inefficient administration and extensive red tape.

Relationships with the neighboring states are generally good, apart from sporadic border disagreements with Uzbekistan. There is little threat of ethnic conflicts between the countries in the region and within Kazakhstan, although there is some tension between Kazakhs and Russians in northern Kazakhstan.

The economy

When Kazakhstan gained independence its economy was highly dependent on the enormous Soviet market and its supply and trade networks, as well as on the markets of the Council for Mutual Economic Assistance (CMEA). During the Soviet period Kazakhstan had a comparative advantage in capital-intensive heavy industry. With the collapse of the Soviet Union and the CMEA there were no immediate alternative markets and all industries fell into deep crisis. Moreover Kazakh products were of low value-added and too undifferentiated to stand up to international competition. The removal of central planning, the loss of protected markets that functioned on the principles of socialist specialization and integration, the disappearance of established patterns of supply and trade, and the cessation of transfers from Moscow caused a sudden and huge fall in output. Companies and industries fell into disarray or disappeared.

There was also a crucial need to bring inflation under control. The adopted measures of macroeconomic stability shrank the economy even further. Macroeconomic stabilization measures adopted proved successful and inflation fell from over 1800 per cent in 1994 to about 11 per cent in 1997. The most significant economic decline occurred in 1994. A few years later the Asian financial crisis had a strong detrimental effect on the Russian financial sector, which in turn stalled the recovery of the Kazakh economy. In 1998 GDP declined by more than 2 per cent due to the fall in oil prices. However in 1999 rising oil prices, the devaluation of the national currency (the tenge) and the good grain crop caused the economy to revive. In 2000 the government launched a national program for economic reforms and privatization. This program encompassed all state-owned productive assets and considerably helped the recovery of the economy. The turning point of the economic recession was 1996, when, after declining continuously for five years the economy began to grow again at a modest pace. In 2002 the US Department of Commerce granted Kazakhstan market economy status (Kazinvest, 2003).

The privatization of productive assets coupled with reform of the legal system and accounting practices have created favorable conditions for business activities. Investments have been made in the development of small and medium-sized enterprises, and in the construction and agricultural sectors. The reforms have led to improved macroeconomic performance and financial stabilization. In 2004 Kazakhstan's country investment rating was 'BBB–' for long-term foreign currency credits and 'BBB' for foreign loans in the national currency (Kazinvest, 2003; USCS, 2005).

Industry is dominated by the extraction and processing of natural resources. Kazakhstan is very rich in oil and natural gas. The production of oil has been growing at a high rate and in 2004 it reached 1.3 million barrels per day. The republic is expected to become one of the world's biggest oil producers by 2020 – it is already the second largest oil producer and exporter after Russia in the Commonwealth of Independent States (CIS). Three large onshore oil fields account for more than half of production. The oil industry is also a major source of export revenues, and the signing of the Caspian Pipeline Consortium Agreement has created an opportunity for increased oil exports. The oil industry is fully controlled by the government. Other important industries are construction and agricultural machinery and military equipment.

Machinery, oil and ore refining, petrochemicals, and food processing now form the backbone of the manufacturing sector. However there is a need to develop value-added production, which would deliver higher export revenues, so a diversification policy has been introduced. An initial move in this regard has been the recent development of a furniture industry.

Since 2000 industry's contribution to the national economy has been fairly steady (Figure 3.1). In 2004 industrial production grew by

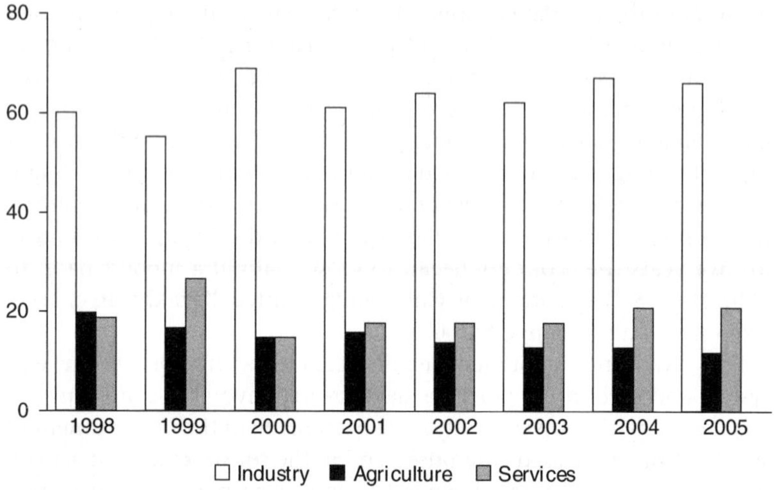

Sources: Statistics Agency of Kazakhstan, National Bank of Kazakhstan.

Figure 3.1 Share of industry, agriculture and services in GDP, Kazakhstan, 1998–2005 (per cent)

10 per cent. Growth was highest in western Kazakhstan, reaching 30.5 per cent. The production of crude oil, iron ore and bauxite ore in 1998–2004 is shown in Figure 3.2.

Due to the rich deposits of lead, wolfram, molybdenum, barite, chromium, manganese and uranium, mining is the second largest

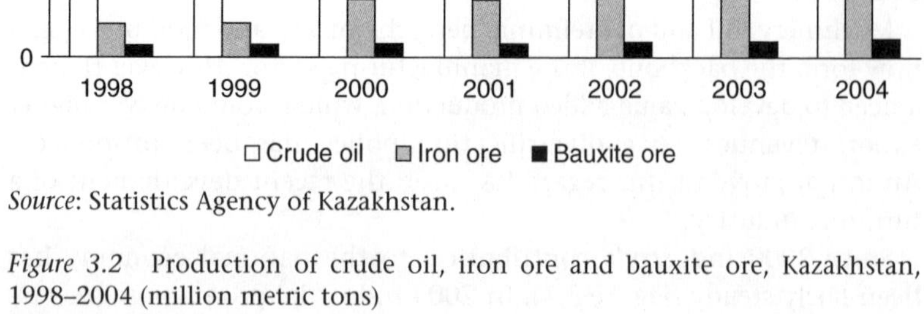

Source: Statistics Agency of Kazakhstan.

Figure 3.2 Production of crude oil, iron ore and bauxite ore, Kazakhstan, 1998–2004 (million metric tons)

industrial sector and accounts for more than 25 per cent of GDP. Mining and metallurgy are vertically integrated and under state control. Foreign capital investment in these sectors takes the form of joint ventures with state-owned companies.

Agricultural production has been declining since 1998 due to sectoral restructuring and the consequent importations of agricultural produce. Nonetheless agriculture contributes about 12 per cent to GDP (Figure 3.1) and provides a livelihood for more than 2.5 million people. Restructuring started in 2003. Livestock farming (cattle, poultry and horses) has been downsized and crop production expanded. Wheat, barley and maize, which are mainly ground in northern Kazakhstan, account for more than 50 per cent of the revenue from agriculture. Other important crops are potatoes, rice and soybeans. Kazakhstan is also the world's largest exporter of pomegranate juice. Figure 3.3 provides a breakdown of agricultural production in 1998–2004.

The contribution made to the economy by the service sector has increased as many new types of service, for example insurance, have found their way into Kazakh life. In 2004 services grew by 6.9 per cent.

The energy sector is well developed but there is still a need for imports. The sector was opened to privatization in 1996 and today about 95 per cent of power-generating facilities are privately owned. However the state has retained control of transmission and distribution.

The transportation infrastructure needs further development and is high on the agenda of the Kazakh government and the governments of other Central Asian countries that are aiming to share and leverage resources and construction capabilities.

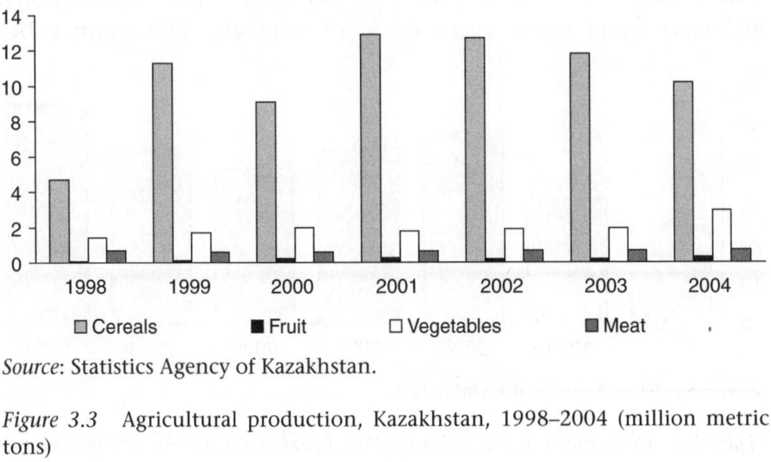

Source: Statistics Agency of Kazakhstan.

Figure 3.3 Agricultural production, Kazakhstan, 1998–2004 (million metric tons)

In the banking sector several commercial bank have been established, both state-owned and private. The sector is still in the process of transformation and consolidation. In 1993 there were 220 banks but by the end of 2001 their number had fallen to 45. The majority of commercial banking services are controlled by four banks: Kazkommerts Bank, Halyk Savings Bank, Turan Alem Bank (part of Astana Holdings) and the Dutch bank ABN-AMRO. Kazkommerts Bank, which has a good reputation for domestic and international banking (*Global Finance*, 2001), is owned by the Kazkommerts Group. The latter also controls pension funds and the airline industry and has international joint ventures in oil refining. After the Russian financial crisis of 1998 the government imposed strict supervisory measures on the operations of the banking sector and the state stock exchange.

Since the late 1990s there has been sustained annual economic growth of about 9 per cent, as measured by annual GDP change, and Kazakhstan has been the fastest growing economy in the CIS. Inflation is less than 7 per cent and unemployment is under control. Government tax revenues are growing and the US$3 billion surplus from oil tax revenues is managed by a national fund. The average annual growth rate of foreign trade is 20 per cent, with export revenues exceeding the value of imports. There has been a consistent effort to increase exports to Russia, the rest of the CIS and China. The contribution of exports to GDP has been on the rise since 2002 (Figure 3.4). Some key economic indicators for the period 2000–5 are shown in Table 3.1.

Kazakhstan's strong and consistent macroeconomic performance and financial viability has enabled it repay its debt to the International Monetary Fund seven years ahead of schedule. The country has

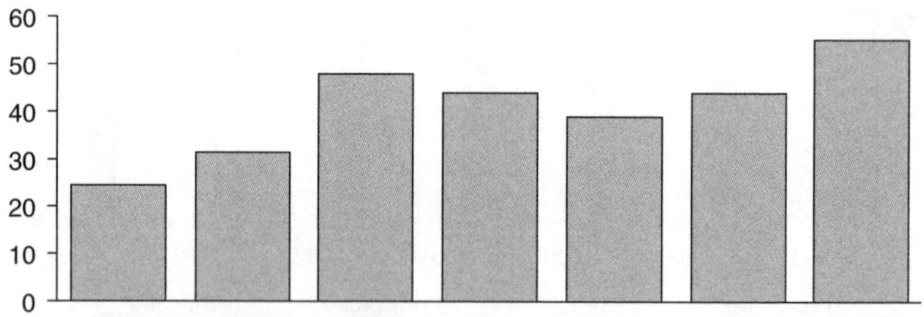

Source: Statistics Agency of Kazakhstan.

Figure 3.4 Contribution of exports to GDP, Kazakhstan, 1998–2004 (per cent)

Table 3.1 Economic indicators, Kazakhstan, 2000–5

	2000	*2001*	*2002*	*2003*	*2004*	*2005*
GDP (US$ billion)	18.3	22.2	24.6	30.8	40.7	54.0
GDP per capita (US$)	1,230.0	1,490.0	1,660.0	2,060.0	2,710.0	3,580.0
Exports (% of GDP)	57.0	46.5	47.2	48.6	56.5	61.4
Inflation (%)	13.4	8.6	6.2	6.5	6.9	7.2
Unemployment (%)	12.8	10.5	9.4	8.8	8.4	7.8

Source: Statistics Agency of Kazakhstan.

demonstrated a commitment to continuous reform of the economy and financial sector, currency convertibility, openness to Eastern and Western foreign investment and effective government control over the means of production and allocation of resources. Its investment credibility has risen and many private and public international financial organizations have been willing to provide business development loans.

Similar to the prevailing Asian economic model, the emphasis is on export-led growth based on fuel and raw materials. This is supplemented by import-substitution through differentiation of the national economy. The approach prioritizes key economic sectors instead of leaving it to the market to determine the developmental path and growth of the economy. The degree of state intervention in the economy has been sharply criticized by the International Monetary Fund and the World Bank, which see it as a major impediment to growth and development. Nevertheless the Kazakh government believes that it should promote local production and support domestic business growth before opening the economy to unrestricted foreign competition.

Domestic conglomerates and conglomerates with domestic and foreign capital have interests in diverse sectors of the economy. For example Astana Holdings has invested in the banking sector, real estate, the automotive industry, and food processing. Apart from its financial operations the Eurasia Bank has investments in the metallurgical industry. The Rahat Group has a highly diverse portfolio that includes sugar refining, liquor production and distribution, media operations, television stations, and significant oil investments. All major domestic businesses strive to improve their international competitiveness by strengthening their financial operations. From a domestic perspective these conglomerates make local businesses financially more viable.

Membership of economic blocs

Kazakhstan is a member of a number of regional blocs: the Organization of the Islamic Conference (OIC), the Economic Cooperation Organization (ECO), the CIS, the Eurasian Economic Community, the Shanghai Cooperation Organization (SCO), the Central Asia Cooperation Organization (CACO), and the Special Program for the Economies of Central Asia (SPECA).

The OIC was set up in 1969 in Morocco to promote Islamic solidarity by fostering economic, political, cultural and scientific cooperation among Islamic countries. Kazakhstan joined in 1995. By 2005 the OIC had 57 members and had made good progress in political, economic and educational cooperation.

The ECO was established in 1985 by Iran, Pakistan and Turkey. In 1992 they were joined by Afghanistan, Azerbaijan, Kazakhstan, Kyrgyzstan, Tajikistan, Turkmenistan, and Uzbekistan. The purpose of the ECO is to achieve sustainable economic development of the member countries through mutually beneficial cooperation. However the results so far have been poor and the effect on the economic development of Kazakhstan has been insignificant. The principal obstacles are the countries' similar degree of economic development and their strong reliance on the production of primary products, which has hampered interorganizational trade.

The CIS, whose headquarters are in Minsk in Belarus, is a community of independent countries that formerly belonged to the Soviet Union. It was founded by the heads of state of Belarus, Russia and Ukraine in December 1991, immediately after the collapse of the Soviet Union. At the end of 1991 Armenia, Azerbaijan, Kazakhstan, Kyrgyzstan, Moldova, Tajikistan, Turkmenistan, and Uzbekistan became members, and when Georgia joined in 1993 this meant that the CIS comprised all the former Soviet republics but the Baltic countries, which are now members of the European Union. The purpose of the CIS is to coordinate the foreign and economic policies of its members while retaining national independence and sovereignty. Since the founding of the CIS a free-market rouble zone has been established and a joint defense force set up. At the CIS summit in 2003 Belarus, Kazakhstan, Russia, and Ukraine agreed to form a unified economic space in which all trade tariffs would be removed and key economic areas harmonized.

The Eurasian Economic Community, which consists of Belarus, Kazakhstan, Kyrgyzstan, Tajikistan, Russia, and Uzbekistan, was set up by Belarus and Russia in 1995. The intention was to integrate the member countries' economic, scientific, educational, cultural, social, political and military spheres while respecting their individual sovereignty. In 1999 the community started to function as a customs union. In 2002 Moldova and Ukraine were granted observer status, as was Armenia in 2003. The proposed merger of the community with the CACO has made little progress to date. Apart from functioning as a customs union the community members have joined forces to secure membership of the World Trade Organization.

In 1994 Kazakhstan, Kyrgyzstan and Uzbekistan created the Central Asia Economic Union (CAEU). When Tajikistan joined in 1998 the CAEU was renamed the Central Asian Economic Community (CAEC), and in 2002 it became the Central Asia Cooperation Organization (CACO). The CACO functions as a customs union but there is also cooperation in the combating of terrorism, in politics and in military activities. President Nazarbayev of Kazakhstan has called for a deepening of the cooperation among the CACO members and for better progress to be made with the unification of the CACO with the Eurasian Economic Community.

The SCO was set up in 1996 by China, Kazakhstan, Kyrgyzstan, Russia, and Tajikistan. Uzbekistan joined in 2001. This cooperative agreement aims to provide the necessary conditions for economic, scientific, technological, educational, environmental and political cooperation. In practice, however, it has focused mainly on regional security and is only gradually expanding into economic activities.

Foreign trade

Kazakhstan's membership of the economic blocs has facilitated its international trade. It is well advanced in its membership negotiations with the World Trade Organization (WTO) and the fact-finding phase of the process was completed in 2003. The major impediment to WTO membership is the slow enactment of key reforms in Kazakhstan's foreign trade regime in order to comply with the WTO's trading norms. Meanwhile many bilateral agreements have been signed, including the US–Kazakhstan Bilateral Trade Agreement of 1993.

The trade regime is gradually being liberalized. Currently the average-weighted import tariff is in the area of 10 per cent. To promote trade, value-added tax (VAT) was reduced from 16 per cent to 15 per cent in 2004. All imported products are subject to VAT on their duty value at the time of importation, except for oil and oil products from Russia because VAT is applied to them before their exportation.

Imported fast moving consumer goods excluding food products are subject to the temporary import regime and may be fully or partially exempt from duties, taxes and non-tariff measures. Food products, industrial waste and consumables are not eligible for duty exemption.

In 2004 Kazakhstan's trade with all its trading partners grew, with exports reaching US$20 billion and imports US$13 billion (a growth of more than 55 per cent in comparison with their values in 2003). Since the mid 1990s there has been a clear reorientation of international trade away from the CIS countries and towards Western Europe. Exports still consist mostly of primary products based on the country's rich raw resources. Meanwhile the importation of goods has not been restricted and imports have gained a substantial share of some market segments, for example imported goods now have an 80 per cent or so share of the clothing market. The major threat to local producers comes from cheap Chinese imports aimed at the mass market and sold in established retail outlets and street markets. Kazakhstan is attempting to develop and upgrade its traditional textile, clothing and shoe industries, food processing and construction as an integral part of its import substitution policy, thus protecting local businesses and making better use of the abundant local resources.

To date Kazakhstan has tailed to develop large-scale trade with Western countries because Kazakh goods are not competitive in the world markets, despite the market and trade liberalization measures introduced in the first half of the 1990s. Currently the government is giving priority to local technological development to improve the competitiveness of knowledge-based industries. In addition revenues from oil exports are being invested in the communications and banking infrastructure to support further diversification into processing industries and the production of final goods with high value-added.

Black market trading of cheap imported goods from China, Kyrgyzstan and Russia by private retailers, also called 'suitcase trade' or *chelnochnaja*, was estimated at US$4 billion in 2002. This has severely damaged the sale of domestic manufactures and many textile, food processing and shoe making enterprises have gone bankrupt.

The main Kazakh exports are oil, precious stones and metals. Imports consist of machinery and equipment, ferrous products and some consumer goods. Kazakhstan's most important export and import partners include Russia, China and Germany. Russia has been a major trading partner since independence (NSA, 2005) and recently the significance of trade with European Union countries and China has increased considerably. The most important destinations for Kazakh goods and

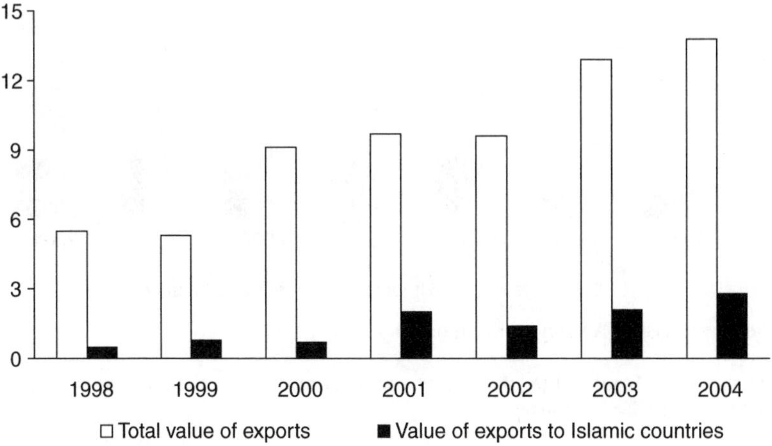

Source: Statistics Agency of Kazakhstan.

Figure 3.5 Value of exports, Kazakhstan, 1998–2004 (US$ billion)

services in 2004 were Bermuda (13.6 per cent of the total value of exports), Russia (13.5 per cent), China (10.2 per cent), Switzerland (9.1 per cent), and Germany (8.9 per cent). The significance of Islamic countries as export destinations has also increased (Figure 3.5). The main import partners in the same year were Russia (35.0 per cent of the total value of imports), China (12.9 per cent), Germany (9.1 per cent),

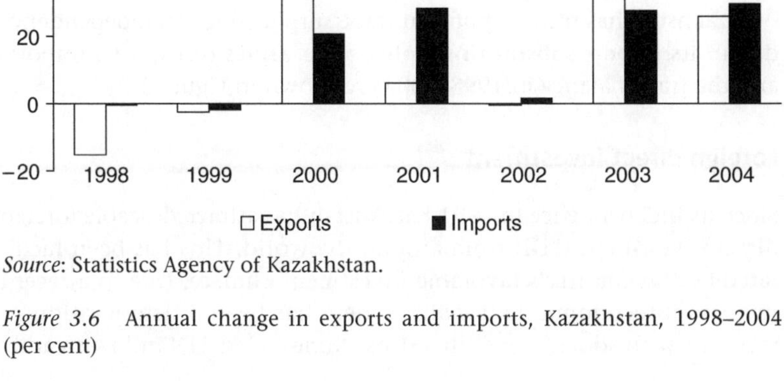

Source: Statistics Agency of Kazakhstan.

Figure 3.6 Annual change in exports and imports, Kazakhstan, 1998–2004 (per cent)

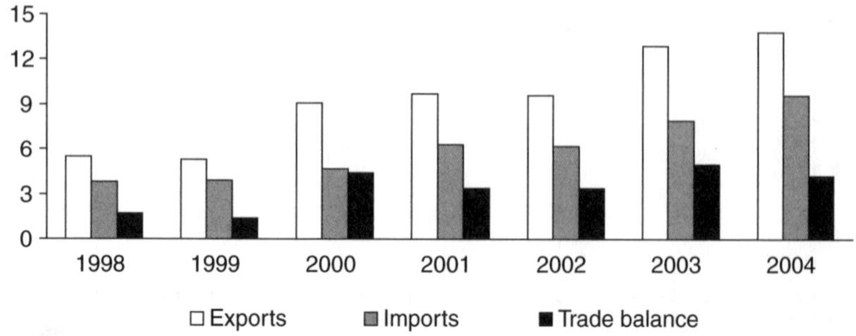

Source: Statistics Agency of Kazakhstan.

Figure 3.7 Total value of exports, imports and trade balance, Kazakhstan, 1998–2004 (US$ billion)

France (6.4 per cent), and Italy (3.4 per cent). Exports and imports have fluctuated considerably since 1998 (Figure 3.6). In 2005 the foreign trade turnover amounted to US$32.9 billion, 54.1 per cent higher than that in 2004.

Because the international competitiveness of Kazakh businesses is limited, policy makers view the country's natural resources as the most important pillar of the national economy in the short to medium term. Currently oil, iron and non-ferrous metals account for approximately 80 per cent of exports, while the share of industrial products in total exports has been in continuous decline. Grain exports vary according to weather conditions. Because of persistent problems in the agricultural sector the share of agricultural products in exports is likely to decline in the long term. Thus exports are being concentrated in an ever narrowing range of product categories with limited or no value added (Ribakova, 1998).

Kazakhstan has run a significant trade surplus since its independence due to its import substitution policy. The values of exports, imports and the trade balance in 1998–2004 are shown in Figure 3.7.

Foreign direct investment

Since its independence in 1991 Kazakhstan has attracted sizable foreign direct investment (FDI) from around the world. This has been facilitated by the country's favorable investment climate. Due to a recent increase in economic nationalism there has been a deterioration of relations with some foreign investors. Nonetheless FDI inflow steadily

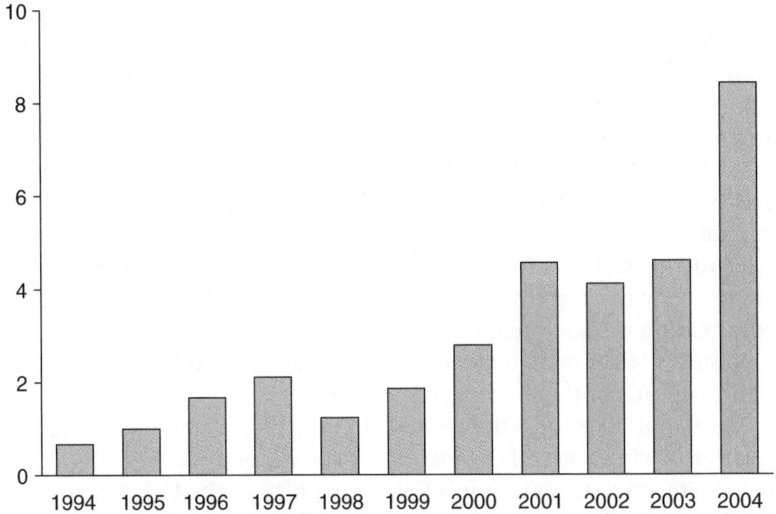

Source: National Bank of Kazakhstan.

Figure 3.8 Net FDI inflow, Kazakhstan, 1994–2004 (US$ billion)

increased over the years, apart from a dip in 1998 (Figure 3.8). The largest annual increases took place in 2001 and 2004.

During the Asian financial crisis and because of the considerable government intervention in the economy some companies became less committed to investing in Kazakhstan or experienced difficulties with their operations. For example in the late 1990s the South Korean company Daewoo, a strategic investor in the state telecommunications company Kaztelecom, ceased to participate in the project.

At the end of 2004, cumulative FDI amounted to more than US$29 billion, or about four fifths of the total FDI flow into the Central Asian region. Cumulative per capita FDI in Kazakhstan at the end of 2005 was more than US$2100, the highest among the members of the CIS. The principal motive for investing in the Kazakh oil, mine and metallurgical industries is to gain access to resources. In processing industries this is combined with a market-seeking drive because of several factors. First, as a stable country that is in transition to a market economy, Kazakhstan is seen as a leading market for the Central Asian region. Second, importing consumer goods to Kazakhstan proved unprofitable because of the high transportation costs (due to the long distances and poor transportation infrastructure) and the low purchasing power of the average Kazakh consumer. Therefore upgrading the existing or creating new local production facilities for consumer products to be sold in the domestic and neighboring markets is now viewed as the most appropriate business strategy by both the Kazakh government and foreign and domestic investors. FDI in the processing industry increased more than 22 told between 1993 and 2003, rising from US$44.7 million to US$1.035 billion, and the processing industry has become the second most popular investment vehicle for foreign capital.

While all sectors of the economy are open to foreign investment there are ownership restrictions in telecommunications, banking and information media: foreign investors are not permitted to have ownership stakes larger than 49 per cent, 25 per cent and 20 per cent in companies in each of these sectors respectively.

The major investor is the United States, which accounts for about a quarter of cumulative FDI, mainly in the oil and gas industry. Two other large investors are South Korea (one fifth of the FDI inflow since 1991) and the United Kingdom, which holds about one eighth of the FDI stock. Russia and China also invest substantial amounts, and China has become the third largest foreign investor in the oil and gas industries.

Around 50 per cent of cumulative FDI (US$15.4 billion) has been poured into the oil industry. Half of this investment has gone into the Tengizchevroil international joint venture in the enormous Tengiz oilfield. The same amount of foreign capital has been injected into the ferrous metal sector. The energy sector, non-ferrous metal and food processing industries have received much smaller capital inflows.

The territorial distribution of FDI is skewed to the west, where the main oil and gas fields are located. Central Kazakhstan, which is rich in ferrous and non-ferrous metals, received about two sevenths of the total FDI inflow. East Kazakhstan, which has abundant deposits of precious metals, mostly gold, received about one ninth of the FDI flow.

Various factors have contributed to the growth of FDI. In the mid 1990s macroeconomic stabilization attracted new foreign investors and additional investment from existing ones. The government's privatization program allowed foreign companies to acquire large state-owned plants and factories at low prices. In addition the government provided various incentives to encourage investment in some high-priority sectors. Joint ventures have been preferred by foreign investors due to restrictions imposed by government policies and the high country risk. In 1999 there were 1,865 companies with foreign capital. By 2003 this number had increased to 6,579 and in 2004 it rose to 7070. Some of these joint ventures were important to the growth of economic activities. Among the major foreign investors are Chevron Texaco, Exxon Mobil, Phillips Petroleum, LG Electronics, Coca-Cola, the Volkswagen Group, Knauf, Samsung Electronics, and Mittal Steel (Kazinvest, 2004).

FDI has also stimulated technology transfer and capacity building. The government requires foreign investors to establish supply relations with domestic firms. For instance the Karachaganak Integrating Organization, a consortium of American, British, Italian and Russian companies, has signed more than 400 contracts with local companies for the supply of goods and services required for the development of oil fields in western Kazakhstan. In the mining industry such relations have led to enhancement of the technological and management capabilities of local companies. Important participants in this regard are the KazZinc and Shymkent Lead Plant (lead and zinc), Aluminum Kazakhstan, which owns two bauxite mines and the Pavlodar Aluminum Plant, and the Kazakh Manganese and Ust-Kamenogorsk Metallurgical Conglomerate (manganese and titanium).

When Kazkhstan gained independence the US oil company Chevron (later Chevron Texaco), which had formerly conducted regular transactions with the Soviet government, signed a production-sharing agreement with the Kazakh government that gave it exploration rights over the bulk of the country's oil fields. In order to counterbalance this monopoly the government encouraged other multinational corporations to invest. Thus in 1993 the newly created Offshore Kazakhstan International Operating Company (OKIOC), consisting of nine multinational companies (BP-Amoco, British Gas, ENI, Inpex, Mobil, Philips, Royal Dutch/Shell, Statoil, and Total), began oil and gas exploration in the northern part of the Caspian Sea. In 2001 the OKIOC was renamed the Agip Kazakhstan North Caspian Operating Company (Agip KCO). In February 2004 a consortium of international oil companies (ENI, Royal Dutch/Shell, Exxon Mobil, Total, ConocoPhillips, and Inpex) invested US$2.9 billion in the development of the rich Kashagan oil field. The total oil reserves of this field are estimated at 13 billion barrels. This venture is expected not only to earn steady revenues for the companies involved but also to deliver high tax payments by the consortium to the Kazakh state.

In 1996 Access Industries of the United States invested more than US$40 million for the upgrading of two coal mines parts of the giant Ekibastuz mining complex owned by the Kazakh government and Access Industries. In 1995 the Dutch LNM Group purchased the Karaganda metal refiming plant (KARMET) for US$225 million and by the end of 2000 had invested US$450 million in technological upgrading and expansion. The plant was later renamed Ispat-Karmet. Today more than 95 per cent of Ispat-Karmet's output is exported to 67 countries worldwide.

Driven by market-seeking motives, in 1993 the US tobacco giant Philip Morris signed an agreement with the Almaty Tobacco Company to invest US$350 million over a period of five years. In 2000 Philip Morris invested a further US$200 million in a new cigarette manufacturing plant in Almaty Oblast with an annual production capacity of over 25 billion cigarettes. In 1993 a US$20 billion international joint venture, Tengiz-ChevrOil (TCO), was set up by Chevron (holding a 50 per cent share) Exxon Mobil (25 per cent), Kazakhstan (20 per cent), and LucArco (5 per cent). The TCO is also a major shareholder in the Caspian Pipeline Consortium that transports crude oil from the Tengiz oil field to world markets via southern Russia and the Black Sea. In line with the terms of the production-sharing contract between the Kazakh government and Chevron the multinational conglomerate has participated in large infrastructural projects in the desert regions of western Kazakhstan.

Foreign companies in the consumer market

Foreign consumer-good companies view the Kazakh market as relatively liberal. They are certainly subject to fewer regulations and constraints than foreign companies that invest in the country's natural resources. A number of foreign multinationals, including Coca-Cola, Colgate-Palmolive, L'Oreal, Nabisco, and Unilever, have gradually established a presence and are providing goods that were previously not available or in limited supply. Foreign multinationals now compete against each other in such product categories as packaged food, cosmetics and household appliances. Promotion and aggressive selling have become crucial to success. The soft drinks market became a battlefield between Pepsi-Co, which had had a well-established position in the former Soviet market, and the world market leader Coca-Cola. By means of a massive promotional campaign that simultaneously targeted Kazakhs, Russians and all other ethnic groups, Coca-Cola managed to gain market share from Pepsi-Co.

Putting a strong emphasis on sponsorship, Procter and Gamble has gained a significant market share by developing an overall brand recognition that is not linked to particular products or product lines. The marketing strategy of the Japanese carmaker Toyota has concentrated on a tailored approach to clients, product reliability and durability, lengthy warranties, excellent after-sales service, and professional servicing and repairs (Smirnov, 2001).

Retailing

Little attention has been paid to the retail sector in Kazakhstan and as a consequence it is still mostly traditional and underdeveloped. There are three principal types of retail outlet:

- Kiosks offering a huge variety of goods can be found in groups in large open-air markets (bazaars). Their major offerings are beverages, snacks, cigarettes, sweets, and toiletries. Most of their goods come from China or Turkey.
- Large state-owned stores selling food, clothing and footwear to low-income consumers.
- Up-market stores selling a wide range of expensive imported goods. The domestic retail chain Butya in Almaty offers branded products from firms such as Adidas, Benetton, Gillette, Hugo Boss, Levi Strauss, Panasonic, and Sony.

Large-scale retail operations targeting the mass market are a fairly recent phenomenon that began in Almaty. The Turkish hypermarket chain Ramstore entered the market in the mid 1990s. It is a joint venture between the powerful Turkish conglomerate Koç Holdings and the domestic group Butya, which has a minority stake in the venture. Butya also has car dealerships, retail outlets and service companies and came into existence soon after Kazakhstan gained independence. It was founded by the Kazakh entrepreneur Bolat Abilov, a relative of the Kazakh president. The state-owned company Detsky Mir has modernized its premises and extended its offerings in order to fight foreign competition. It has also entered a franchise agreement with the Italian retailer Moschino. In Almaty and several other large cities there are Joop and Gianfranco Ferre franchises agreements. The Kazakh retailer Dastarkhan has a strong position in the consumer market of Almaty. The virtual lack of competition and the undersupplied market mean that there are good opportunities for foreign companies in the retailing sector.

Promotion

When Kazakhstan was a constituent republic of the Soviet Union promotional activities were informative and limited to radio and the print media. In the late 1950s television broadcasting began in the area of the former capital, Almaty, and advertisements became regular part of the programming. By the end of the 1960s television covered most of the urban areas of Kazakhstan. Color television was introduced at the beginning of the 1980s. Radio and television were broadcast in Kazakh and Russian languages. Programs for minority groups were provided at certain scheduled times on a weekly basis. By the 1990s three minority languages were spoken regularly in broadcasts: Uygur, German and Korean (Barlybaeva, 1995). All the media were state-owned and were managed, directed, coordinated, and monitored by officials in Moscow. When *Perestroika* was introduced by Mikhail Gorbachev in the 1980s a limited degree of local management became possible.

Since Kazakhstan's independence there has been a constant increase in the number and variety of promotional media. Liberalization and privatization resulted in significant changes in content and format and the ownership divisions between the media began to blur, with holding companies owning a portfolio of television, radio, print and outdoor media. Nowadays all the media are controlled by large conglomerates but there is little information on their ownership structure.

Television has been and still is the most important promotional medium. After independence the state-owned and controlled Kazakh State Television and Radio Broadcasting Company owned two television channels and three radio stations. Inter-Channel and the National TV Channel provided 18 hours of broadcasting a day. In 1993 a private television channel was set up, with its own transmitter and studio. Initially it only covered the Almaty area but six years later it achieved national coverage. Two other private television stations, Tan-TV and TVIN, were established but these were limited in terms of programming, air time and terrestrial coverage.

Since the mid 1990s the most influential domestic television broadcaster has been Khabar TV, whose programs reflect government policy. A number of television stations owned by Russians, Uzbeks and Kyrgiz broadcast in the respective languages. These are also several cable and terrestrial commercial stations that cover the major urban conurbations and in recent years rural towns have attracted the attention of media investors. The media are generally perceived as conforming to the interests of those in state power (Mukatayev, 1995).

The print media and television are the most popular means of promotion, followed by radio. The most important radio station is the government-owned Kazakh Radio, which broadcasts in nine languages that are spoken in Kazakhstan or neighboring countries. Private radio stations have mushroomed and by 2005 there were more than 50, all with national coverage. According to official estimates there are about 400 radio sets per 1000 inhabitants.

The last 15 years have witnessed the rise of a new medium: the video salon. Video salons, representing exhibitions of movies and videos with massive advertising have become quite popular with Kazakhs and by the end of 2004 there were more than 5000 in 12 cities. Print media are very popular – about 50 daily newspapers and 30 monthly or quarterly magazines are published in Almaty alone. In spite of the low purchasing power of the average Kazakh consumer, brand awareness is high due to the intense advertising campaigns conducted by the large multinational companies that serve the Kazakh market. The most influential advertisements are believed to be those that appear in the Russian editions of the magazines *Playboy* and *Marie Claire*. Every regional city has at least one daily newspaper and dozens of weekly periodicals. Small domestic businesses often cannot afford the cost of advertising so the government provides subsidies for the purpose. Moreover all television and print media are exempt from value added tax (IREX, 2003).

The daily newspaper *Zhas Alash*, established in 1921, is published in Kazakh and has a circulation of 135 000. The most widely circulated dailies in Russian are *Kazakhstanskaya Pravda* and *Karavan*. The weekly *Karavan* has the largest readership and is the best vehicle for advertising consumer goods for the mass market. The daily *Times of Central Asia* and the *Almaty Herald*, both of which are in English and are widely read, provide political information and carry some advertisements for consumer products of interest to foreign residents of Kazakhstan.

There are no periodicals that specialize in advertising but all have a section dedicated to advertisements. Advertisements in daily newspapers target the mass market while those in magazines target people with particular lifestyles or special interests. They are mostly to do with fashion, sport, health, and hobbies.

Advertising has recently been introduced in cinemas, but its impact is limited to young cosmopolitan consumers. There is some outdoor advertising on billboards, rooftops and pylons but this has negative connotations in that it is associated with the ideological propaganda, slogans and image of the Soviet era. Only about 10 per cent of the population has access to the Internet and the latter is only available in the big cities. Consumers in small towns and villages rely mostly on information provided by the state-controlled television and radio stations.

As implied earlier the media strongly reflect the economic and political interests of the state. The Ministry of Information oversees all media activities and is in change of registering, licensing and accrediting private media operations. Broadcasting licenses are awarded by tender. The Media Law regulates the advertising industry. There are strict rules for television and radio advertising and Internet advertising is closely monitored too. Advertisements must not take up more than 15 per cent of a specified broadcasting time and must not interrupt statements by state officials or educational, religious and children's programs. The advertising of alcohol is prohibited and tobacco can only be advertised on the inside pages of print media. Such government restrictions are intended to protect consumers from advertisements that are insensitive to local cultural norms.

Reardon *et al.* (2005) argue that Kazakh consumers have a high degree of ethnocentrism and show animosity towards advertising and foreign branded products. It can be suggested that this is due to the country's lower level of economic development, the early stage of the transition to a market economy, limited consumer exposure to foreign advertisements, and a preference for advertisements that focus on the quality and functional properties of products rather than appealing to the emotions.

Western companies operating in the Kazakh market tend to engage in aggressive advertising applying sophisticated marketing techniques. For instance when Unilever entered the market it advertised massively on television and in the print media, and engaged in public relations campaigns, direct sales, and outdoor advertising for several months. This helped the company gain a significant market share in a short period of time.

In 2005 the revenue from advertising was estimated at US$130 million, three quarters of which was generated by television advertising. The bulk of television expenditure is accounted for by multinational corporations and large Kazakh companies such as Air Kazakhstan. Media conglomerates provide most of the work for advertising agencies. Private businesses also support small-scale advertising companies that mostly promote private business interests. Advertising in the regional media generates about 10 per cent of television advertising revenues and up to 6 per cent of newspaper and magazine revenues.

Market research agencies are available but are barely affordable by small and medium-sized companies. Due to the high costs only multinationals and a few domestic conglomerates use the services of market research agencies on a regular basis. The market is dominated by the media group owned by the president's daughter, Dariga Nazarbayeva.

This includes Khabar, Kazakh Telekompany, National Telekompany, and ORT of Kazakhstan. Advertising and public relations agencies are a relatively new arrival but their number has increased substantially since 2000.

Kazakhstan hosts annual trade shows, the most important of which is the Kazakhstan International Oil and Gas Exhibition, which is held every October in Almaty. Others are the Consumer Expo in April, the Kazakhstan International Health Exhibition in May, and the Kazakhstan International Telecommunications Exhibition in June.

Procurement

Most procurement for public institutions is conducted by government-organized tender. Under the terms of the national procurement legislation, small domestic companies have preferential treatment in the tendering process. Newspapers carry invitations to tender one or two months before the closing date. The application must be written in Russian or Kazakh. Foreign companies need to have a local distributor or agent with good government contacts to monitor tender announcements in the press and participate in the tendering process. Procurement is also conducted by major foreign investors, mainly in the oil sector. These investors are expected to develop facilities in the areas in which they operate including facilities for healthcare and social and recreational activities.

Distribution

Developing a marketing strategy that is tailor-made for the Kazakh market is of crucial importance to the success of businesses. Foreign firms must pay special attention to local market requirements and provide support to their local representatives in terms of marketing intelligence and financial backing.

Currently there are about 30 well-established importers and wholesale distributors, which are mostly located in Almaty or Astana. The distribution of many product categories is controlled by state-owned companies, for example the distribution of newspapers and magazines is handled by the state-owned company Kazbaspasoz. Many importing companies provide their Russian-based distribution representatives with the exclusive right to distribute throughout the CIS. In terms of both consumer and industrial products, Kazakhstan is regarded as a small market with limited potential so Russian-based foreign distributors tend to pay little attention to it. This has resulted in considerable grey- or black-market trade throughout the country. Thus engaging local distributors is highly recommended. Recently the distribution and telecommunications networks have been expanded and improved.

Foreign companies operating in Kazakhstan use a variety of marketing methods, including direct marketing, working through a countrywide distributor or agent, making contractual arrangements with more than one local area distributor or agent, and distributing or selling products directly from a centrally located warehouse. Direct marketing has recently gained in popularity, especially in the large cities. Popular forms of direct marketing are the provision of free samples at points of sale, organizing and selling at major cultural events, and door-to-door sales. Mail order retailing is of limited appeal as the country's postal system is regarded as unreliable by foreign investors.

Franchising

Franchising is a new concept in Kazakhstan and is still in the introductory phase. The government has officially sanctioned franchising as a desirable and useful strategy for business development. Assistance is provided by several organizations, including the Kazakhstan Franchise Association, which helps with the formation and functioning of franchise operations.

However the nature of the Kazakh market puts limits on the development of franchising. For example the small population is spread over a vast territory, which restricts market reach and prevents the full realization of market potential. Also, setting up a franchise operation requires significant effort and expense in terms of training and educating local partners. Moreover the Kazakh certification and standardization systems set limits on the transfer of any technological equipment needed for a franchise as it has to comply with the local testing requirements and national standards. Despite all this there are many advantages to franchising, including the opportunity it offers for business expansion by using Kazakhstan as a good stepping stone to the large market of Central Asia.

The legal terms for franchising are still being developed. The Law on Franchising, which was passed in June 2000, addresses the legal right of the franchisor to control the franchisee's business operations and the franchisor's right to purchase the franchise back from the franchisee should the latter decide to cease operating. Intellectual property rights and compensation for damages in the event of confidential information being disclosed to third parties are also covered by the law. However the law is seen as rather lax and lacking important provisions on key areas of international franchise agreements. Because of this it has attracted strong domestic and international criticism. As there are not provisions in Kazakh law to address dispute settlements the Kazakhstan Franchise Association (KFA) recommends that the International Arbitrage Center of the World Intellectual Property Organization be approached to resolve disputes over franchise contracts.

In 2004 the KFA estimated that there were 55 franchise businesses in Kazakhstan, most of them in Almaty. They include RamButya, (a Ramstore retail chain operated by the local retailer Butya), World Class (fitness centers) and Bhs (a clothing retailer).

To aid the establishment of franchise operations the ATF Bank, in cooperation with the KFA, offers low-interest loans to domestic franchises. In 2004 the bank started to provide funds to Kazakh companies that wished to obtain licenses for international branding.

Company marketing

Marketing at the company level started in the mid 1990s with the entry of foreign businesses. The strong governmental control over the functioning of the economy has had an adverse effect on the application of the marketing concept and the creation and use of marketing departments by domestic and foreign companies serving the Kazakh market. Kleindl and Liu (2005) have studied the marketing practices and market orientation of companies operating in China, Hungary, Kazakhstan, and the United States. A summary of their findings on the market orientation of companies in Kazakhstan is presented in Table 3.2.

It is clear that market orientation is in its infancy in Kazakhstan and that companies are still with mostly production orientation. A sales orientation is gradually taking root in the rather underdeveloped service sector and limited marketing is being conducted by companies in the extraction, mining, manufacturing and service industries.

Companies tend to price their products according to what the market can stand. As the average purchasing power of the population is low, prices are also low by Western standards. On the whole, imported or locally produced Western consumer products and brands are more expensive than equivalent goods produced by domestic firms and firms from Central Asia, Southeast Asia, and Russia. Thus the average Kazakh consumer's ability to purchase Western products and brands is severely limited, and when developing their marketing

Table 3.2 Market orientation of companies in Kazakhstan

	Characteristics	*Comparative evaluation*	*Reasons for the observed characteristics*
Company management	No significant customer focus, low customer orientation	Lower customer orientation than in China and Hungary	Largely state controlled economy
Management commitment	Low to very low	Lower than in China and Hungary	Unrecognized need
Environmental analysis	Very limited	Similar to practices in China	Unrecognized need
Level of competition	Low	Similar to that in China	Limited number of competitors (mostly oligarchic or monopolistic industrial structure)
Environmental stability	High	Higher than in China and Hungary	Significant preservation of the former economic structures and substantial government control over economic activities
Impact of ownership on market orientation	No change	In Hungary private firms perform substantially better than state-owned companies	Prevailing state ownership

Source: Based on findings in Kleindl and Liu (2005).

strategy Western companies must take into account the strong competition from other countries.

Key components of price that should be considered by foreign companies intending to enter the Kazakh market are transportation costs, import duties, certification payments, and the costs associated with the high expectation of profits by importers and distributors. The average import tariff is about 10 per cent, but specific aspects of the border-crossing procedures have substantial financial implications. All imported products are subject to a value added tax of 15 per cent, and this has to be paid on top of all customs duties and excise taxes at the time of customs clearance. Customs regulations tend to change constantly. That is, international trade-related procedures, lists of goods that are subject to mandatory licensing, and technically specific issues are under constant revision and customs officials tend to apply regulations selectively and arbitrarily. While the State Customs Committee has recently begun to computerize the customs operations, considering all the problems associated with customs clearance, importers are advised to use the services of a customs broker.

Conclusion

Kazakhstan is an emerging market that is attractive to foreign investors because of its abundant natural resources. Its economic potential mostly lies in the extraction and processing industries but the developing manufacturing sector offers opportunities for diversification. The government has firm control over all economic activities and imposes restrictions on modes of market entry and foreign ownership. The economy is dominated by diversified conglomerates with national and foreign capital.

The international competitiveness of Kazakh products is limited as the low value-added outputs from the manufacturing sector find it difficult to meet international quality standards. The government has recognized that the technological and innovative capabilities of domestic industries are deficient and has therefore encouraged foreign participation in ventures that involve the transfer of technology and know-how. The foreign presence in Kazakhstan is mainly restricted to joint ventures with local businesses, although some franchises are now being established.

Kazakhstan is a member of several regional blocs that are designed to promote cooperation in economic, political, social and military projects. Future membership of the WTO will boost international trade and investment. Exports of natural resources go to Europe and the United States, and to satisfy China's rapidly growing demand for fuel and raw materials. Manufactures and agricultural exports predominately go to the CIS members, other Islamic countries and China. The latter has also recognized the investment potential offered by Kazakhstan and by the end of 2005 it had become the third largest source of FDI.

The consumer market is relatively small and scattered over a vast territory. The infrastructure is underdeveloped, the purchasing power of consumers is low and their response to marketing campaigns is somewhat limited. Kazakhs tend to be very price sensitive, highly ethnocentric and express animosity toward foreign brands, apart from a small number of affluent consumers.

Distribution and retailing are a mixture of facilities from the Soviet past, traditional open-air bazaars and new retail chains in the large urban areas. Foreign presence in retailing is insignificant and predominantly takes the form of franchising. The only foreign retailer that has entered the market via FDI is the Turkish company Koç Holdings, which has set up the Ramstore hypermarket chain via a joint venture with the domestic group Butya. The retail market is expected to grow in line with the purchasing power of consumers.

References

Barlybaeva, S. (1995) 'Radio and television of Kazakhstan: a review in context in the Asian communication system', *Journal of Development Communication*, 2 (6), pp. 48–55.

Dailey, M. and V. Cardozier (1989) *Higher Education in Russia* (www.utexas.edu/students/heaspa/library/rus.htm).

International Research and Exchanges Board (IREX) (2003) *Media Sustainability Index: Kazakhstan* (www.irex.org/msi/2003/MSI03-Kazakhstan.pdf).

Kazakhstan Investment Promotion (Kazinvest) (2003) *Investor's Guide 2003* (Almaty: Kazakhstan Investment Promotion Center).

Kazakhstan Investment Promotion (Kazinvest) (2004) *Investor's Guide 2004* (Almaty: Kazakhstan Investment Promotion Center).

Kleindl, B. and S. Liu (2005) *Marketing practice in transition economies: A four-nation study of market orientation* (www.mis.org.sg/ajm2005/AJM0405).

Mukatayev, A. (1995) 'The press of independent Kazakhstan needs help and support', *Journal of Central Asian Media Studies*, 1 (1), p. 23.

National Statistics Agency of Kazakhstan (NSA) (2005) *Statistics Bulletin* (Astana: NSA).

Rao, D. and L. Rybina (2004) *Kazakhstan, capitalism and conscience: Metamorphosis of a former Soviet republic's business education* (www.ciber.gatech.edu/workingpaper/2003/04-020.pdf).

Reardon, J., C. Miller, I. Vida and I. Kim (2005) 'The effects of ethnocentrism and economic development on the formation of brand and ad attitudes in transitional economies', *European Journal of Marketing*, 20 (7/8), pp. 737–54.

Ribakova, T. (1998) 'Export performance of the economy of Kazakhstan', *Kazakhstan: Economic Trends*, 1 (1), pp. 20–31.

Smirnov, S. (2001) 'Is Tokyo problematic? The problem can easily be settled'. *The Globe* (Almaty), 5 October.

United States Commercial Service (USCS) (2005) *Doing Business in Kazakhstan: A Country Commercial Guide for U.S. Companies* (Washington, DC: USCS).

4
Marketing in the Maghreb Region

Marin Marinov

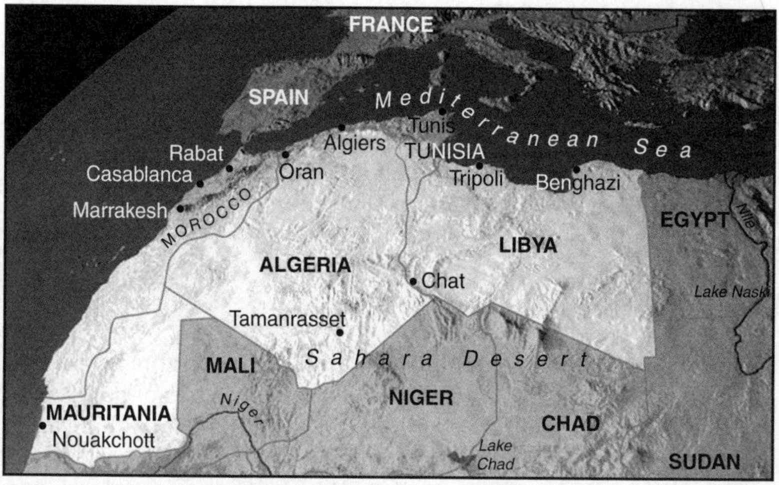

Source: www.maghreb-studies-association.co.uk/pix/map.jpg.

Map of the Maghreb region

Brief historical background

'Maghreb' is the old Arabic name for north-west Africa. The region consists of Algeria, Libya, Mauritania, Morocco, and Tunisia and is isolated from the rest of the African continent by the natural boundaries of the Sahara Desert and the Atlas Mountains.

The Maghreb was first inhabited by Cro-Magnoids and in about 8000 BC peoples of Afro-Asiatic descent, such as the Berbers, settled in.

Subsequently the Phoenicians, Carthaginians, Romans, Vandals, and Byzantines fought for power and dominance over the Maghreb coastline territories, where they set up their own provinces.

Following the Arab conquest in the eighth century AD and the spread of Islam, trade across the region flourished. In addition caravan stranding in salt, gold, ivory, and slaves travelled to and from Sub-Saharan Africa, the Middle East, and Europe.

From the late Middle Ages until the beginning of the nineteenth century most of Maghreb was ruled by the Ottoman Empire. This was followed by a period of colonization by France, Spain and Italy, which expanded their territory in search of resources and international influence. Algeria, Morocco, Mauritania, and Tunisia were French colonies until they gained independence after World War Two. Libya was annexed by Italy in 1912, placed under military government by the Allies during World War Two and became an independent monarchy at the beginning of the 1950s. In 1969 a military coup led by Colonel Muammar Abu Minyar al-Qaddafi established an Islamic state based on socialist principles. Only Morocco is ruled by a monarch. Algeria, Mauritania and Tunisia are republics. Thus the Maghreb peoples and cultures have Middle Eastern, European and African roots and influences, but nowadays are either Arabic- or Berber-speaking Muslims.

The regional economy

The economic and demographic indicators of the Maghreb countries are presented in Table 4.1. The largest country in terms of population and the strongest economy in the region is Algeria. For all indicators Mauritania is the poorest country in the region.

After gaining independence, all the Maghreb countries developed centrally planned economies based almost exclusively on the exploitation of raw materials. While Algeria adopted radical socialism and

Table 4.1 Economic and demographic indicators, Maghreb countries, 2004

	Population (million)	*GDP (US$ billion)*	*Real GDP growth (per cent)*	*Per capita GDP (US$)*
Algeria	32.5	83.1	5.0	2,620
Mauritania	2.8	1.2	4.1	443
Morocco	30.8	49.6	3.7	1,620
Tunisia	9.9	28.1	5.7	2,830

Sources: National statistics.

Tunisia a socialist ideology, Morocco opted for monarchic control. There was a high level of illiteracy and a lack of skilled workers in the countries so their economies depended on the exportation of raw materials and goods with very low value-added. That of Algeria relied mostly on oil and some agricultural exports.

In the 1970s the rising world prices of raw materials led to increased revenues and the beginning of industrial development, which in Algeria was combined with nationalization of the oil industry. Industrial development was largely based on import substitution and the protection of national industries. Financial policies encouraged investment by imposing negative real interest rates on savings deposits. Substantial investment in education and training upgraded the quality of the workforce. Economic growth was achieved via the extensive use of production factors rather than productivity improvements.

The terms of international trade deteriorated in the 1980s and caused considerable economic difficulties. The substantial economic distortions resulting from the import substitution policies led to reduced foreign trade. This situation was exacerbated by the falling prices of raw materials and the reduced global demand for agricultural and artisanal products. To overcome the crisis market principles were introduced. In the 1980s the Maghreb governments agreed to conform to International Monetary Fund's structural adjustment programs. This was met with discontent in some quarters because it involved the elimination of subsidies for local business development. The aim of the programs was to improve the competitiveness of Maghreb businesses and industries. Privatization programs were implemented and fiscal and monetary policies were made more transparent.

In the 1980s and 1990s some foreign capital made its way into the region, but Algeria resisted this and preferred to maintain its economic independence. Morocco and Tunisia created free trade zones to facilitate foreign trade and adjusted their investment laws to encourage foreign direct investment (FDI). However the limited domestic markets, political volatility, serious regulatory impediments and corruption acted as impediments to FDI. Foreign participation was mostly in the form of joint ventures or partially owned subsidiaries. There was very little greenfield investment in wholly owned subsidiaries. Algeria received a small amount of foreign investment in its hydrocarbon sector. Morocco enjoyed more significant FDI through privatization (the privatization of Maroc Télécom in 2001 raised US$2.1 billion) and the conversion of debt into investment. The clear winner in the FDI

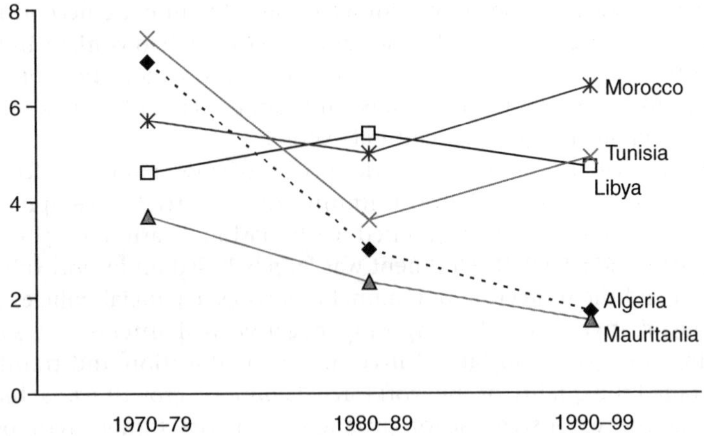

Sources: IMF statistics.

Figure 4.1 Average annual GDP growth rate, Maghreb countries, 1970–99 (per cent)

competition was Tunisia, which received more than 40 per cent of the cumulative foreign investment in the Maghreb region in 1980–2003.

Because of high unemployment and low living standards there are sizable informal sectors in all the countries and these are not reflected in the national statistics (Figure 4.1). Macroeconomic performance has been relatively stable over the last ten years. Inflation has been mostly kept at bay and the average annual growth of GDP has been in the range of 4–5 per cent. The economy in Algeria is dependent on oil revenues, whereas in the other countries it is based on a broader range of export items. The economies are relatively similar in respect of per capita GDP, apart from Mauritania, which has had a comparatively low annual growth rate. Algeria is in the lead, but Morocco and Tunisia are not far behind (Figure 4.2).

Unemployment continues to be a significant problem for all the regional economies. The limitations on trade and investment and the structural economic imbalances have restricted not only business development but also the creation of new jobs. The nomadic way of life of many people and women's confinement to running the household have also affected educational progress and employment. In 2004 the average unemployment rate for the Maghreb countries was 25.5 per cent, with Algeria and Mauritania having the highest rates (Figure 4.3).

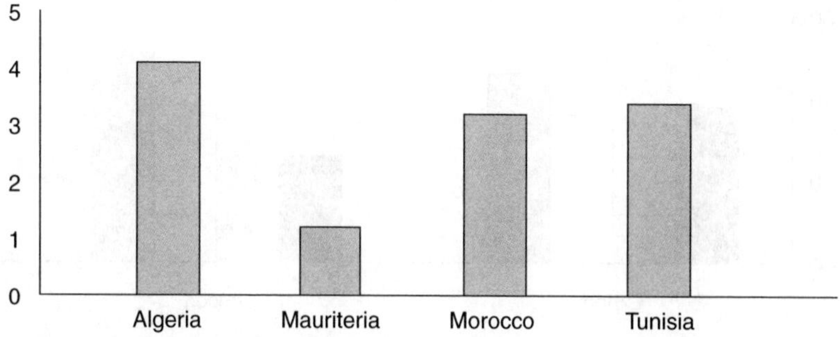

Sources: National statistics.

Figure 4.2 Per capita GDP growth, Maghreb countries, 2004 (per cent)

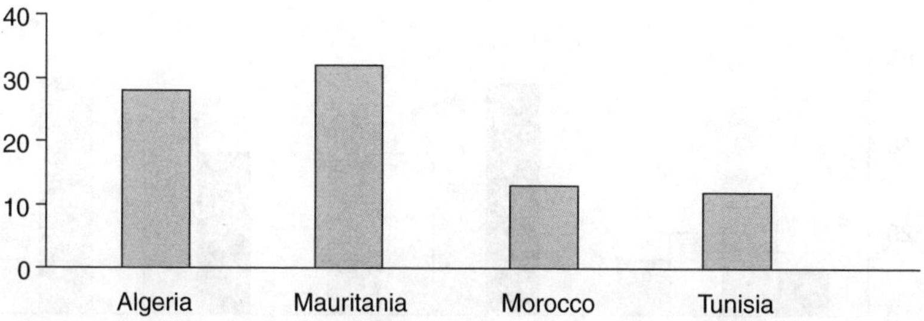

Sources: National statistics.

Figure 4.3 Unemployment rate, Maghreb countries, 2004 (per cent)

Because of the limited international competitiveness, maintaining a positive trade balance has proved difficult for the Maghreb countries. In 2004 only Algeria had a trade surplus. Mauritania had the highest trade deficit as a percentage of GDP but in absolute numbers Tunisia's deficit was the highest. (Figure 4.4)

The economic structure of the Maghreb countries differs and the relative contribution of agriculture, industry and services varies (Figure 4.5). The Algerian economy depends heavily on the industrial sector whereas the Mauritanian, Moroccan and Tunisian economies are mainly service based. Agriculture is a significant sector in Mauritania and least significant in Algeria.

The Algerian economy

Crude oil extraction has gradually increased in Algeria and the government predicts a further rise from 1.4 million barrels per day at the end

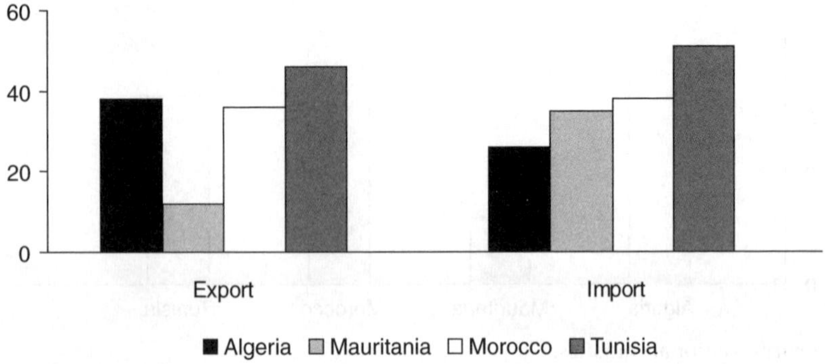

Sources: National statistics.

Figure 4.4 Exports and imports, Maghreb countries, 2004 (percentage of GDP)

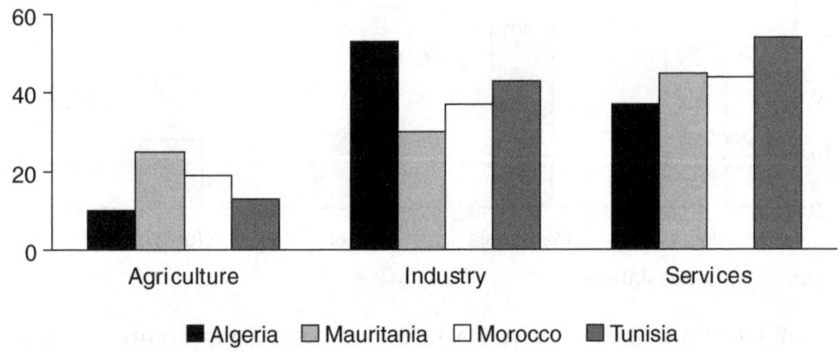

Sources: National statistics.

Figure 4.5 Structure of GDP, Maghreb countries, 2002 (per cent)

of 2004 to 2.0 million barrels by the end of 2010. Natural gas extraction is also expected to increase by more than 45 per cent in the same period, reaching 95 billion cubic meters per annum in 2010. Oil and gas are the main sources of export revenue (Table 4.2).

Table 4.2 Main exports and imports, Algeria, 2003 (US$ billion)

Exports	*Value*	*Imports*	*Value*
Crude oil	11.85	Capital goods	5.03
Natural gas	6.11	Food products	2.73
Condensate	4.18	Semifinished goods	2.44
Refined products	3.34	Consumer durables	2.23

Source: Algerian Ministry of Trade.

Table 4.3 Principal trading partners, Algeria, 2003 (percentage of total exports/imports)

Exports		*Imports*	
Italy	18.9	France	32.9
USA	17.9	Italy	10.2
France	13.2	Spain	6.5
Spain	10.9	Germany	6.1

Source: Algerian Ministry of Trade.

Imports for industry and the consumer market mostly come from Europe. Algeria's political, economic and cultural ties with France have resulted in the latter being its major trading partner, followed by Italy. In 2003 France, Italy, Spain, and Germany provided more than 55 per cent of imports in terms of value (Table 4.3). Similarly in 2003 more than 60 per cent of Algerian exports went to Italy, France, Spain, and the United States.

A 4300 kilometer gas pipeline, one of the longest in the world, is currently being constructed between Nigeria and Europe via Algeria. Utilities within the country are being expanded and a new electricity plant, scheduled to begin operating at the end of 2006, will satisfy 28 per cent of Algeria's energy requirement. Meanwhile the telecommunications industry is being modernized with investment from Kuwait and a huge factory for telecommunications equipment is being constructed with the help of Chinese joint venture capital. Foreign capital for joint ventures has also been provided by Germany for vehicle servicing facilities and by Kuwait for the upgrading of a vast state-owned pharmaceutical plant. However other flows of FDI to Algeria have been limited by terrorist threats and the low qualifications of local workers. Although unemployment has fallen in recent years it remains higher than the regional average.

Much of the economy is owned and run by the state, although it is planned to liberalize the largest sector – oil and gas – and transfer some ownership to private capital. The banks are controlled by the government and loans are mostly channeled to the loss-making public sector. The revenues from oil and gas sales are used for infrastructural improvements, to raise living standards and for investment in the manufacturing and service industries to improve their international competitiveness.

Algeria has an Association Agreement with the European Union and expects to become a member of the World Trade Organization in the near future. It is also a member of the Arab Maghreb Union, along with Libya, Mauritania, Morocco, and Tunisia. This union has had limited success because of political tensions and territorial disputes, mainly between Algeria and Morocco over Western Sahara.

Agriculture, most of which is in private hands, contributes 12 per cent to GDP and provides employment for 30 per cent of the Algerian workforce. Nevertheless Algeria imports more than 75 per cent of the food consumed in the country, spending over US$2.5 billion per year. The government provides financial help for the upgrading of internationally competitive small and medium-sized agribusinesses.

Most Algerians prepare and cook traditional food at home, although changes are slowly taking place in urban areas where mainly young households are adopting Western lifestyles. Many affluent urban consumers purchase home-cooked meals from housewives who need to supplement the family income. About 15 per cent of the population, mostly in rural areas, lives in extreme poverty on an income of less than US$35 per month.

Algeria has suffered gravely from Islamic insurgency. At present the situation is largely under control, with the exception of recurrent violence in the Berber region of Kabyila. The government is determined to suppress the fundamentalist forces.

The Libyan economy

The economy of Libya weakened during the 1990s and the early 2000s because of serious international confrontations and Libya's presence in the list of terrorist states. The economy is entirely dependent on oil. Oil export revenues have risen sharply in recent years, reaching US$28.3 billion in 2005. This was a five fold increase over the 1995 value. The lifting of the US and UN sanctions that were imposed on Libya after the bombing of Pan Am flight 103 over Lockerbie in Scotland has allowed a vast improvement in Libya's economic performance, producing a trade surplus of US$17.3 billion in 2005.

In 2005 GDP grew by about 6.7 per cent and consumer price inflation was below 3 per cent. Unemployment remains high. Control over the economy is highly centralized, which is impeding to foreign investment and more significant economic growth. The country has applied for membership of the World Trade Organization. Some liberalization and privatization has been attempted but with little success to date.

Libya intends to reduce its dependence on oil by investing in agriculture, fisheries, mining, natural gas, and tourism. Agriculture contributes less than 15 per cent to GDP but employs one fifth of the workforce. It mainly caters to the domestic market. This sector is a top priority of the government and it has invested US$30 billion in a project to bring water from aquifers beneath the Sahara to the Mediterranean coastal area. Crude oil exports go mostly to Europe. Crude oil and its derivatives account for almost 95 per cent of the value of total exports. Other exports include natural and manufactured gas, hydrocarbon products, and fertilizers. Imports mainly consists of industrial supplies, machinery, fresh and processed food, consumer durables, and transportation equipment.

Libya's main trading partners are Italy, Germany, Spain, France, and Turkey. Trade with its Maghreb neighbors, although important, is limited to about 7–8 per cent. Oil exports and imports of technological products dominate European trade, which accounts for about two thirds of the total. Recently there has been a gradual reorientation of trade towards China and India.

The Mauritanian economy

The Mauritanian economy relies totally on iron mining and processing, agriculture, and fishing. The country receives substantial foreign aid because of its poor economic conditions. Until the mid 1980s Mauritania had a foreign trade surplus but since then it has accumulated a significant trade deficit and an enormous foreign debt. Per capita GDP is less than US$500. However a significant part of international trade is based on barter and it has been estimated that about a third of foreign goods are smuggled into the country, so the GDP figure may be higher in real terms.

Mauritania is among the poorest countries in the world and most people lead a primitive life. The few affluent members of society are concentrated in the capital, Nouakchott, and have a comparable lifestyle to the middle class in developed countries, but with lower purchasing power.

The severe drought in recent years has made the old nomadic lifestyle far less tenable and caused many people to move to urban areas. It should be noted that the infrastructure in Mauritanian towns is the same as in the villages.

The Moroccan economy

The Moroccan economy has been in the process of restructuring since the 1980s in the interest of sustainable development and long-term growth. This process has covered reform of the financial sector and currency convertibility, the privatization of state-owned enterprises, the reform of government spending and development of the service and industrial sectors. The agricultural sector is considerable but highly dependent on rainfall as there are limited irrigation facilities. High temperatures and drought can have a severe impact on agricultural output and the overall economic growth rate.

Despite the fact that the economic reforms have stabilized Morocco's macroeconomic performance and inflation has been kept to about 2 per cent, economic growth has been poor, with a negative effect on the employment rate. Foreign investment would boost the economy as domestic capital is limited and the government is having to repay a substantial foreign debt of almost US$19 billion. The country is rich in phosphate and its deposits account for two thirds of the world's phosphate reserves. Phosphate exports account for more than 50 per cent of GDP. Textiles and clothing head the list of exports, although electronic components have recently grown in importance (Table 4.4). France, Spain, Italy, Germany, and the United Kingdom are Morocco's principal trading partners and account for about half of the value of its foreign trade (Table 4.5).

Morocco has a relatively liberal trade regime and has arranged free trade agreements with the United States and the European Union. The latter will take effect in 2010. The geographic proximity of some

Table 4.4 Main exports and imports, Morocco, 2003 (US$ billion)

Exports	*Value*	*Imports*	*Value*
Textiles and clothing	2.01	Consumer goods	3.55
Electronic components	0.60	Semifinished goods	3.38
Phosphoric acid	0.57	Capital goods	3.28
Phosphate rock	0.42	Fuel and lubricants	2.31

Source: Moroccan Ministry of Trade.

Table 4.5 Principal trading partners, Morocco, 2003 (percentage of total exports/imports)

Exports		*Imports*	
France	26.1	France	21.2
Spain	16.4	Spain	13.6
United Kingdom	7.0	Italy	6.7
Germany	5.4	Germany	6.5

Source: Moroccan Ministry of Trade.

Table 4.6 Main exports and imports, Tunisia, 2003 (US$ billion)

Exports	*Value*	*Imports*	*Value*
Textiles and clothing	3.31	Textiles and clothing	2.29
Electrical equipment	0.93	Machinery	1.43
Petroleum and derivatives	0.80	Electrical equipment	1.31
Leather and leather products	0.49	Petroleum and petroleum products	1.13

Source: Tunisian Ministry of Trade.

European countries and the efforts by the European Commission to develop trade with Africa, place Morocco in a favorable position. However the government is under pressure to deal with drug-related economic activities, which take place mostly in the north of the country.

The Tunisian economy

Tunisia has the most diverse economy in the Maghreb region. The main sectors are textiles and clothing; food-processing, mechanical and electrical manufacturing; and tourism. There is also some phosphate mining and oil extraction. The structure of the main exports and imports is shown in Table 4.6.

Agriculture and fishing are important for the domestic market but have little export significance. Saudi Arabian, Italian and US investors have made some small investments in the economy, while a large joint venture with Iranian and Tunisian capital is helping the development of the fertilizer industry.

The government's long-term plan for economic development includes incentives to encourage domestic and foreign investment via the privatization of state-owned companies and reform of the financial sector. However the economy will continue to be under government control due to state ownership of most productive assets.

Tunisia became a member of the World Trade Organization in 1995. It also has an Association Agreement with the EU, and this is reflected in its trading partnerships (Table 4.7). Recently trade with the United States has increased and it is expected that the latter will eventually become one of Tunisia's main trading partners, thereby diminishing its dependence on the EU countries.

Other bilateral arrangements are a free trade agreement with Turkey and a trade and technological agreement with Norway. Under the

Table 4.7 Principal trading partners, Tunisia, 2003 (percentage of total exports/imports)

Exports		*Imports*	
France	35.6	France	31.2
Italy	22.8	Italy	23.4
Germany	12.0	Germany	10.0
Libya	5.4	Spain	6.0

Source: Tunisian Ministry of Trade.

latter, Norway provides Tunisia with credit for importing Norwegian products and Norwegian companies invest in and provide technological transfers for joint ventures with Tunisian partners.

Tunisia has made good progress with eradicating poverty and now less than 9 per cent of the population lives below the poverty line (set at an income of US$60 per month). As in Algeria, poverty is mostly associated with rural areas.

Internationalization

Agriculture accounts for about one third of regional GDP and, apart from Algeria, Libya, and Tunisia, the Maghreb economies rely mainly on the export of agricultural commodities and minerals. The majority of regional businesses are small family-owned enterprises that operate individually or as members of cooperatives, mutual benefit societies or development associations.

Tunisia produces mainly textiles, clothing, food, beverages, tobacco, and chemicals. About half of the manufacturing workforce is employed in the production of textiles and clothing. In general exports from the Maghreb are labor-intensive, low value-added products, the majority of which go to EU countries. Capital-intensive businesses export their products to other emerging markets, mostly outside the region, and to some developed countries. Such exports have increased lately and now account for about 25 per cent of Moroccan and 29 per cent of Tunisian exports. Morocco and Tunisia are among the world's main exporters of textiles and clothing, and these make up a significant part of their total exports (Table 4.8).

Agricultural exports are not significant to the region's total export revenues but the contribution of agriculture to the GDP of individual countries is important, particularly in Morocco, where production is based mainly on cooperatives. Some of the countries have successfully

Table 4.8 Exports of textiles and clothing, Morocco and Tunisia, 2003 (percentage share of total)

	Total exports	*World market*	*EU*	*USA*
Morocco	33.0	5.5	32.0	0.6
Tunisia	42.5	5.1	41.5	0.5

Source: World Trade Organization statistics.

developed technology-based manufacturing that is capable of competing in world markets. For example the electrical and electronic industries form the backbone of the Tunisian economy.

During the last decade all the Maghreb countries have taken steps to attract foreign direct investment, but the response has been patchy and relatively low. This can be attributed to political instability in the region and the sluggish economic growth rates. Most foreign investment has come from EU countries.

The various national governments are still prone to protecting domestic products by imposing high customs duties and tariffs. Lengthy and non-transparent customs procedures and red tape serve as further impediments. However the establishment of free trade zones and the upgrading of port facilities, for example in Tangiers, have had a positive effect on the participation of the region in international trade.

As a result of industrialization in the 1980s and 1990s the predominantly rural countries of Algeria, Morocco and Tunisia became urbanized. Mauritania, despite some drought-spurred migration to urban areas, is still mainly rural.

Tunisia spends about 7 per cent of its GDP on education and the adult literacy rate is the highest in the region – about 75 per cent. Algeria follows with 70 per cent, while Mauritania has a low 30 per cent because the government spends less than 0.6 per cent of GDP on education.

With the aid of foreign investment Morocco and Tunisia have diversified their economies by developing the tourism sector, the textile industry and financial services, whereas the Algerian economy has remained strongly natural-resource dependent. In Morocco and Tunisia the textile industry now employs almost half of the workforce. However since the mid 1990s textile exporters have faced growing competition from Asian textile manufactures, mostly from China.

Intraregional trade is negligible in comparison with the trade between the Mahgreb countries and the European Union (Table 4.9).

Table 4.9 Trade among the Maghreb countries and between them and the EU, 1990–2002 (US$ billion)

	Exports		*Imports*	
	Maghreb	*EU*	*Maghreb*	*EU*
Algeria	1.6	68.9	1.3	63.4
Morocco	1.7	62.9	1.5	56.8
Tunisia	2.3	79.9	1.7	74.7

Source: IMF statistics.

Liberalization of their trade regimes would benefit their future foreign trade operations. In terms of international competitiveness Tunisia seems to have the best prospects, followed by Morocco.

Conclusion

The Maghreb countries are upgrading and restructuring their economies and improving the living standards of their people. Apart from Algeria and Libya, which are strongly dependent on oil, the regional economies are based mainly on agriculture and manufacturing. The region has a high degree of homogeneity because of its common history, cultural heritage and religion, but regional economic integration is hampered by the similarity of the economies and their dependence on trade and economic cooperation with more developed countries, mostly EU states.

Business and marketing practices are similar across the region due to the significant part played by the governments in the functioning of the economies and the shared culture and language. Apart from some income differences the social strata and consumer bases are similar. Therefore a uniform approach can be taken when doing business and marketing in the region, with some minor adjustments for economic and sociodemographic particularities.

5
Marketing in Morocco

Lyn S. Amine and Kenneth R. Gray

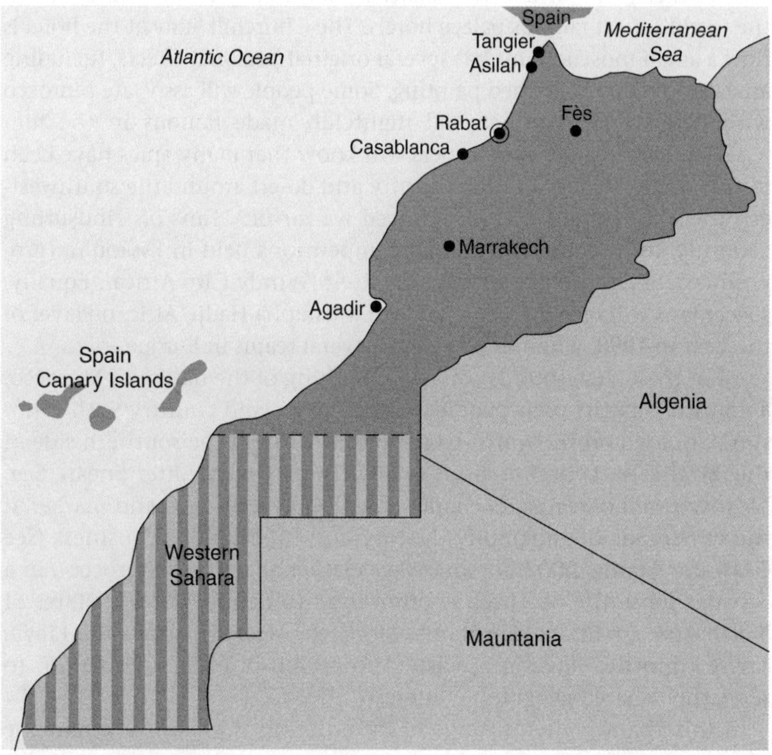

Source: www.universes-in-universe.de.

Map of Morocco

Introduction

To some non-Moroccans *'al-Maghrib'* (pronounced al-mah-grib), the local name for Morocco, is known mostly for being an ally of the United

States in the Gulf War, the war in Iraq and the war on terrorism. Followers of the 2004 Olympics will know that Hicham El-Guerrouj, the four-time world champion, won two gold medals for the 1500 meter and 5000 meter races. Readers of *Forbes* magazine may recall the extravagant seventieth birthday party that the late Malcolm Forbes, founder of the magazine, held at his villa in 1989 in Tangiers, the northern port and holiday resort. Elizabeth Taylor was his guest of honor. Those interested in history will know that Sir Winston Churchill, former prime minister of Britain, spent time painting in the crystal clear air and light of the southern city of Marrakech. Usually he stayed at La Mamounia, one of the world's most famous palace hotels. The Churchill Suite at the hotel is now a small museum and has several original personal effects, including an easel and an unfinished painting. Some people will associate Morocco with Rick's Café, the fictional nightclub made famous in the film 'Casablanca'. Regular moviegoers will know that many epics have been filmed in the Moroccan high country and desert around the southwestern town of Ouazarzate (pronounced wa-zar-zat). Fans of windsurfing certainly know about the annual competitions held in Essaouira (pronounced ez-ah-wee-ra), which calls itself 'Windy City Africa'. Equally, soccer fans will recognize the name of Mustapha Hadji, African Player of the Year in 1998, who has played for several teams in Europe.

All of these descriptions convey something of the nature of Morocco, a country that its own people describe as a 'cold country with a hot sun'. Situated on the north-west tip of Africa, on the southern side of the Straits of Gibraltar at the mouth of the Mediterranean Sea, Morocco well deserves its characterization as a country and market at the crossroads of geography, history and international business (see Gray and Amine, 2002, for an earlier market analysis of Morocco). In a broader sense the Maghreb is often used to denote the five states of North Africa, namely Mauritania, Morocco, Algeria, Tunisia and Libya. These countries have long wished to establish a Maghreb Union to serve their shared geographic interests.

In this chapter a wide range of information is presented about the Moroccan environment and its impact on marketing practices. It discusses recent changes in the local market and offers some guidelines on how to approach business in Morocco. Much of the information presented here is the result of research by the two authors, who have a combined experience of over fifteen years of living in Morocco. Various aspects of life and business are discussed in order to give the reader a good feel for the special characteristics, opportunities and challenges of marketing in Morocco.

First the macro-environment is discussed with reference to the highly important part played by the monarch, King Mohamed VI, in trying to improve the quality of life of his people. Then a brief review of Morocco's history and cultural legacies is presented to familiarize the reader with the Moroccan people's sense of heritage. This is followed by a discussion of the current political scene.

In the second section Morocco's trade links with the world are explored in terms of participation in regional market blocs; physical and electronic links to the world through transportation, telecommunications and e-commerce; and tourism as a key source of revenue for the Moroccan economy.

The third section addresses marketing practices in Morocco, first with regard to marketing to the consumer and then in respect of business-to-business practices. The chapter concludes with a brief summary of the key points and the future prospects for business and marketing in Morocco.

The macro-environment of business

Following the widely accepted model of environmental analysis in the field of international marketing (see Cateora and Graham, 2005), this section discusses aspects of Morocco's economic, political, historical and cultural environments in order to give readers a clear understanding of Morocco's unique features.

The role of the monarch

King Hassan II of Morocco died in the summer of 1999. His funeral was attended by many heads of state, including US President Bill Clinton, and it put Morocco on the front pages of leading newspapers and television news broadcasts throughout the world. Part of the reason for this extensive coverage was the crucial part played by the late king as a peacemaker between Israel and the Palestinians. His role as a moderate political intermediary has since been taken up by his son, King Mohammed VI.

A less well-known reason for the A-list attendance at King Hassan's funeral was the three-century friendship between Morocco and the United States. Morocco was the first country to recognize the newly independent United States of America. This fact was recalled and commemorated in a double-page advertisement in *The Economist* (March 1999) that was signed by 109 senators and members of the US House of Representatives.

The king of Morocco is not only the secular head of state but also serves as Commander of the Faithful (*Amir al Mouminine*, pronounced ameer-al-mou-mee-neen). In other words the monarch is the highest religious authority in the country. Because Islam does not have a central authority (such as the pope is for Catholicism), each Muslim country has developed its own religious hierarchy. Thus any ruling by the king of Morocco is not only a matter of state but also a religious decree. The year 1999 was a turning point in Morocco's modern history as government by royal fiat began to give way to democratization and the protection of human rights. In November 1998 and 1999 the new King Mohammed sponsored weeklong nationwide campaigns to support the destitute, entitled *Unis pour aider les démunis* (unite to help the helpless). The campaigns were aimed specifically at rural women, who suffer disproportionately from the burdens of illiteracy, unemployment and poor health care (Gray and Amine, 2002). The king is building a name for himself as an innovator, a person of social conscience, a leading defender of human rights, an advocate of democracy, and a strong supporter of women's rights in the family and workplace (see Gray, 2001).

In recent years Moroccan family law (*moudauana*, pronounced moo-dah-wahna) has been one of the most hotly debated and divisive issues in the country. The traditional law, based on the Islamic Shari'ah, put women in a very vulnerable position: men were able to divorce and evict their wives with ease but it was very difficult for women to escape even abusive relationships. In 2003 the king announced a landmark reform of the law governing women's position in the family. Although many Moroccan women in their twenties, thirties and forties work outside the home, the majority are still primarily home makers. Recently an historical precedent was set when the elected parliament convened with 33 women members, the largest number ever (United Nations, 2003).

Changes to the law have given greater rights to women on matters of marriage and divorce. Married women now have property rights and both spouses have equal authority within the family. Divorce has been made easier for women, and the minimum age of marriage for girls is to be raised from 15 to 18. Polygamy will not be outlawed, but it will become much more difficult as a man will require the consent of his wife before marrying another.

The king's positive attitude towards women's rights has been evidenced by his permission for his marriage to be publicly televised, the revelation of his wife's name (Salma Benani) and his pride in the fact that she has career in computer engineering (MAP, October 31, 2001; BBC, 2002). In 2003 in Marrakech the king presented a message of welcome to the delegates at the Global Summit of Women (MAP, June 28, 2003), outlining numerous government initiatives and programs to improve the status and education of women in Morocco.

In the light of these important developments the people of Morocco have great expectations for the future of their country. There is a perceptible feeling of change and innovation, and an end to 'business as usual' in the political and administrative spheres. Privatization, deregulation and administrative reform are all being implemented as part of an ambitious national strategy of structural adjustment. Targeted sectors include justice, government administration, the business legal environment, employment legislation, the customs regime and the financial system (MAP, December 11, 2003). Thus any business person contemplating doing business in Morocco should be aware that this is a country in transition and, as in many developing countries with young populations, change may come very quickly. (For a discussion of other Arab nations in transition see Amine and Cavusgil, 1986.)

Historical cultural legacies

Present-day Morocco has been shaped by centuries of interaction between the original Berber population and the foreign peoples who successively invaded the country. Morocco's history is essentially a tale of a conservative society that triumphed against most attempts at conquest, with especially fierce resistance by the Berbers in the mountain regions, while absorbing technical and spiritual innovations from other cultures (see Abun-Nasr, 1975; Munson, 1993). Morocco's historical cultural identity was frequently likened by King Hassan II to a desert palm: rooted in Africa, watered by Islam, and rustled by the winds of Europe (MAP, October 15, 2003).

The first great change in Morocco's culture occurred in about 1000 BC, when Phoenician traders brought agriculture and urban civilization to Morocco. The second came in the eighth century AD, when the cavalry armies of the Muslim Caliphate introduced Islam, Arabic and the advanced culture of the Middle East. Arab military rule lasted only a few decades but the spiritual and social message took deep root, with subsequent rulers of Morocco claiming direct descent from the Prophet Mohamed as 'Commander of the Faithful' (L'economiste, 2004a). The third great change took place from 1912, when Morocco became a protectorate of France and the French introduced modern scientific, medical and administrative methods. In 1956 the protectorate came to a peaceful end and a constitutional monarchical government was formed under Sultan Sidi Mohamed, who became King Mohamed V, grandfather to the present king.

As noted above, the original inhabitants of Morocco were the Berbers, and nowadays various Berber communities live in the mountains and southern areas around the port of Agadir. There are several tribal groups, each with its own geographic area of origin, culture, history, and traditions. The most well known are the Chleuch (pronounced sh-loo-h) and the Soussi (pronounced soo-sy). The Soussi have a quasimonopoly over the corner-shop grocery sector in Morocco.

With the encouragement of King Mohamed VI who is himself half-Berber (MAP, October 31, 2001), several Berber languages are now being written down and taught, such as the Amazigh dialect (pronounced am-ah-zeer). The new English-language university and business school, Al-Akhawayn University (pronounced al-ah-ha-wane) in Ifrane (pronounced ee-fran), a small town in the Middle Atlas Mountains, is doing pioneering work that will bring greater recognition and status to the Berbers. In 2001 the king created by royal decree the Royal Institute of Amazigh Culture, also located in the Middle Atlas Mountains.

Until the mid 1990s it had been illegal to treat the Berbers as a separate group from other Moroccans. This was due to fear that they might try to assert their independence. However in 1994 King Hassan ended this law by royal decree, and King Mohamed now describes his country as 'a genuine melting pot ... the most blended North African country'. It 'has a plural yet cohesive identity, made up of several elements, Amazigh, Arab-Islamic, Andalusian, and African' (MAP, October 15, 2003).

The Sahara

In 1958 King Mohamed V spoke of the 'Moroccanity of the Sahara' (MAP, October 31, 2001), and in the 1970s King Hassan II reasserted Morocco's claim to the Spanish Sahara, a protectorate of Spain since 1884. He sent 350 000 Moroccan civilians on a 'Green March' to proclaim Morocco's sovereignty. In 1976 Spain withdrew its troops, leaving the Algerian-supported guerrillas of the Polisario Front to contest ownership of the region, which had been divided between Morocco and Mauritania. In 1979 Mauritania withdrew and Morocco laid claim to the entire region (now renamed the Western Sahara) and its resources, causing relations with both Algeria and Mauritania to deteriorate. The conflict between the Polisario and Morocco continued until a ceasefire was declared in 1991. The UN is still trying to gain the approval of all parties for a referendum on the status of the territory that might lead to a permanent settlement. In the meantime the border between Algeria and Morocco remains closed, and any maps that do not show the Western Sahara as part of Morocco are considered illegal.

In 2004 the minister of foreign affairs and cooperation, Mohamed Benaissa, admitted that the dispute over the Sahara was preventing any move towards completion of the proposed regional trading entity, the Union du Maghreb Arabe (MAP, August 14, 2004).

The political scene

The political scene in Morocco can be characterized by reference to the type of government, its challenges, and new initiatives.

Type of government

The 1972 constitution vested supreme executive power in the king, who appoints a prime minister according to the results of elections. The independent judiciary is headed by the Supreme Court, which is also appointed by the king. The country has universal adult suffrage, and women are provided with an important voice in government through the 33 elected female representatives. The parliament has two chambers: the members of the first are nationally elected, while the second is composed of members elected by local councils and professional organizations.

The traditional religious role of the king as Commander of the Faithful is carefully preserved by King Mohamed VI. Morocco has never witnessed a split between the religious Islamic hierarchy (ulema) and the determinedly secular government in the way that some other Arab states have. Each election has brought improvements to the democratic process, with the goal of achieving political pluralism. Indeed, in 2002 Morocco was internationally praised for its fair and transparent elections, and the mass media actively report and comment on political affairs. Greater freedom and independence for the press and the media are key concerns of the present monarch and are often mentioned in his speeches to the Moroccan people. In 2002 the king proclaimed November 15 as National Press and Communication Day, in recognition of the values of freedom and accountability. He also announced that an annual National Press Prize would be awarded from 2003 (MAP, November 15, 2002).

Challenges

After the terrorist attacks on the United States on September 11, 2001, Muslim fundamentalism surfaced in Morocco on May 16, 2003 with the simultaneous bombing of six locations in Casablanca, the principal port and commercial center. The economic impact of these events on international investment and tourism has not yet been calculated.

While Islamic extremism has not gained widespread support in the country, the rapid increase in urban poverty has led to some growth of the Islamist movement, as demonstrated by the attacks on May 16. A more recent phenomenon has been the emergence in urban slums of gangs of Islamic youths who are willing to use violence to enforce their concept of religiously correct behavior. While there is no accurate information upon which to base an estimate, it is likely that *non-violent* Islamists probably account for nearly one fourth of the population. They are divided between those who cooperate with the government and those who do not. The former are represented in parliament by the Party of Justice and Development. The latter have a disciplined organization but remain outside the realm of political legitimacy. Their activities are closely circumscribed by the authorities.

New initiatives

One innovation by King Mohamed VI that was of great significance for Moroccans was the creation of a human rights reparations committee to pay compensation to victims of political oppression or their surviving family members. This constituted explicit recognition of the past mistreatment of citizens and was an important step towards the official establishment of respect for human rights. Commitment to the defence of human rights is a prerequisite for membership in the European Union (EU), which has long been a major goal of Morocco.

In order to reduce the 23 per cent unemployment rate (quoted as 11.69 per cent by the Moroccan government) and improve the living standards of the 19 per cent of the population who live below the poverty line, ambitious projects for local economic development have been implemented. For example there is a national program to rehouse 860 000 households living in shanty towns around major cities, at a cost of US$555 million (MAP, July 30, 2004). Another project is to create jobs in the tourism sector as a key part of Morocco's overall strategy for sustainable development. By 2010 it is hoped to attract 10 million tourists a year, through a combined effort to build new facilities and conduct marketing campaigns (MAP, February 12, 2004).

The economy and trade links

Clearly Morocco cannot afford the economic price of terrorism so the government, under the king's leadership, is working hard to strengthen security and create jobs by seeking greater cooperation in trade with other countries, as well as membership in several market groups. Morocco's strategic geopolitical location on the Atlantic coast and at the mouth of the Mediterranean Sea provides easy access to markets in North America, Europe, Africa, and the Middle East. Not surprisingly its chief trading partners are France, Spain, the United States, Britain, Italy, and Germany. Capital and semifinished goods, fuels and consumer goods lead the nation's imports, while exports include agricultural commodities, phosphates, phosphoric acid, and clothing.

In terms of economic activities, Morocco boasts the world's largest phosphate reserves, a diverse agricultural sector, rich ocean fisheries, a growing manufacturing sector (especially in clothing and electronics), a dynamic and deregulated telecommunications sector and a sizable tourist industry. The following sections look at current initiatives to achieve greater participation in both regional and global markets, to create new linkages with world markets and to promote tourism as a major driver of economic growth.

Participation in regional and global market blocs

Foreign trade as a proportion of GDP has increased in recent years but Morocco has continued to incur trade deficits. Customs duties provide the bulk of state revenue, while foreign exchange comes from three major sources: exports of phosphates, tourism and remittances from Moroccan workers overseas (Gray and Driouchi, 2000). The king has urged Morocco's 31 million people to think critically about the wide range of trade reforms and innovations that are needed to ensure a brighter future. Some of these initiatives are reviewed below.

European Union–Morocco Free Trade Agreement

Morocco's Free Trade Agreement (FTA) with the EU took effect in March 1999 and has already spurred the development of manufacturing in Morocco. With an illiteracy rate of 43.7 per cent, great importance is attached to this agreement as it is hoped that business development will facilitate social and educational reform (Ministry of Commerce and Industry, 2004).

Morocco's request for EU membership

Full membership in the EU has long been sought by Morocco, based on continuous cooperation with Europe since 1969. However hope was dashed when the EU welcomed ten Eastern European members in 2004, rather than Morocco and Turkey. These two nations are Muslim, yet have secular governments. Both are also net exporters of guest workers who remit considerable funds from Europe and Canada. These two factors – religion and population movement – are viewed unfavorably by decision makers in the EU. A further deterrent to membership is the persistent illegal production and export of cannabis from the northern Rif Mountains of Morocco.

Moroccans are increasingly aware that their best business opportunities may lie outside the EU. This has been a painful realization because most of Morocco's trade has traditionally been with Europe, with France alone accounting for about a quarter of Morocco's imports and a third of its exports. More promising and rewarding opportunities may be found in other markets bordering the Mediterranean, across the Atlantic in North America, elsewhere in Africa, in Arab markets across North Africa (the Maghreb), and in the Middle East. In 2003 at a public colloquium on the 'Arab World and Africa', King Mohamed VI asserted that 'Morocco will remain at the forefront of the Arab–African dialogue and will continue to be actively engaged in other forums, especially the Islamic, the European, and the American ones, as well as in South–South dialogue' (MAP, October 15, 2003).

The role of the monarch in the economic development of Morocco

King Mohammed VI has continuously followed a reform policy since his ascent to the throne. Its aim is to accelerate the process of economic and social development and provide Morocco with new business opportunities, especially in the tourism sector, where expansion and development offer considerable promise. The king has also provided strong support for Morocco's privatization program. He associates its implementation with special emphasis on the incorporation of public entities with significant national importance, such as Royal Air Maroc and la Banque Populaire.

Euro-Mediterranean Association Agreement – the 2010 Agenda

In 1996 Morocco signed the Euro-Mediterranean Association Agreement with the EU. This eased trade barriers with Europe and provided access to certain EU development funds. Under the so-called

Barcelona Process of regional cooperation around the Mediterranean, an enormous free trade area is planned by 2010. This framework is called the 2010 Agenda. The new FTA will extend from Sweden in the north to Morocco in the south-west and Turkey and Egypt in the south-east. An important provision will allow the free circulation of capital for direct investment in Morocco, as well as the possibility of repatriating capital, profits, income and savings (MAP, February 12, 2004).

The US–Morocco Free Trade Agreement

The US trade representative has described the 2004 free trade agreement (FTA) with Morocco as the best market access package and the strongest intellectual property protection of any FTA that the United States has signed so far with a developing country (MAP, July 16, 2004). The agreement has special significance for the United States because it constitutes a first step towards implementation of the plan for a Middle Eastern FTA, led by the United States.

Morocco has already signed bilateral FTAs with several North African countries in preparation for implementation of the 2010 Agenda. The Agadir Declaration, a four-country agreement, was signed in May 2001. This provides for a free trade zone to be established between the Arab countries of Morocco, Tunisia, Egypt, and Jordan. Eventually the FTA will include a further six Arab countries, namely Algeria, Libya, Mauritania, Syria, Lebanon, and Palestine (Arabic News, 2001).

The significance of the US FTA for Morocco lies in the fact that Morocco is the first country on the African continent to sign an FTA with the United States, and only the second Arab country after Jordan to do so (MAP, August 17, 2004). The agreement is consistent with the king's vision of Morocco as a 'buffer zone, an airlock' between East and West (MAP, October 31, 2001).

The FTA provides US producers of several agricultural products with increased access to the Moroccan market, while complementing Morocco's agricultural reform program. It will eliminate tariffs on 95 per cent of bilateral trade in consumer and industrial products, with all remaining tariffs to be eliminated by 2013 (MAP, July 16, 2004).

The New Economic Partnership for African Development

Morocco is part of the New Economic Partnership for African Development, which seeks to achieve sustainable development across Africa. As an expression of its support Morocco has canceled the debts owed to it by the least developed African countries. It also grants those countries preferential treatment with regard to customs duties on their exports (MAP, October 15, 2003).

Agenda 21

King Mohamed VI is a staunch supporter of sustainable development, both as a goal for all countries and as a method of doing business. When he addressed the opening session of the meeting of heads of state and government at the World Summit on Sustainable Development in Johannesburg in 2002 (MAP, September 2, 2002) he recalled the crucial importance of Agenda 21, which had been developed at the 1992 Earth Summit in Rio de Janeiro (United Nations, 1992).

Morocco faces environmental challenges caused by climatic change, drought and desertification (MAP, September 2, 2002). Important goals include the protection of biodiversity, the preservation of places of historical and national interest, education and training, and improvements in people's quality of life.

Physical and electronic links to world markets

This section discusses new links between Morocco and the rest of the world by mode of transportation, telecommunications, and e-commerce.

Transportation links

Over the centuries relations between Spain and Morocco have been checkered. However in January 2004 the governments of the two countries signed a landmark agreement to cooperate in a series of studies of the possibility of constructing a rail tunnel under the Straits of Gibraltar to join Morocco and Spain. This link would be an exciting addition to the air and sea routes to Europe. It would also carry forward the 2010 Agenda for a free-trade area stretching from northern Europe through to Africa by providing a continuous rail link between the continents. The tunnel would certainly have a positive impact on the Moroccan transportation, trade, tourism and telecommunications sectors.

Construction of the tunnel is planned to start in 2008. While finance for the preliminary studies has already been secured, the EU will be asked for financial assistance with the implementation of the project. There are to be two tunnels with a connecting service tunnel in the middle. The tunnels will be 24 miles long and are expected to cost somewhere between three and ten billion euros. The route is likely to be between Punta Paloma (west of Gibraltar) and Punta Malabata (close to Tangiers).

The tunnel promises to be as historic an achievement as the Channel Tunnel (connecting Britain to the continent of Europe) was in 1994, or as the Spanish minister of development has put it, the tunnel will be in the twenty-first century what the Suez Canal was in the nineteenth century and what the Panama Canal was in the twentieth century.

With regard to road and rail transportation inside Morocco, there are ambitious plans for highway and railroad construction (L'economiste, 2004a) to improve access to rural areas. In addition major new roads will be constructed from north to south, linking Tangiers, Marrakech and Agadir, and from north-west to north-east, linking Fez to Taza and on to Oudja, which lies close to the border with Algeria. A second major infrastructure project in the north is the construction of a new port in Tangiers and a surrounding industrial and commercial park.

In line with the EU's 'open skies' program, which facilitated competition between national flag-carrying airlines and newer start-up carriers, Morocco is reforming its airline industry (MAP, February 12, 2004). To date this has been dominated by Royal Air Maroc. Price competition, new routes and charter flights will make Morocco more accessible and promote opportunities for business and tourism (L'economiste, 2004a).

Telecommunication links

Somewhat surprisingly for a developing country, Morocco has an excellent telecommunications network with the latest fiber optic technology, allowing for up to 722 mbps and a completely digitized transmission network. By leapfrogging generations of technology this sector has changed dramatically in just two years, thanks to effective implementation of the government's liberalization and privatization reforms.

In addition an effective product launch strategy has resulted in the rapid adoption and diffusion of cellular phones throughout Morocco. Consumers are able to purchase phones and operate them using inexpensive prepaid cards, rather than enter into the complex contractual arrangements typically found in the United States. A unique feature of the telephone card is that cellular phones can continue to receive incoming calls for several months after expiry of the prepaid quota of minutes, which means that even the poor and elderly can afford the new technology. This is an interesting example of marketing success based on a simple idea.

In 1998 the Secrétariat d'Etat aux Postes et Technologies de l'Information (SEPTI) was created. The mission of this government agency is to develop an integrated national IT strategy that will enable Morocco to enter the information age and become a knowledge-based economy (SEPTI, 2004). Strategic objectives include the development of human capital, infrastructure and the application of IT strategies (NICI, 2004).

E-commerce links

Morocco's FTA with the EU represents an initial step towards globalization, which will require domestic companies to become much more competitive. One means to improve efficiency is the Internet. However e-commerce in Morocco is hampered by problems relating to the Moroccan currency, the banking system and the use of credit cards.

As an export-oriented economy, export revenues have traditionally been used to build up foreign currency reserves by retaining 80 per cent of export proceeds through the banks. As a consequence the Moroccan dirham is non-convertible in commercial transactions. (The exchange rate is roughly ten dirhams to one US dollar.)

The use of credit and debit cards has been hampered by banking restrictions, the unsophisticated domestic interbanking system, technological backwardness, and the absence of regulatory framework for e-commerce transactions. For example encryption and electronic signatures have yet to be established.

Despite these problems Morocco is the most computerized country in North Africa and ranks second in Africa as a whole, after South Africa. It is expected that the liberalization and rapid expansion of the IT sector will boost the sales of computers and peripherals by 35–40 per cent per year. At the end of 2000 the annual growth of Internet traffic was estimated to be more than 300 per cent and the domestic Internet community had more than doubled in size. However there are still only about 300 000 Internet users, a penetration rate of just six per thousand. The number of dial-up subscribers is estimated at 45 000, of which 25 per cent are firms based mainly in Casablanca and the capital, Rabat. There is only one network operator, Maroc Telecom, which is also an Internet service provider. Privatization of this company and the award of new operating licenses are expected to stimulate Internet use and e-commerce in Morocco (SEPTI, 2004).

Government offices, banks, and 55 per cent of the larger companies have web sites, but they mainly use the Internet for email and to provide information. Less than 10 per cent use the Internet for e-commerce.

Demand for website design is expected to grow rapidly as small and medium-sized companies start using e-commerce. A few government offices, such as the Customs Office, provide government-to-business information services on the Internet. A pilot program has been set up in the small university town of Ifrane, under the aegis of the research faculty at the English-language Al-Akhawayn University, to provide local people with government information and access to records. This is a prototype for the larger portal system that is planned for the major city of Fez. The project has been cofinanced by a Canadian agency (Centre de Recherche pour le Développement International) and the British Embassy in Rabat (L'economiste, 2004b). It is interesting to note that Al-Akhawayn University has operated as a 'paperless' campus almost since its inception in the 1990s, with heavy reliance on electronic communication for campus announcements.

Cybercafés have quickly become very popular in Morocco. They cater to about 40,000 users and generate revenues of approximately US$7 million. It was estimated that the number of Internet users in cybercafés would reach three and a half million by 2008 or about 12 per cent of the population, constituting a market worth of US$5 billion.

IT businesses expect to generate US$2 billion of sales per year by 2008. Given that more than half of the population of 30 million are below the age of 20 and lack variety in their leisure-time activities, demand should flourish for Internet applications such as research, entertainment, music, computer games, and chat rooms. In order for these projections to be realized, public and private entities such as SEPTI, the Customs Office, the Exchange Office, banks and professional associations are addressing the inconvertibility of the national currency and the viability of bank cards issued in Morocco for e-commerce. Laws are being dratted to regulate credit card transactions, the choice of protocols and software, the authentication of documents, the use of consumers' personal data, the physical delivery of goods and the question of ethics in e-business.

The expansion of tourism

In 2001 the Tourism Framework Agreement (TFA) was signed by tourism operators in the public and private sectors, creating what is called the 2010 Vision. Objectives include increasing the current annual number of tourists from 2.5 million to 10 million, generating US$8 billion in hard currency sales (up from just US$2 billion in 2000), providing 80,000 new hotel rooms and investing US$5.5 billion in tourism-related infrastructure. The focus will be on beach holidays, with six new beach resorts (MAP, February 12, 2004), as this is expected to bring higher revenues than cultural tourism in the interior of the country. The state is subsidizing 50 per cent of the cost of land acquisition and will help with the cost of off-site infrastructural development. Special tax advantages will be available for development projects whose investment value exceeds US$20 million.

Successful Moroccan businesses and brands

Most domestic producers are unable to compete successfully with multinationals that serve the Moroccan market. However some, such as Azbane Cosmetics, have taken a greater market share of soaps, perfumes, and skincare products as a result of Moroccan's recent shift in preference towards domestic products.

Another example is Aïcha, a very successful family-owned business. It is the largest producer of marmalade, olive oil, and tomato puree in Morocco, as well as the world's most significant purveyor of the rare white terfess truffle. Aïcha is a very strong traditional brand and is on a par with the global brands Coca-Cola and Tide soap powder.

Marketing practices and opportunities

This section is designed to give the reader a feel for how marketing is conducted in Morocco, in both the consumer and the business markets. It highlights particularities of Moroccan consumers and the market, focusing on trends, challenges, and opportunities.

The consumer market

Marketing to consumers in Morocco will be discussed here in terms of market challenges, segmentation, target marketing, and marketing mix opportunities.

Moroccan consumers

Recently there has been a clear increase in urbanization in Morocco. This is associated with worsening desertification and very low living standards in rural areas. As a result of this population movement, products that are used predominantly in urban areas have exhibited strong growth trends that are expected to continue in the future.

Until recently the majority of married women were confined to the domestic sphere and were financially dependent on their husbands.

However this traditional feature of Moroccan society is changing and a growing number of women are joining the workforce. Consequently the disposable income of the average Moroccan household is on the rise, allowing the purchase of products that were previously considered luxury goods, including disposable wipes and kitchen towels. As employed women have less time for domestic chores such as washing nappies, this has added to the demand for disposable products.

Market challenges

Sales volumes and revenues have recently declined for many imported cosmetics, skin-care products, and fragrances due to a strengthening of Islamic values among the majority of Moroccan consumers. In addition most middle-income employed Moroccan women have shifted to traditional beauty products such as ghassoul and henna in protest against the US–British-led invasion of Iraq in March 2003 and the failure of the United States to stop Israeli–Palestinian violence. There has also been an unofficial boycott of other US products and brands and the majority of consumers prefer to buy non-US goods, especially French.

In spite of this, foreign multinationals continue to dominate the consumer market due to brand loyalty among affluent consumers, the high quality of foreign products, and aggressive advertising campaigns.

Segmentation and target marketing

Important psycho-demographic segments include the 'old rich,' the *nouveaux riches*, the young and modern (Amine and Cavusgil, 1986), religious traditionalists and those at the 'bottom of the pyramid' (for a discussion of marketing to the latter see Prahalad, 2005). Conspicuous consumption is important among the fashion conscious in Morocco, and status symbols at various price ranges are popular with all demographic segments. As new households are constantly being set up by younger members of the population the demand for all manner of consumer products and services is growing.

Presently half of the Moroccan population live in rural areas, and market segmentation has to take account of the urban–rural divide in terms of income, education and purchasing behavior. More than half of Moroccans are under the age of 25 and the size of the middle class is growing. Another trend is reduced household size. About 20 years ago there were as many as 20–25 children in a household but today there are just three or four in urban areas. Young Moroccans in the large urban areas are gradually adopting a Western lifestyle, influenced by Europeans in general and the French in particular.

Language is another important factor in marketing. Voice-overs in television and radio commercials are mostly in Moroccan Arabic but some advertisements are produced in three versions to target those in the middle class who speak both Moroccan Arabic and French, the mass of consumers who speak Moroccan as their first language, and the inhabitants of northern Morocco who speak Spanish as a result of historical links with Spain. Illiteracy in the rural population is very high and is estimated to be about 85–90 per cent.

Opportunities for products and services

During the twentieth century North Africa was known as the 'Near East,' suggesting an exotic, non-European character. Yet ironically the Arabs of the Gulf countries in the Middle East refer to Morocco and its two neighbors in North Africa – Algeria and Tunisia – as the 'European Arabs'. This term recognizes the pervasive influence of Europe, and particularly France, on the three cultures of North Africa. France's influence on culture and business in Morocco, a legacy of Morocco's time as a French protectorate, is increasingly being whittled away by creeping Europeanization distinct from the influence of France and Americanization. This is a direct result of global satellite broadcasting and advertising. Many global brands are available in Morocco, especially in the case of clothing, cosmetics, personal care products, consumer electronics, and cars (L'economiste, 2004c). Increasingly, the English language is taking hold in Morocco through business contacts and the spread of global communications and entertainment. American fast-food franchises have opened in a number of places, with McDonald's (known as 'McDo') competing with Kentucky Fried Chicken, Subway, Dunkin Donuts, and Dairy Queen, to name but a few.

Private and public institutions of higher learning are increasingly offering American-style BBA and MBA courses, led by Al-Akhawayn University in Ifrane, which has partnership agreements with numerous US and European companies and institutions (Al-Akhawayn University, 2004).

Advertising and promotion

Several advertising agencies operate in Morocco but the small scale of their operations reflects the underdeveloped state of the local advertising industry. However McCann Erickson and a joint operation by Leo Burnett and Darcy Masius Benton & Bowles provide state-of-the-art resources for new product launches.

Television has overtaken the print media as the most popular vehicle for advertising, generating more than 70 per cent of advertising revenues. Food, hygiene products and beverages are the most common goods advertised on television, with global companies such as Procter & Gamble and Coca-Cola ranking among the biggest advertisers. Newspapers and periodicals provide advertising space for a variety of products and services, but the lack of reliable data on subscriptions and circulation numbers makes it difficult to gauge their cost-effectiveness. Added to this is the high illiteracy level. Billboards, advertising everything from state-of-the-art cellular phones to coffee, have dramatically increased in recent years. Advertisements frequently feature local celebrities such as actors, athletes, singers, and musicians, who provide background music. Sponsorship of musical and sporting events, conferences and exhibitions is a very popular way of promoting soft drinks.

'Slice-of-life' and product demonstration advertisements are very common. The family is typically depicted as a married couple with at least two children, and the wife is often portrayed as a modern working woman who is time-pressured and values convenience. Some product demonstration advertisements contrast old methods, such as washing clothes by hand with a bar of soap and a washboard with the convenience of using an automatic washing machine and powder detergent. Problem solving also features, as for example in the case of shampoos to control dandruff. Advertisements using fear appeals are much less common. The new approach to advertising is due to the primary need to build brand recognition and to establish the product benefit message in a specific market where there is a high rate of illiteracy and need for consumer education.

A notable tendency among local marketers is their copycat behavior with regard to advertising and promotion. This reflects the belief that 'good ideas are worth copying' and 'if it works for you, it will work for me'. There is little concern about diluting the effect of a creative advertising campaign by overexposure of very similar offers. Foreign marketers should therefore be prepared for their advertisements to be copied, particularly if their campaign has been successful (Gray and Amine, 2002).

Distribution and retailing

The retail market is very fragmented and dominated by small grocery stores, although few supermarkets have appeared in large urban areas. A recent phenomenon is the establishment of modern self-service retail outlets, including convenience stores.

Other retail innovations include department stores, global brand-name chains such as the Spanish Zara, open-air and enclosed shopping malls, large discount cash and carry stores such as Aldi and Makro, and convenience stores along the highways. There are also many traditional family-run businesses such as corner-shop groceries, restaurants, clothing and jewelry stores, as well as open-air markets for meat and produce. A significant number of retail clothing stores in the major cities are owned and operated by migrant entrepreneurs from India.

Even consumers who live far from urban centers typically have regular contact with retailers through visits to weekly open-air markets on the outskirts of towns. Therefore national distribution of branded products and services is important, even though purchasing power in rural areas is modest. Bottom-of-the pyramid marketing opportunities are attractive, based on very frequent (even daily), small-volume, low-priced sales.

Pricing policies

Price sensitivity and awareness, and comparison shopping characterize consumer behavior in Morocco at all income levels. The traditional haggling over prices persists in the traditional retail sector, but set prices have become widely accepted through the influence of international retail chains such as McDonald's and Makro.

In order to protect the poorest consumers, price controls are maintained on staples such as gasoline, vegetable oil, sugar, and subsidized flour. Otherwise the market is free to determine commodity prices without government intervention. In June 2003 Morocco introduced a new tariff system for grain (barley, wheat and corn) that resulted in a significant increase in the tariff for bread wheat. The October 1998 tariff system is still applicable to oilseeds and sugar.

Seasonal price promotions are very popular, particularly during Ramadan, the holy month of daytime fasting. Food products, kitchen equipment, clothing and gifts are put on sale at special prices to capitalize on the many parties and social events that take place during the night-time hours of Ramadan.

The entry of international Internet service providers and Maroc Telecom's efforts to provide connections to a larger population have combined to reduce the cost of Internet access. In 2004 the monthly connection fee for consumers was about US$5.31 for unlimited access at 64 kbs, with telephone fees of about US$1.45 per hour. These rates make Morocco an attractive Internet market. Computer vendors, in partnership with credit loan banks, are promoting uptake by offering packages that include Internet access and computers for US$30–40 per month. Nonetheless a survey by the Ministry of Industry and Commerce has shown that price is still the biggest hindrance to the adoption of computers by consumers in Morocco.

The Moroccan soft drink market

The soft drink market in Morocco is significant but its potential for growth is somewhat limited by the low purchasing power of the average Moroccan consumer. In 2003 the annual growth was about 8 per cent. The largest sellers are carbonated drinks, which are very popular among Moroccan consumers because they cost less than bottled water and are suited to the hot climate. The fact that Islam forbids the consumption of alcohol is another reason for the success of these drinks.

The strongest brands are Coca-Cola and Pepsi-Cola. A recent entrant, Mecca-Cola, is named after the holy Islamic city of Mecca in Saudi Arabia. The purchase of this by Orthodox Muslims has been restricted by the fact that the use of sacred religious symbols for commercial purposes is frowned upon. Thus Mecca-Cola has had limited success in penetrating the market as many Moroccan consumers perceive it to be an unethical product of poor quality.

Bottled water is predominately consumed by the upper and middle classes. Health consciousness and imitation of French drinking habits are the main factors in this. Bottled water is also very popular with tourists and foreigners living in Morocco. Les Eaux Minérales d'Oulmès is the most significant producer and supplier.

The business market

This section provides details of the Moroccan industrial base and discusses managerial values and the world of work.

Industry and agriculture

Business and industry are concentrated on the Atlantic coast around Casablanca, Rabat, and Kenitra. About 15 per cent of the population is employed in phosphate processing and agriculture. Leading products are olives, olive oil, flour, milk, fish, fruit, flowers, and vegetables. A second tier of industry includes cement works, tire and textile factories. The mining and construction industries employ another 15 per cent of the population, with smaller numbers of workers in tourism, public utilities and the civil service. Traditional crafts such as hand weaving, leather work, metal work, pottery, and carpet making are widely distributed among towns and cities. The government is encouraging the development of industries outside Casablanca and has liberal rules on foreign investment (Government of Morocco, 1999). For details of the evolution of aspects of the marketing environment see Amine and Cavusgil, 1986, and Amine, 1990a, 1990b, 1990c).

About a quarter of the workforce belong to trade unions. The leading unions are the Union Marocaine du Travail, the Union Générale des Travailleurs du Maroc and the Conféderation Démocratique du Travail. In accordance with an initiative by the king, employment conditions and laws are currently under review and a new social contract is planned. It is expected that a new employment code will reform the right to strike and allow for the provision of social assistance and health insurance, as well as alleviating some poverty (L'economiste, 2004a).

Managerial values and the world of work

Underlying Morocco's multicultural society are some deeply held traditional values, beliefs and ways of thinking and behaving, as summed up by the French phrase *la mentalité marocaine*. This mentality can cause some frustration when doing business in Morocco, particularly if one comes from Europe or North America. Moroccans are used to very large power distance (see Hofstede, 1991). They are highly deferential to people in authority and are unwilling to question orders from above. Action will not be taken unless specifically commanded by a superior, and only that action will be taken – no more, no less. Thus a business person who is used to delegating responsibility, assigning problem-solving tasks to employees, and expecting initiative to be taken when appropriate may feel confused. The best solution is to make friends with your Moroccan counterparts and try to see the world through their eyes. These new friends will then go above and beyond the call of duty to help you (Gray and Amine, 2002).

Morocco is a country where emotions are easily roused and openly displayed. People will break into tears at another's misfortune, they will laugh till they cry when they hear a good joke, they will clap their hands in the air at another's success, and they will shout at children or low-status employees. This behavior can be quite disconcerting at first for managers from low-context cultures (see Hall, 1979) who are used to more self-restraint, but the emotional outburst soon passes. If a visiting business person is unsure about a person's status or connections it is better to err on the side of caution by greeting everyone formally with a handshake, rather than risking snubbing someone by being too casual and just saying 'Hi'. (For information on aspects of Moroccan culture, see Hargraves, 1996, and the country 'culturegrams' produced by Brigham Young University and eMSTAR, 1999.)

As a people with a long tradition of hospitality Moroccans do not like to disappoint others, be they coworkers, compatriots or visitors from abroad. From bosses down to their secretaries and office messengers, no one feels comfortable about saying no to a request. This results in the common practice of promising to take action in order to save face and to satisfy the needs of the moment. This habit of over-promising and underdelivering can lead to lost business if foreign visitors lose patience with the failure to deliver.

Conclusions and prospects for the future

This chapter has tried to present a balanced picture of Morocco as a developing country that is fast becoming an important market in terms of production and consumption, as well as in respect of regional and international trade relations. The part played by King Mohamed VI has been discussed in detail, along with his many policy initiatives to modernize and improve business conditions in Morocco. Specific marketing opportunities have been identified, particularly with reference to construction projects, the promotion of e-commerce, and consumer and business marketing. Market segmentation, targeting, and marketing mix have also been discussed, along with aspects of general business conditions.

Throughout the discussion we have aimed for an even-handed appraisal of business in Morocco. It is fair to say that some Moroccan business people despair of ever seeing any change in *la mentalité marocaine*, which they believe may hinder foreign business relations. Others are excited by the growing momentum of modernization as young people go abroad to study and come home with new ideas, and as foreign investors bring not only capital investment but also new technology and new management methods. As a people Moroccans typically welcome progress and quickly adopt innovations that can improve the quality of life and bring success for their country in world markets.

Morocco is looking closely at its options for future growth in trade and economic development. Opportunities to work in multilateral groups based around the Mediterranean, such as the Euro-Mediterranean Association Agreement and the so-called '5+5' group, are being actively pursued. The 5+5 group is composed of the five Maghreb countries plus the Mediterranean coastal countries of France, Italy, Malta, Portugal, and Spain (MAP, December 5, 2003).

Bilateral trade with distant countries is also growing. In 1999 the Chinese premier, Ziang Zemin, visited Morocco to explore the possibility of establishing trade relations; the US–Morocco free trade agreement has opened new possibilities for trade across the Atlantic; and the New Economic Partnership for African Development provides a forum for Morocco to work with African trading partners. Thus on the basis of all the evidence presented here, we conclude that Morocco offers promising market opportunities in a rapidly changing business environment.

References

Abun-Nasr, J. (1975) *History of the Maghrib* (Cambridge: Cambridge University Press).

Al-Akhawayn University (2004) Partners, Office of International Programs (www.alakhawayn.ma).

Amine, L. S. (1990a) 'Marketing environment in the Middle East and North Africa', in H. Thorelli and S. T. Cavusgil (eds) *International Marketing Strategy*, 3rd edn (New York: Pergamon Press), pp. 229–48.

Amine, L. S. (1990b) 'Demand estimation in a developing country environment', in H. Thorelli and S. Tamer Cavusgil (eds) *International Marketing Strategy*, 3rd edn (New York, NY: Pergamon Press), pp. 305–26.

Amine, L. S. (1990c) 'Production-sharing in Mexico and Morocco: a comparative study of problems and opportunities', *Advances in Business Studies: An Irish Review*, 2 (2), pp. 18–36.

Amine, L. S. and S. T. Cavusgil (1986) 'Marketing environment in the Middle East and North Africa', *Advances in International Marketing*, 1, pp. 115–41.

Arabic News (2001) 'Signatory Countries of Agadir Declaration on Arab FTA Hold Meeting in Amman', (www.arabicnews.com/ansub/Daily/Day/011228/2001122823.html).

BBC (2002) 'King of Morocco weds', (news.bbc.co.uk/1/hi/world/africa/1886812.stm).

Brigham Young University and eMSTAR (1999) (www.culturegram.com).

Cateora, P. R. and J. L. Graham (2005) *International Marketing*, 12th edn (Boston, Mass.: Irwin McGraw-Hill).

Government of Morocco (1999) *Five-Year Development Plan 1999–2003* (Rabat: Government of Morocco Printers).

Gray, K. R. (2001) 'Women entrepreneurs in Morocco', *The Journal of North African Studies*, 6 (4), pp. 64–74.

Gray, K. R. and L. S. Amine (2002) 'Doing business in Morocco', *Thunderbird International Business Review*, 44 (3), pp. 379–98.

Gray, K. R. and A. Driouchi (2000) 'Globalization and Morocco', in *The Global Economy and Society: A World Survey*, Proceedings of the Professors' World Peace Academy Eighth World Congress, pp. 110–15.

Hall, E. T. (1979) 'Learning the Arabs' silent language', *Psychology Today*, August, pp. 45–53.

Hargraves, O. (1996) *Culture Shock! A Guide to Customs and Etiquette – Morocco* (Portland, Oreg.: Graphic Arts Center Publishing).

Hofstede, G. (1991) *Cultures and Organizations: Software of the Mind* (London: McGraw-Hill).

L'economiste (2004a) 'Texte Intégral du Discours de SM le Roi à l'Occasion de la Fête du Trône' (www.leconomiste.com).

L'economiste (2004b) 'Regain d'Intérêt pour l'Habillement Qui Tient le Haut du Pavé des Implantations' (www.leconomiste.com).

L'economiste (2004c) 'C'est l'Université Al Akhawayn Qui Mène Ce Projet Financé par le CRDI-Canada' (www.leconomiste.com).

MAP (Maghreb Arabe Presse) (October 17, 2001) Speech by King Mohamed VI when setting up the Royal Institute of the Amazigh Culture (www.map.co.ma/mapeng/speeches_interviews.htm).

MAP (October 31, 2001) *Paris Match* interview with King Mohamed VI (www.map.co.ma/mapeng/interviews/match_eng.html).

MAP (September 2, 2002) Royal speech at the meeting of heads of state and government at the World Summit on Sustainable Development (www.map.co.ma/mapeng/speeches/johannesburg.html).

MAP (November 15, 2002) Message by King Mohamed VI on National Press and Communication Day (www.map.co.ma/mapeng/speeches/Press_speech2002.html).

MAP (June 28, 2003) Full text of the royal message to the Global Summit of Women, Marrakech, June 28, 2003 (www.map.co.ma/mapeng/speeches/women_summit_message.html).

MAP (October 15, 2003) Full text of the address by King Mohamed VI to the Colloquium on 'The Arab World and Africa: Today and Future Challenges' (www.map.co.ma/mapeng/speeches/arabworld_africa.htm).

MAP (December 5, 2003) Full text of the speech by King Mohamed VI at the 5+5 Summit in Tunis (www.map.co.ma/mapeng/speeches/5+5summit.htm).

MAP (December 11, 2003) Text of the message sent by the sovereign to an international conference on 'Investment, Cultures and Civilizations: Links and Impacts' (www.map.co.ma/mapeng/speeches/invest_culture.htm).

MAP (February 12, 2004) Full text of the royal message to the Third National Tourism Convention (www.map.co.ma/mapeng/speeches/assises_tourism_4.htm).

MAP (July 16, 2004) 'FTA with Morocco to Reinforce Relations with Longstanding Partner, Bush'. (www.map.co.ma/mapeng/home_dep/h_depmay1979.htm).

MAP (July 30, 2004) 'Economic takeoff impossible without healthy social climate' (www.map.co.ma/mapeng/home_dep/Spain_throne.htm).

MAP (August 14, 2004) 'M. Benaissa: L'Algérie Détient Les Clés du Règlement de la Question du Sahara qui Fait Obstacle au Projet de l'UMA' (www.map.co.ma/mapfr/depeches_2004bis/benaissa-cles-sahara.htm).

MAP (August 17, 2004) 'Le Président Bush Signe le Décret d'Application de l'Accord de Libre Echange USA-Maroc' (www.map.co.ma/mapfr/depeches_2004bis/bush_libre_echnage_ma.htm).

Munson, H. (1993) *Religion and Power in Morocco* (New Haven, CT: Yale University Press).

NICI (2004) Morocco. 'National Information and Communication Infrastructure' (www.uneca.org/aisi/nici/country_profiles/Morocco/morocpol.htm).

Prahalad, C. K. (2005) *The Fortune at the Bottom of the Pyramid: Eradicating Poverty Through Profits* (Upper Saddle River, NJ: Pearson).

SEPTI (2004) Secrétariat d'Etat auprès du Premier Ministre Chargé de la Poste et des Technologies des Télécommunications et de l'Information (Secretary of State in charge of the Post and Telecommunications and Information Technologies) (www.uneca.org/aisi/nici/country_profiles/Morocco/morocpol.htm).

United Nations (1992) 'UN Conference on Environment and Development' (www.un.org/geninfo/bp/enviro.html).

United Nations (2003) *Arab Human Development Report 2003: Building a Knowledge Society* (Amman, Jordan: National Press).

6
Marketing in the Middle East

Marin Marinov

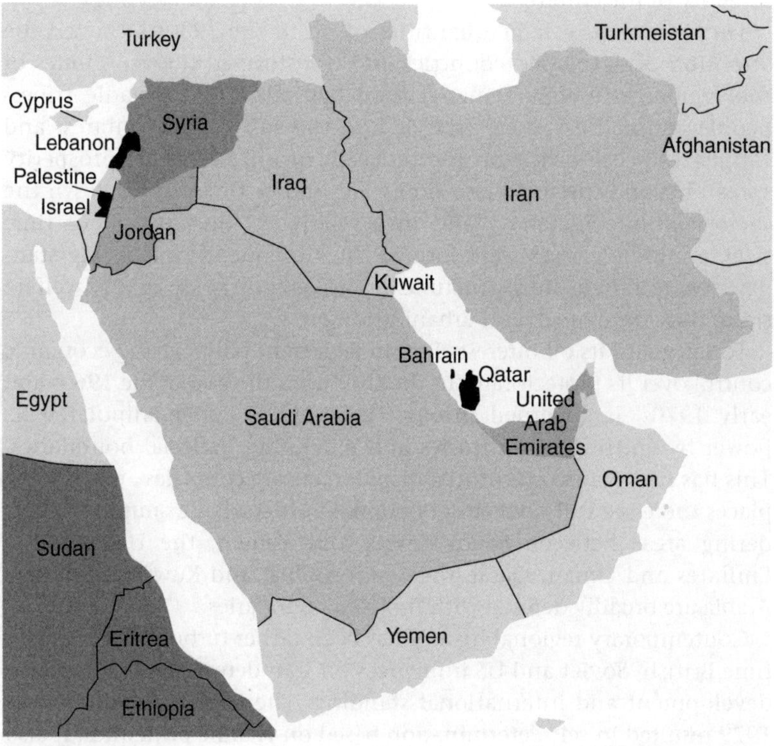

Source: www.universes-in-universe.de.

Map of the Middle East

Brief historical background

People have been living in the Gulf area since the Stone Age and about 5000 years ago it was home to advanced civilizations. Many of the contemporary countries of the Middle East, for example Bahrain, Kuwait, Qatar, Saudi Arabia, and Yemen, were established in the eighteenth or nineteenth centuries by nomadic tribes that shared a common identity. Others, such as Iran and Oman, are ancient empires with a rich historical heritage. The Ottoman Empire ruled most of the region from the eleventh to the nineteenth century. In the mid 1800s its influence diminished because the activities of local tribes destabilized the integrity of the empire.

The discovery of large quantities of oil in the 1930s attracted the attention of developed countries and transformed the economies of the region, although Yemen lagged behind. Poor nomadic tribespeople adopted a settled lifestyle and the sultanates, emirates, and caliphates became rich on the proceeds of oil. Economic prosperity spread beyond the royal and noble families to those lower down the socioeconomic hierarchy and in a relatively short period of time sizable middle classes were formed. In subsequent years living standards were raised, infrastructural improvements were made, welfare states were developed, and urbanization grew.

To safeguard its oil interests Britain kept tight political and economic control over its protectorates in the Gulf until the end of the 1960s and early 1970s. It governed through local rulers and manipulated its power by cutting off territories and redefining national boundaries. This has since caused territorial disputes among countries and in some places there are still no distinct national borders. For example the bordering areas between Saudi Arabia and Yemen, the United Arab Emirates and Oman, Qatar and Saudi Arabia, and Kuwait and Saudi Arabia are broadly defined with no fixed boundaries.

Contemporary regional history has been rather turbulent. For a long time British, Soviet and US influences on Iran determined its political development and international standing. The Islamic Revolution of 1979 resulted in self-determination based on Islamic principles. It also gave rise to Islamic fundamentalism and strong ethnocentrism. The border dispute between Iran and Iraq escalated into full-scale wars that continued for most of the 1980s. The Iraqi invasion of Kuwait in 1990 and the consequent Gulf War in 1991s reshaped regional attitudes and relationships. More recently the Iraqi War has further destabilized the region. There are sharp contrasts between the attitudes of governments and peoples of the region towards the Western world in general and the United States in particular. Iran and Syria have an anti-Western stand, as do some groups in Iraq, which presently is in complete disarray. Kuwait, Saudi Arabia, and the United Arab Emirates have good relations with the West and are more receptive to Western political doctrines. This has had a positive effect on their economic development.

The rapidly improving living standards and employment opportunities in the oil-rich countries have caused an unprecedented movement of people within and into the Middle East. Today the population of Kuwait includes more non-Kuwaiti than Kuwaiti nationals. Non-Kuwaitis from the Arab world and Western countries are mostly well-educated professionals with highly paid jobs, while the majority of immigrants from the Indian subcontinent have little education and engage in low-skill labor.

Bahrain and the United Arab Emirates compete for the status of the most important business hub in the Middle East. Both countries have liberal economies and attract domestic and foreign investment and professionals, workers, and tourists from all over of the world. At the other end of the spectrum, Yemen struggles to provide jobs and improve its economic growth, and it is rife with social and political uncertainties.

The economy

The share of oil in the GDP and exports of the oil-rich economies in the Middle East are shown in Table 6.1. Fluctuations in oil prices can be damaging to the economy so the national governments have followed a variety of economic diversification strategies in order to reduce

Table 6.1 Percentage share of oil in GDP and exports, Middle East, 2000

	Share of GDP	*Share of total exports*
Kuwait	42	88
Qatar	41	72
Bahrain	33	26
Oman	32	90
Saudi Arabia	30	93
United Arab Emirates	28	69
Iran	17	85

their dependency on oil revenues. These mainly involve the development of gas-related and heavy industries, services, and tourism. Industrialization has been aided by state investment in import substitution production and the imposition of tariff barriers on industrial imports. The exploitation of natural gas is greater in Iran, Qatar, Saudi Arabia, and the United Arab Emirates, which together have about a third of world's reserves. This involves gas processing, electricity generation, and related industrial production activities (Fawzy, 2000). Investment in heavy industries such as steel, aluminum, petrochemicals and so on is most substantial in Iran, Oman, Saudi Arabia, and the United Arab Emirates. Many of the recent ventures have involved foreign investment, technological assistance and knowledge transfer. The service sector, with its value-adding activities, has grown at great speed in Dubai and Bahrain, which act as major re-exporting and banking centers for Africa and the Middle East. They attract financial investments from all over the world and have become popular destinations for business people and tourists.

The use of import substitution production for the purpose of industrial diversification has been weakened by the Gulf countries' membership of the World Trade Organization (apart from Yemen and Iran). However there is still government protection in sensitive areas such as agriculture and food processing, where reliance on imported inputs is rather substantial.

In their move towards economic diversification, key challenges for the Gulf countries are to enlarge the scope and increase the rate of technological transfer and to create a knowledge base to foster the development of knowledge-intensive industries to offset the resource skewed structure of the national economies. Despite their differing cultures and traditions, the geographic position of the Gulf countries as a crossroad for international trade between Asia, Africa, and Europe, combined with their favorable investment climate and natural resources, should have a positive effect on business development, innovation and knowledge creation.

Between 65 per cent and 82 per cent of the demand for industrial and consumer goods in the Middle East is met by imports. There are numerous retail outlets, the majority of which are traditional in style and small in size. The governments do not tax most goods and services, apart from the *zakat*, a mandatory tax imposed under Islamic law. Bahrain, Kuwait, Oman, Qatar, Saudi Arabia, and the United Arab Emirates host about four fifths of foreign retail operations in the Middle East and account for 80 per cent of the value of imported goods and services.

Living standards vary significantly across the region. The oil-rich countries have a high per capita GDP in absolute terms and in purchasing power parity, but the nominal per capita GDPs of two of the countries – Qatar and Yemen – are more than a hundred times apart. The Middle East also has a higher per capita GDP than other developing regions. For example it is more than three times higher than in Latin America and more than 15 times higher than in Sub-Saharan Africa. Moreover annual GDP growth exceeds population growth, with the per capita income consequence that increases by about 5 per cent per annum. However here too there are regional disparities. While in Qatar it averaged about 23 per cent in 2000–4, in Syria and Yemen it averaged 1.5 per cent in the same period and in Iraq it fell by about 15 per cent.

In 2004 Bahrain, Iran, Iraq, Kuwait, Oman, Qatar, Saudi Arabia, and the United Arab Emirates accounted for almost two thirds of the world's oil extraction and three quarters of oil exports. Non-oil exporting Middle Eastern states such as Egypt, Israel, and Syria have diversified economies with a strong or moderate degree of technological development, which Jordan, Yemen, and Lebanon, whose economies are less developed or unstable, have become providers of the workers required by Bahrain, Kuwait, Oman, Qatar, and the United Arab Emirates. Saudi Arabia also has a large number of foreign workers in absolute terms but if taken as a percentage of the workforce its reliance on foreign labor is less marked.

The economic bases of the Middle Eastern countries have some complementarities in terms of factor endowment and factor development, but these are too limited to act as a driver of regional economic integration. One factor that favors integration is the region's strategic position between Europe and Asia, and between Africa and Asia. Another is the similar ethno cultural fabric of the countries that comprise the region, apart from Israel, which is non-Islamic and differs not only in its historical associations but also in its cultural and economic characteristics and Iran, which is Islamic but non-Arab and Farsi rather than Arabic is spoken there. However integration is hampered by strong competition between groups of economies, their rather uniform natural resource bases and the turbulence created by international, ethnic and religious tensions, as manifest in wars, skirmishes, guerilla fighting, and terrorist acts. Thus little real progress has been made towards full regional integration.

Six countries belong to the Cooperation Council of the Arab States of the Gulf, formerly known as the Gulf Cooperation Council: Bahrain,

Kuwait, Oman, Qatar, Saudi Arabia, and the United Arab Emirates. Its economic and social objectives include common regulatory policies in the fields of economics, finance, trade, legislation and administration, the fostering of scientific and technological progress, and intraregional capital investment. A long-term objective is to coordinate and integrate the national economies by introducing a common currency. Yemen is negotiating entry to the council but Iran, Iraq, Jordan, Syria, and Egypt have not applied.

In recent years the governments of many of the countries have implemented significant privatization programs and adopted microeconomic policies aimed at minimizing price distortions. This is part of economic liberalization and the opening of the economies to foreign participation, which is expected to boost their international competitiveness.

Since the 1990s European Union (EU) member countries have invested significant amounts in the Middle East. British, French, German and Dutch investments account for more than 90 per cent of the total EU flow into the Middle East to date.

The regional market

In terms of population and size of nominal gross domestic products Iran and Saudi Arabia are the most populous and strongest regional economies (Figure 6.1) and they both have sizable markets. Investors

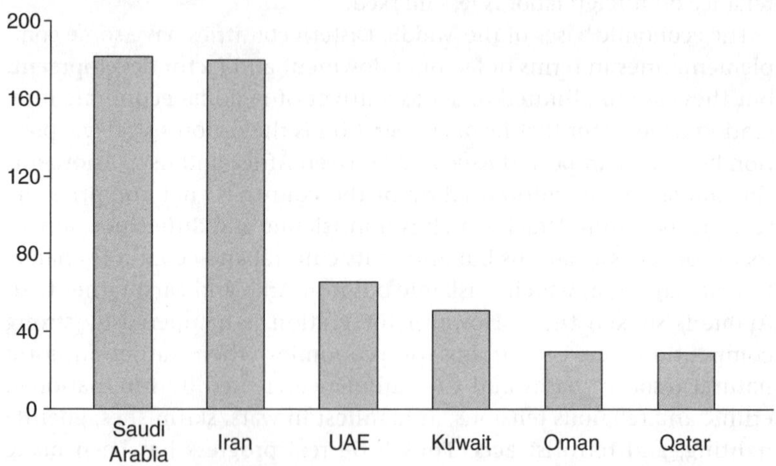

Sources: National statistics.

Figure 6.1 Nominal GDP, Gulf countries, 2003 (US$ billion)

with no experience of doing business in the region perceive the Middle East as politically risky, and even companies that are already established in the region fear that their operations will be disrupted by political forces, the instability of social structures, the complexity of the regulatory climate, and unforeseen problems such as terrorist attacks and social unrest. This is especially the case for companies that have invested resources in order to gain market entry. The political situation in Iraq, Syria, the Palestinian territories, and Iran has had a negative impact on investors' confidence. However other markets, many of which are small in size, have shown stable growth and attracted large investments, mostly in oil and oil-related industries. The markets of the United Arab Emirates, Kuwait, Bahrain, Qatar, and Saudi Arabia are all considered relatively stable and promising for international marketing operations.

The regulatory environment also acts as a major deterrent to market entry. According to O'Driscoll *et al.* (2002) there is little economic freedom in the majority of Middle Eastern countries. The varying degree of volatility restricts the choice of market entry modes, limits the formation of joint ventures, and requires companies to spend considerable time lobbying local government and business officials.

Nominal per capita GDP in the region generally reflects the possession or otherwise of oil reserves. Oil-rich Bahrain, Kuwait, Qatar, and the United Arab Emirates have the highest per capita GDP, while Egypt, Syria, and Yemen, which are less well endowed with natural resources, have a very low per capita GDP (Figure 6.2). Qatar has the highest purchasing power, based on average nominal per capita GDP, followed by the United Arab Emirates, Kuwait, Bahrain, Oman, and Saudi Arabia.

When estimating purchasing power using the purchasing power parity (PPP) index the average price differences are taken into account. This means that the average purchasing power in Iran, for example, increases nearly fourfold because of the lower value of its PPP index (Figure 6.3). Low in per capita income is viewed by social scientists as a major factor in social tension and political instability, as can be seen in the more volatile Middle Eastern countries: Lebanon, Jordan, Egypt, Syria, and Yemen. The fact that this instability deters foreign investors exacerbates the problem of low economic growth and slow social development.

The uneven economic performance in the region is the 1990s was due to fluctuating oil prices. The Kuwaiti economy performed best with an average GDP growth rate of 5.2 per cent per annum. In most of the

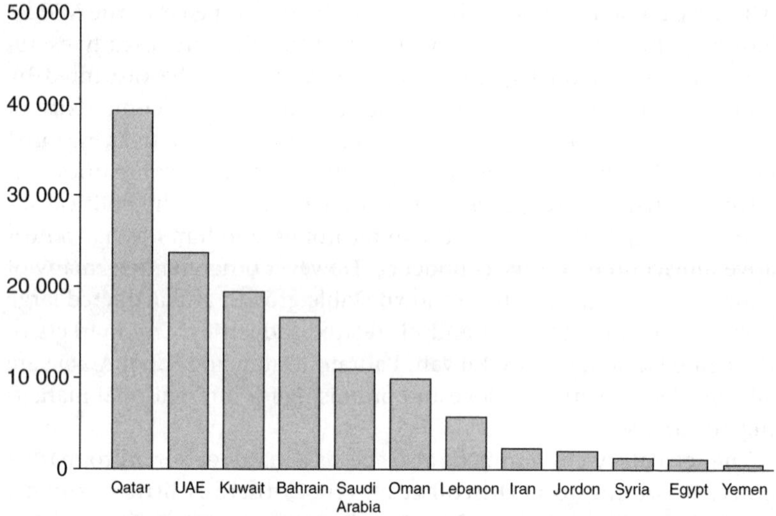

Source: International Monetary Fund (2005).

Figure 6.2 Nominal per capita GDP, selected Middle Eastern countries, 2004 (US dollars)

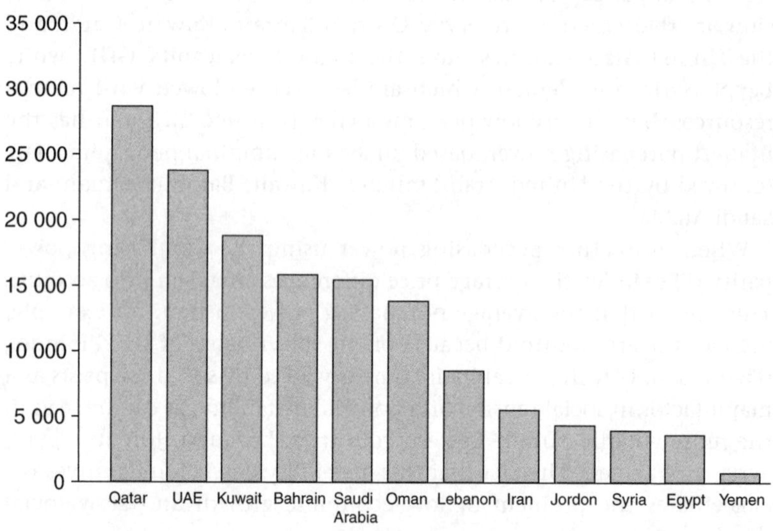

Source: International Monetary Fund (2005).

Figure 6.3 Per capita GDP in PPP, selected Middle Eastern countries, 2004 (US dollars)

countries inflation has been kept low by imposing financial restrictions and covering budget deficits by issuing bonds. In countries where there has been high inflation it has been caused by shortages brought about by war or cross-border tensions.

The generally high population growth rate – substantially higher than the global average – is the consequence of a high birth rate and a continuous inflow of migrant workers. The age structure in the Middle East is typical of developing countries, with more than two thirds of the population under the age of 25 and more than half under the age of 15. The expatriate population is substantial, ranging from more than three fourths of the total population in Qatar and the United Arab Emirates to about a third in Oman and Saudi Arabia. The majority of immigrant workers come from the Indian subcontinent, followed by Southeast Asia, other Middle Eastern countries, and Western states. Indians account for about a third of the population in the United Arab Emirates and Pakistanis and Bangladeshis for more than a fifth (Jeffreys, 2000). Presently Iran hosts more than five million unskilled refugee workers, mostly from Afghanistan and Iraq.

The size of the middle and upper-middle classes in the oil-rich countries is growing and there are currently about 8–12 million people in these classes in the region as a whole. This has spurred the development of franchised retail outlets and fast-food restaurants such as McDonald's, Burger King, Chili's, and Hardee's (Ramseyer, 2001). Franchises are an ideal way of establishing a presence in the Middle East because their operations and offerings can be adapted to Islamic values (Young, 2001).

The other common mode of market entry is to set up a joint venture with a local firm. Many local business people are very interested in forming joint ventures with Western companies and travel across the world in search of foreign partners. The members of the Cooperation Council of the Arab States of the Gulf offer conducive conditions for entering their markets and therefore competition among foreign entrants is fierce.

Cultural characteristics

The overall culture of the Middle East is strongly embedded in the nomadic way of life and Islam. While all the Arab countries have a common language and religion and a similar social structure, Iran, Egypt, Syria, and Iraq have differentiated themselves from the Gulf states. In the historical development of the region there have been confrontations and animosity based on local conflicts and foreign intervention. The discovery and exploitation of oil brought a change to international relations due to the global economy's dependence on oil. It also resulted in drastic improvements in income, living standards, industrialization, and infrastructure (Abbasi and Hollman, 1993). However it also brought a degree of Westernization, which clashed with the traditional Arab culture and Islamic religion. For Arabs Islam is the foundation of all aspects of life – political, economic, social and business. Modern interpretations of the Islamic Holy Scriptures, fostering separation of the followers of Islam, represent new reasons for contradictions that affect cultural unity in the region (Ali, 1993).

As well as religion, national particularities determine the culture of the countries in the region. For example Kuwaitis have great respect for tribal associations and value systems, are very traditional and submissive to higher authority (Yasin and Stahl, 1990), while Saudi Arabians are authoritarian and strongly believe in conformity (Ali and Al-Shakhis, 1986). Contemporary Middle East is seen by many authors (see, e.g., Kassem, 1989) as possessing unique cultural traits when compared to other parts of the world. However according to Hofstede's (1980, 1991) cultural dimensions there is a high degree of homogeneity among the countries in terms of high power distance, collectivistim, masculinity, and risk aversion. Using the contextual features of cultures developed by Hall (1976), the Arab cultures of the Middle East can also be described as having high context specificity. Risk aversion means that foreign companies entering the market must display a strong commitment and consumers set demanding standards for products and their modification or adaptation. Masculinity is expressed in gender segregation, as laid down in Islamic teachings. Segregation can be extremely strict, with separation in the provision of education, banking services and so on, plus gender-specific retail outlets and hotel facilities. Gender segregation reaches its extreme in Saudi Arabia but is more liberal in Bahrain, Kuwait, and the United Arab Emirates. In general women are now participating more in economic, social and political life.

Consumer behavior

Consumers in the Middle East are demanding and expect high-quality products and services (Fry, 2001). Moreover many are well-informed due to satellite television, international travel, and the Internet. There is a sizable middle class with strong brand recognition and a growing appetite for foreign products and services.

Religious beliefs are often taken as the starting point in consumer segmentation. Rice and Al-Mossawi (2002) argue that this applies both within countries and across the Middle East. The influence of Islamic values on purchasing behavior and marketing mix preferences is strong among all age groups and social strata. Moreover the conflicting forces of traditionalism and innovativeness (Jordan, 1998), technological embracement and conservatism, desirable and desired (Rice, 1999) are emotionally embedded in Middle Eastern consumers. All this presents a great challenge to marketers that are attempting to design a differentiated approach to consumer markets.

There are certain differences in purchasing behavior among and within the countries of the region, so whilst universal values generally determine the marketing approach an understanding of country- or market-specific factors can be crucial to its success (Siddiqi, 1999). For one thing the ethnic diversity in the region means that demands differ in terms of the nature of goods and services and their quality and price. Retailers often address this by employing managers and shop assistants from a variety of nationalities. This facilitates a customized service with cultural sensitivity. Establishing brand recognition among the various ethnic groups and social strata can be difficult, but brand sensitivity is relatively high in the case of fashion and fast moving consumer goods. Young consumers are the most brand conscious (Martin, 1999) and spend heavily on high-end foreign brands. Currently the fashion sector has the fastest growth rate. However it is becoming difficult to maintain brand loyalty.

Apart from Islam, politics can have a marked effect on consumer behavior. Consumers who oppose certain countries' foreign policies tend to boycott products from these countries. This is the case with US products in Iran, Syria, and Yemen, and even in Saudi Arabia and Jordan, where consumers have been generally receptive to US goods. Consumers now tend to purchase Japanese, German and French products. Hence, the combined influence of political and religious attitudes and beliefs can be a powerful factor for a company's market position in the region, based on consumer associations of the company's country of origin and brand.

As the Middle Eastern states are relatively new to consumerism and consumer protection, vendors are often perceived as having the upper hand and arguments often break out between buyers and sellers when the former's expectations are not met.

Product choice depends heavily on purchasing power. Affluent consumers tend to buy high-quality products from all over the world while the growing middle class leans towards value-for-money products from developed countries and local food items. The majority of consumers have a limited income and mostly shop in bazaars where they can bargain with the traders. Their attitude towards Western products is mostly negative and associated with perceived social injustice and resource exploitation. Despite this, when it comes to consumer durables they aspire to products from Western and other developed economies. Hence marketing strategies that emphasize firms' social commitments to improving people's lives and uplifting them from the trappings of poverty have a much greater chance of attracting those at the bottom of the consumer pyramid.

According to a study published by Al-Khatib *et al.* (2005) conducted by the NFO WorldGroup in 2002, Bahrain, Kuwait, Oman, Saudi Arabia, and the United Arab Emirates are the most Westernized of the Middle Eastern countries and in general there is a growing tendency for individualism and a move towards nuclear rather than extended families. About 25 per cent of the respondents were young, moderately traditional and would consider trying imported goods and brands. While abiding by Islamic values they were reasonably open minded, progressive and more oriented towards the nuclear than the extended family. They tended to be receptive to Western influences, were hard working and had a comparatively liberal view of the role of women in society.

In contrast another 25 per cent of those surveyed, mostly elderly people, maintained strong traditional and family values and refrained from purchasing modern Western goods and brands. Most of these consumers were risk-averse, had a paternalistic view of the family and the role of women in society, and were ethnocentric in respect of products and brands.

Thus the traditionalists that made up half of the market had different approaches to purchasing decisions. While the majority of the elderly consumers subordinated their needs to those of their families and relatives, younger traditionalists were mostly income earners and made their own decisions about purchases.

The largest group consisted of people aged 25 years to middle age (about 35 per cent of those surveyed). These were career-oriented liberal individualists whose purchasing decisions were related to the nuclear family. While their actions accorded with Islamic values they had a need for self-realization. Women in this group tended to aspire to higher education, good job opportunities, and greater personal freedom.

The smallest segment (15 per cent), the 'rebellious' group, consisted of teenagers and individuals in their early twenties who tended to be individualistic and self-interested. Those from well-off families had Western shopping habits and preferred reputable expensive brands. Most of them respected family ties but preferred to socialize with friends. They liked fashion, luxury and glamour, and their self-indulgence made them a good target for brands that suggested status and style.

There were no apparent differences in the purchasing power of the four groups, so each one was an attractive target for products and services that could address its preferences. The consumers in the first two groups were mostly product-led or influenced by the functional characteristics of a brand. Those in the last group responded positively to the emotional facets of a brand and the promises it offered.

Al-Khatib *et al.* (2005) have studied the ethical standards of consumers in Kuwait, Oman, and Saudi Arabia and found that the majority adhere strongly to Islamic moral and cultural values. Al-Khatib *et al.* label the largest group (39 per cent of the respondents) 'principled purchasers'. These are characterized by consistently high ethical behavior and exhibit a significant degree of trust, although they fear that people will not deal with them in a trustworthy way. The next group, 'suspicious shoppers' (37 per cent), mistrust people and are afraid they will be cheated or exploited. They themselves refrain from actions that could hurt others. These characteristics are particularly typical of less educated Kuwaiti consumers. The smallest group, 'corrupt consumers'. (24 per cent), are suspicious of the intentions of others and are very cautious when dealing with people. Consumers in this group are likely to exploit advantageous situations and relationships to meet their needs.

The relationship-based culture in the region and Islamic values require innovative marketing strategies that combine satisfaction of consumer preferences with relationship marketing. Such an approach would help to counter the avoidance by consumers of US and other Western brands and products because of their negative associations, and to promote the purchase of good-quality products from emerging economies.

Marketing strategies for Middle Eastern markets

The shared religion and value system in the Middle Eastern countries has led some to believe that they can use a standardized marketing strategy and marketing mix throughout the region (Melewar *et al.*, 2000). However this fails to take account of cultural differences and the consequent formation of different market segments. Siddiqi (1999) suggests that marketers should differentiate between core values and the peripheral ones that are unique to each country. He goes on to say that even though some consumers have the same core values they may be influenced in different ways by marketing messages. This argument can be extended to the consumption of products and the use of relationships for distribution, as well as attitudes towards the various types of distributor. The fundamental core values defined by Islam should certainly be reflected in companies' marketing mix elements or market penetration strategy. This would not only improve the effectiveness of their ventures but also prevent them from making culturally insensitive blunders. Thereafter market segmentation could be based on income, psychographic differentiation, and the differing preferences of ethnic groups. The perception of Saudi Arabia, Kuwait, the United Arab Emirates, Lebanon, and Egypt as a homogenous market prone to a high level of standardized marketing operations is well in line with the desire of international companies to exercise control over their international marketing strategies, objectives and positioning across markets. It has been recognized that Islam determines the behavior of people in the Gulf states of Saudi Arabia, Kuwait, Qatar, Bahrain, the United Arab Emirates, and Oman, and advertising can be and is often used to show the virtues of Islam (Al-Makaty *et al.*, 1996).

The necessity for local adaptation applies particularly to advertisements, which should consider the degree of adherence to Islamic practices as well as brand and country of origin preferences. Whilst there is a strong religious commitment (Amin, 2000) throughout the Middle East, in Iran the teachings of Islam have become fundamental to state policy whereas in Dubai the situation is more *laissez faire*. Advertisements aimed at female consumers should also be tailored to the country in question. In some countries the women portrayed in advertisements should be veiled, while in Egypt, Lebanon, and the United Arab Emirates, for example, it is permitted to show the face (Al-Olayan and Karande, 2000) although the rest of the body must be covered. There are also income differences to consider. In the United Arab Emirates, Kuwait, Bahrain, and Oman many women are more affluent than their counterparts in the more conservative Gulf states because the more liberal social attitudes mean that women now hold senior management or professional positions. People's general attitude towards advertisements is hostile in some countries, for example Egypt, whereas in the United Arab Emirates and Bahrain they are more receptive to them.

The Middle East is one of the most promising retail markets in the world because of the population's relatively high average purchasing power. The high population growth rate and the existence of rich young consumers with cosmopolitan tastes are also favorable factors.

West European and US retail companies started to enter large urban areas in the region at the beginning of the 1980s. Their presence has gradually led to changes in the structure of the retail market. The first to enter were Arcadia, Monsoon, Bhs, and Next, followed by Debenhams, Marks & Spencer, Liberty, and Harvey Nichols. Mothercare has also established a presence and has numerous retail outlets in Saudi Arabia. Shopping malls began to be built in the late 1980s and since then have grown in number, size and sophistication (Young, 2001). Retailing has been one important means of diversifying the economies in the region.

Conclusion

The large Middle Eastern region is rich in oil, gas, and other natural resources that have attracted foreign companies and led to rapid economic development and improved living standards in many of the countries. Economic diversification has somewhat reduced some of the countries' dependence on oil and gas revenues.

The varying degrees of economic development among the countries limit the opportunities for regional integration, so economic relations with the rest of the world are crucial to development. Outside the oil sector the entry of foreign companies, mostly via the establishment of joint ventures with local businesses or individuals, is usually related to the countries' need to import consumer goods.

Islam lies at the heart of state arrangements and governs consumer behavior, although the richer countries have been Westernized to varying degrees. While the older generations have remained traditional and are strict followers of Islamic principles and values, the younger generations have adopted certain Western norms and patterns of behavior.

The Middle East is the largest region with Islamic population that has another unifying cultural trait for most of it, the Arab language, which has had strong influence on the behavioral characteristics of consumers in the region.

The Middle East is important not only as a source of crude oil and natural gas but also as a large market with considerable potential.

References

Abbasi, S. and K. Hollman (1993) 'Business success in the Middle East', *Management Decision*, 31 (1), pp. 55–9.

Ali, A. (1993) 'Management theory in a transitional society: the Arab experience', *International Studies of Management and Organization*, 20 (3), pp. 7–35.

Ali, A. and M. Al-Shakhis (1986) 'The relations between administrators' attitudes and needs in Saudi Arabia', *Proceedings of the Academy of International Business Southeast Chapter*, Atlanta, GA, USA, pp. 210–32.

Al-Khatib, J., A. Staton and M. Rawwas (2005) 'Ethical segmentation of consumers in developing countries: a comparative analysis', *International Marketing Review*, 22 (2), pp. 225–46.

Al-Makaty, S., G. van Tubergen, S.Whitlow and D. Boyd (1996) 'Attitudes toward advertising in Islam', *Journal of Advertising Research*, 36, pp. 16–26.

Al-Olayan, F. and K. Karande (2000) 'A content analysis of magazine advertisements from the United States and the Arab World', *Journal of Advertising*, 29, 69-83.

Amin, G. (2000) *Whatever Happened to the Egyptians?* (Cairo: American University Press).

Fawzy, H. (2000) 'Dolphin', paper presented at the conference 'The Gulf 2000: Energy, Infrastructure and Finance', Abu Dhabi, 28–9 March.

Fry, A. (2001) 'Pushing into Pan Arabia', *Campaign Report on World Advertising*, 8 June, p. 21 Washington, DC: US Advertising Association.

Hall, E. (1976) *Beyond Culture* (New York: Doubleday).

Hofstede, G. (1980) *Cultural Consequences: International Differences in Work-Related Values* (Beverly Hills, CA: Sage).

Hofstede, G. (1991) *Culture and Organizations: Software of the Mind* (New York: NY McGraw-Hill).

International Monetary Fund (2005) *World Economic Outlook* (Washington, DC: IMF).

Jeffreys, A. (2000) *Emerging Emirates 2000* (London: Oxford Business Group).

Jordan, B. (1998) 'Kid's stuff?', *Gulf Marketing Review*, 52, pp. 6–9.

Kassem, M. (1989) 'Services marketing: the Arabian Gulf experience', *Journal of Services Marketing*, 3 (3), pp. 61–71.

Martin, J. (1999) 'Franchising in the Middle East', *Management Review*, 88 (6), pp. 38–42.

Melewar, T., S. Turnbull and G. Balabanis (2000) 'International advertising strategies of multinational enterprises in the Middle East', *International Journal of Advertising*, 19, pp. 529–47.

O'Driscoll, G., K. Holms and M. O'Grady (2002) *Index of Economic Freedom* (Washington, DC: Heritage Foundation).

Ramseyer, R. (2001) 'Middle-East piece', *Restaurant Business*, 100 (12), pp. 29–35.

Rice, G. (1999) 'Islamic ethics and the implications for business', *Journal of Business Ethics*, 18, pp. 345–58.

Rice, G. and M. Al-Mossawi (2002) 'The implications of Islam for advertising messages: the Middle Eastern context', *Journal of Euro-marketing*, 11 (3), pp. 71–96.

Siddiqi, S. (1999) 'Strategic geographic and strategic corporate challenges: a regiocentric perspective to the Middle East', *Managerial Finance*, 25 (2), pp. 45–62.

Yasin, M. and M. Stahl (1990) 'An investigation of managerial motivational effectiveness in the Arab culture', *International Studies of Management and Organization*, 20 (3), pp. 69–78.

Young, J. (2001) 'Retailers opt for a market full of eastern promise', *Retail Week*, 31 August, p. 14.

7

Marketing in Kuwait

C. P. Rao and Adel Al-Wugayan

Source: www.globalsecurity.org/military/world/gulf/kuwait-maps.htm.

Map of Kuwait

Introduction

Marketing is a contextual activity. While it is often argued that the basic concepts, theories, tools and techniques of marketing are universal in nature, effective marketing depends very much on a clear understanding of the context in which it is undertaken. Hence marketing practices vary from country to country. It is essential for the marketing context in the country in question to be clearly understood both by domestic and international marketers so that they can customize their approach to achieve the desired results. This chapter considers the unique market characteristics of and typical marketing practices in the State of Kuwait.

Geographical and historical background

Kuwait is an independent Arab country located at the westernmost point of the Gulf. It is rich in oil and has about a tenth of the global deposits. It is a member of the Gulf Cooperation Council, the Arab League, and the Organization of the Islamic Conference. The country borders the Kingdom of Saudi Arabia to the south and south-west, and Iraq to the north and north-west. Kuwait has always resisted the territorial aspirations of its large and powerful neighbors – Iraq, Iran, and Saudi Arabia – and their attempts to influence its political development. Since independence, the sovereignty of the country has been guaranteed by the West via special arrangements based on the fact that Kuwait is a major supplier of oil to the United States and Western Europe. Since the Gulf War of 1991 Kuwait has been protected by large contingents of British and US troops.

The territory of Kuwait consists of flat sandy desert sloping down the Gulf. Its location makes it a natural gateway to and starting point from the Arabian Peninsula, which gives it strategic and commercial importance. For many centuries the country was a crossroad for nomadic tribes and the ancestors of present-day Kuwaitis engaged in trade with other countries in the region. Some descendants of the important merchant families who played a significant role in this trade are highly influential in the political, economic and social life of Kuwait today.

Kuwait occupies just 17,818 square kilometers (about 7,000 square miles) of the mainland and owns several tiny uninhabited islands in its territorial waters. The island of Failaka is quite attractive and is popular with tourists due to its Stone Age excavations. The farthest distance from north to south is about 200 kilometers (124 miles) and from west to east it is 170 kilometers (100 miles). The infrastructure of this compact country is well developed.

The area occupied by contemporary Kuwait has been inhabited since ancient times. The city of Kuwait was established about three hundred years ago, when a number of clans from the Al Aniza tribe migrated to the northern shore of the Gulf from Arabia. These settlers created an oligarchic merchant entity, the economic prosperity of which was based on fishing, pearling and trade. In 1756 a sheikhdom was created by Sabah al-Awal and the Al Sabah dynasty took control of the country. Although the sheikhdom was a part of the Ottoman Empire it enjoyed considerable independence. In the eighteenth and nineteenth centuries the British Empire aspired to make Kuwait its protectorate, which eventually happened in 1899. The application of British policies and the presence of British military forces in the sheikhdom guaranteed stability and international recognition. Oil was discovered in 1938, and in 1946 the British–US Gulf Oil Corporation began oil extraction. From 1951 the sheikhdom received half of the oil revenues and used it to develop the country's infrastructure and provide welfare services. Together with Iran, Iraq, Saudi Arabia, and Venezuela, Kuwait was a founding member of the Organization of Petroleum Exporting Countries (OPEC), which was created in 1960 to protect the oil interests of the member states.

When Kuwait declared independence in 1961, the sheikhdom was turned into an emirate. Iraq strongly objected and expressed territorial claims. In July 1961 Kuwait joined the Arab League; in 1963 it became a member of the United Nations; and in 1981 it was a founding member of the Gulf Cooperation Council. In 1975 the Kuwaiti government took full charge of the revenues from Kuwaiti oil.

With its abundant oil wealth the State of Kuwait prospered during the 1970s and 1980s and became one of the major economic and trading centers in the Arab world. However, during the Iran–Iraq War (1980–88), when Kuwait supported Saddam Hussein's Iraqi regime, the Kuwaiti oil installations were frequently bombed by Iran. Military help was received from the United States and the Soviet Union to protect Kuwait against Iranian military incursion. In August 1990 Kuwait was invaded and annexed by Iraq, and many Kuwaitis were killed or kidnapped. Substantial economic and ecological damage was caused by the war and the burning of oil wells by withdrawing Iraqi troops following their defeat in the 1991 Gulf War.

In the years after liberation the economy was successfully rebuilt and Kuwait became one of the most affluent countries in the world. In October 1992 the first parliamentary elections were held, and in

January 1995 Kuwait became a member of the World Trade Organization. During the first months of the Iraqi War, which started in March 2003, Kuwait was an important staging point for the deployment of British and US troops. The conflict has a somewhat negative effect on the country's economy and trade.

In the harsh and hostile desert of the Arabian Peninsula the summers are long, extremely hot, and dry, with frequent dust storms and high humidity. The winters are short, warm and rarely rainy. Consequently for most of the year Kuwaitis rely heavily on air conditioning to withstand the brutal heat. Moreover the absence of fresh water has necessitated the construction of water desalination plants, although these also have the advantage of producing electric power. The Kuwaiti government subsidizes water and energy prices by roughly 90 per cent. Some water shortages have been experienced recently due to consumption outweighing production, so the government is considering removing the subsidies. It is expected that this would create huge demand for energy-saving alternating current machines.

Structure of the economy

As well as several large export-oriented petrochemical enterprises and oil refineries there are small manufacturers and large water desalinization, ammonia, desulfurization, fertilizer, brick, block, and cement plants. During the Iraqi invasion in 1990 troops looted all moveable equipment of value, especially high-technology items and small machinery. Much of this has been replaced with newer equipment. The government has extended its economic relations with the United States in order to attract foreign investment in industry, thereby diversifying the otherwise oil-dependent economy. Agriculture is insignificant because of the lack of water and arable land. Moreover most of the soil that was suitable for farming in south-central Kuwait was destroyed when the Iraqi troops set fire to the oil wells, thereby creating vast oil lakes. The government has since had some success with hydroponic food production (Figure 7.1).

Fish and prawns are abundant in Kuwaiti's territorial waters, and large-scale commercial fishing takes place locally and in the Indian Ocean. Manufacturing is mostly focused on food processing and packaging. The local production of building materials and furniture, complement the imported products and materials required by the construction sector. Petroleum extraction and refining, fertilizer and chemicals production, and water desalination account for 60 per cent of the

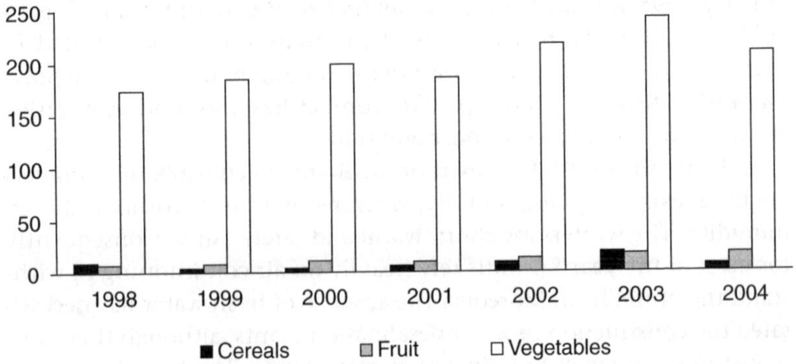

Source: Ministry of Planning and Census, Kuwait.

Figure 7.1 Agricultural production, Kuwait, 1998–2004 (thousand metric tons)

country's GDP; services account for 39 per cent, and the contribution of agriculture is miniscule.

The Kuwaiti dinar is a strong currency pegged to a basket of currencies in which the US dollar has the most weight. There is a balance of payments surplus. The government provides foreign economic assistance to other states through the Kuwait Fund for Arab Economic Development, an autonomous state institution created in 1961 on the pattern of Western and international development agencies. In 1974 the fund's lending mandate was extended to all developing countries.

Demographic profile

At the end of 2001 the population of Kuwait was 2 309 102, of which Kuwaiti nationals accounted for just 38 per cent. The remaining 62 per cent consisted of migrants from different parts of the world. While there is a close gender balance among Kuwaitis (49.3 per cent male, 50.7 per cent female), among non-Kuwaitis males outweigh females by 33.4 per cent. This is because more non-Kuwaiti males than females move to Kuwait to seek work, and because the Kuwaiti immigration laws restrict family immigration in order to reduce pressure on the public utilities, mostly energy and drinking water. In general Kuwaiti citizens are more affluent than non-Kuwaitis.

It is estimated that 92.8 per cent of Kuwaitis are literate. About 17 per cent of the population has post-high school education and almost 10 per cent hold university degrees. This high literacy rate has significant implications for the type of marketing required to attract consumers.

According to the most recent census the overwhelming majority (71 per cent) of the country's population is below 29 years of age, so there is a demand for products and services that are geared to younger consumers. Entertainment products such as television, DVD players, electronic games, and Internet-related services have enjoyed substantial growth in the past few years, as have communication services and equipment such as mobile telephones. Moreover, given that 18 year-old are permitted to drive, the demand for cars is growing fast. The same applies to motorcycles, off-road vehicles and water jet-skis.

The market for consumer goods

The Kuwaiti market offers a wide variety of consumer goods, many of them imported. Most consumers spend around 25 per cent of their income on food and beverages. The percentage of monthly expenditure on various products and services by household is shown in Table 7.1. Kuwaiti and non-Kuwaiti households are two distinct segments of household markets. In order to provide an overall picture of the structure of domestic trade in goods and services, Table 7.2 shows the number of companies in each business sector and the sector's profitability. The net profit to capital ratio also indicates the competitive nature of each of the sectors.

Consumer behavior

Islamic and Arab cultural traits, values and norms characterize consumer behavior in Kuwait. From a marketing perspective Kuwaiti con-

Table 7.1 Monthly expenditure per household, Kuwait, 2001 (per cent)

	Kuwaiti households	*Non-Kuwaiti households*	*Average*
Food and beverages	27.61	28.56	28.06
Clothing	8.82	7.39	8.14
Rent and fuel	7.76	24.05	15.51
Household equipment	14.99	6.93	11.16
Medical expenses	0.79	0.63	0.71
Transport and communications	16.32	10.9	13.74
Education and recreation	4.24	6.18	5.16
Transfer payments	7.67	6.79	7.25
Other	11.8	8.57	10.26

Source: Kuwaiti Institute of Banking Studies (2002).

Table 7.2 Number and profits of Domestic trade and service companies, Kuwait, 2001

	Number of companies	*Net profit to capital (per cent)*
Food	64	74
Clothing and accessories	154	301
Furniture and electrical	127	80
Information and recreation	58	33
Construction materials	50	5
Equipment and machinery	78	93
Contracting	125	35
First aid products	31	42
Mixed activities	261	96
Agriculture and livestock	59	23
Commercial services	145	24
Professional services	2	21
Marketing, exchange and hotel	1,007	26
Consulting	42	23

Source: Kuwaiti Institute of Banking Studies (2002).

sumers exhibit both modernism and cultural conservatism. There are two distinct consumer segments. Non-Kuwaitis comprise a diversity of cultures, ethnicities, and nationalities. Kuwaiti consumers exhibit the cultural traits of a collectivist society. Table 7.3 compares the cultural dimensions of Kuwaitis as compared to consumers in the United States.

There are several characteristics of Kuwaitis that distinguish them from other Arab and Islam consumers, as well as from foreigners residing in the country. First, the country has experienced a long period of Westernization and Kuwaitis have benefited from generous oil-revenue handouts from the government. This has enabled them to become more business oriented and develop a spirit of competition whilst preserving the traditional traits of group cohesiveness and obedience (Ali,

Table 7.3 Comparison of US and Kuwaiti consumers using Hofstede's cultural dimensions

	US consumers	*Kuwaiti consumers*
Power distance (out of 110)	40	85
Uncertainty avoidance (out of 95)	46	66
Masculinity (out of 112)	62	50
Individualism (out of 91)	91	38

Source: Al-Wugayan (1998).

1988). Second, economic prosperity has allowed the recruitment of a large number of foreigners most of whom work in privately owned businesses, leaving Kuwaitis free to pursue entrepreneurial activities that provide them with a large and easy income. Third, the fact that foreign business people need a Kuwaiti national or company to guarantee their operations gives Kuwaitis legal rights over foreign businesses and an alternative way to amass wealth. All these factors have encouraged Kuwaitis to take affluence for granted (Al-Kazemi and Ali, 2002).

Based on income group and behavioral patterns, three consumer segments can be identified, as discussed below.

High-income consumers

This consumer group consists mainly of Kuwaiti citizens and a small proportion of non-Kuwaitis. They are affluent and either have their own business or work in highly paid professions. Individuals in this group have a net worth of one million dinars. Their principal characteristics are as follows:

- A good education at the high school level and beyond.
- The ability and inclination to travel abroad for leisure and shopping.
- A large expenditure on the most advanced electronic products.
- The purchase of leading global brands that represent a luxurious lifestyle.

Despite the lack of data on income distribution in Kuwait, proxy measures indicate that the size of this segment is small but growing. Inherited money, which is not taxed in Kuwait, can dramatically increase the wealth of younger Kuwaitis. The members of this group display a preference for American, Western European and Japanese products and brands.

Many invest large amounts overseas: official estimates put private foreign investment by Kuwaiti nationals at more than US$60 billion at the end of 2000.

Medium-income consumers

Extensive government employment programs that guarantee a steady income have bolstered the growth of this segment. The Kuwaitis and non-Kuwaitis in this category are mainly highly paid professionals with jobs in the public or private sector. The Kuwaitis in this group have the following characteristics:

- A moderate to high level of education.
- Spend a large amount of money on electrical and electronic goods.
- Prefer established and well-known brands.
- Take out bank loans for house and car purchases.
- View the high-income consumer group as an aspirational benchmark.

The non-Kuwaitis differ slightly in that they spend moderately on electrical and electronic goods, and demonstrate price sensitivity. They also devote a high proportion of their income to savings and house purchases in their home country.

Low-income consumers

The Kuwaiti consumers in this group have a low to moderate education, spend relatively little on electrical and electronic goods, devote a low to medium proportion of their income to clothes and footwear, and usually avoid branded and fashionable products. The non-Kuwaitis have a similar educational level to their Kuwaiti counterparts but spend less on clothes and footwear. Because the male workers in this group tend to have families in their home countries a large proportion of their income is remitted home.

The non-Kuwaiti population (numbering approximately 1,450,000) consists of many nationalities with differing consumption patterns that depend on their country of origin, especially in the case of basic household products. The majority come from India, Pakistan, the Philippines, and Arab countries, mostly Egypt, and the rest come from a number of Asian and Western countries. Prior to the Iraqi invasion in 1990, the non-Kuwaiti population consisted mainly of Palestinians, Yemenis, and Sudanese. These groups, especially the Palestinians, lived with their families and had settled in Kuwait. Hence their income was not remitted abroad but used for immediate consumption. After the Iraqis were ejected in February 1991 these groups were no longer welcome and their number fell from over 500,000 to 80,000. Thus in postwar Kuwait the demand by non-Kuwaiti for luxury and high-quality goods declined and consumers on the whole became more price sensitive.

Another sizable group comprises stateless non-Kuwaitis, who are estimated to number about 60,000. The government regards them as violators of the immigration law yet allows them to remain in the country, but without any citizenship privileges. They mostly work in the private sector and to a lesser extent in the government-owned military sector.

Charitable institutions provide some aid to those living below the subsistence level.

Characteristics of marketing management

The marketing of goods and services in Kuwait involves systematic management of products, prices, promotional activities, and distribution channels based on the unique characteristics of the Kuwaiti market.

Product management

Products and services need to be targeted at each consumer segment with a clear understanding of consumption patterns in that segment. Affluent consumers put great store on brand reputation, product quality, country of origin, and good after sales service. They prefer well-known brands from developed countries to products from less developed countries. For example they would rather buy Sony products manufactured in Japan than similar products from developing countries such as Malaysia. At the lower income levels adjustments in product quality and accompanying services have to be made.

Kuwait imports practically all the consumer and industrial products required in the country. Because there is free market access and import tariffs are low (4 per cent on average), products come from all parts of the world. Hence foreign marketers experience fierce competition in the Kuwaiti marketplace and have to find new ways of distinguishing their product offerings and making them more attractive to potential customers. The experience of General Motors (GM) clearly illustrates the need for strategy adaptation. GM has been a major supplier of cars to Kuwait for more than 60 years. However in the past two decades Japanese carmakers have penetrated the market with products that are more attractive in terms of both quality and price. Recently South Korean and some West European car manufacturers have entered the market. In an effort to regain market shares GM started increasing the variety of its product offerings. This strategy failed to produce significant results so GM shifted its focus to fleet sales to the police, the military, and car rental companies. This strategy has been more successful and has increased the visibility of GM cars on the roads which in turn has stimulated further demand.

Products also have to be adapted to the climatic and cultural conditions of Kuwait. While the climate is temperate for eight months of the year, from June to September the temperature rises as high as 50 degrees Celsius (about 120 degrees Fahrenheit). Products such as cars, household appliances, electronic goods, and a multitude of consumer goods have to be able to withstand not only this extreme heat but also problems caused by violent sand storms and the high humidity in the coastal areas.

Price management

The prices that Kuwaitis are willing to pay correspond largely to their income level. As already noted, those in the upper income bracket prefer well-established, high-quality brands and are willing to pay premium prices for them, while those with lower disposable incomes choose to buy less expensive versions of the same products and are less concerned with country of origin. However even affluent consumers are price sensitive and all income groups have a tendency to bargain, despite the fact that the majority of outlets have fixed prices.

Most Kuwaiti families are large and therefore wish to buy many products in bulk. In pricing terms this often requires multiple-unit prices to appeal to the target markets.

Promotion management

Promotion management deals with various communication programs aimed at consumers and/or distributors. All consumer and channel communications are in Arabic, but since there is a sizable number of English-speaking expatriates it is necessary for marketers to provide both Arabic and English versions of their advertisements, sales literature, and product instructions.

Given the fact that Kuwait has the cultural traits of a collectivist society, personal relationships, interpersonal communications, and especially word of mouth can have a greater influence on purchasing decisions than mass media communications. In line with this, personal selling and sales promotion play a significant part in the promotional mix. Sales people from non-Arab countries may develop a working knowledge of Arabic over time but they cannot be expected to understand or convey all its subtleties and nuances.

While there are numerous printed vehicles for advertising, in the form of newspapers and magazines, the effectiveness of the audiovisual media is somewhat limited, especially in terms of targeting different market segments. Outdoor advertising media are utilized extensively. Consumer goods companies often conduct promotional campaigns that involve giving free gifts or free meals to children in an effort to associated themselves with socially entrenched family values.

In all marketing communications marketers have to adapt their message to the specific societal and cultural values, norms and behavioral patterns of the target audience. International companies that advertise on television and the print media are usually given advice on the text and audiovisual format of their advertizements so as to avoid making cultural blunders.

Distribution of channels

The distribution system in Kuwait is dominated by a number of import trading companies, some of which are large and family owned. Each of them imports a wide variety of products for wholesale and distributes them to retail outlets throughout the country. These companies also engage in other business activities, such as construction, real estate, investment, and government contracting.

The structure and functioning of retail outlets exhibit characteristics of both the developed and the developing world. At one end there are large-scale retail establishments such as supermarkets, privately owned and cooperative societies, and department stores. There are four hypermarkets generating US$250 million per annum in sales. Supermarket sales amounted to US$125 million in 2004. Up-market specialist stores carry well-known premium international brands and fashion items, primarily from the United States and Western Europe. These establishments are typically confined to modern shopping malls such as Sharq, Marina, and Kuwait-Magic. At the other end of the spectrum, small retail establishments carrying lower-quality merchandise at lower prices are typically located in local souks or markets. Their merchandise is imported from various Southeast Asian countries and some cater to different nationality groups residing in Kuwait. There is only occasional bargaining in upper-end stores with fixed prices, but bargaining is typical in the souks. Discounted sale prices are commonly offered by stores during important festival periods, including the holy month of Ramadan and the annual festival called Hala.

Direct marketing is not common in Kuwait, although some European and US companies offer home shopping from catalogs. This form of shopping is favored by some women for reasons of convenience and privacy. Therefore fashion catalog companies such as the German Otto and Quelle and the US Freeman have managed to gain a market share. IKEA has also been successful in attracting interest in its furnishing catalogs. Direct marketing by means of flyers, special offers on the Internet and newspaper inserts is also used by companies. The cold calling of randomly selected individuals is not popular with consumers.

The physical distribution system in the country is very well developed, with good roads and a sophisticated network of warehouses. In this regard the standards are similar to those in developed countries.

Government regulations for international companies

Businesses in Kuwait have to comply with rigid government regulations, and a variety of laws and regulations govern the establishment and operations of marketing enterprises. Before establishing a business enterprise it is necessary to obtain the appropriate license either from the municipality or the relevant government agency. Non-Kuwaitis have to have a Kuwaiti sponsor, who often becomes a partner in the venture.

Political volatility in the region in the 1980s and 1990s discouraged foreign direct investment (FDI), with the result that Kuwait has received only about 1 per cent of the total FDI stock in all Arab countries. The annual net FDI flows were less than US$100 million for the period 1996–2000, most of which went to the oil sector. On average annual FDI is only 1.4 per cent of the national GDP.

To encourage FDI the Law for Direct Investment of Foreign Capital in the State of Kuwait was passed in 2001. This allows majority foreign ownership, and under certain conditions this can reach 100 per cent. Since 2002 multinational corporations such as BNP Paribas, Dow Chemicals, Dnata Agencies, BarterCard International, and Duboats have invested in the emirate. FDI originates mainly from the United States, United Kingdom, United Arab Emirates (UAE), France, and the Netherlands. Since 2002 US FDI has accounted for 24 per cent of the total FDI inflow, the UK for 20 per cent, and the UAE for 16 per cent. In the last two years FDI has been mainly targeted at property development, business and tourism, financial services, consumer goods, and heavy industry. There are also laws aimed at facilitating the privatization and liberalization of the Kuwaiti economy

Kuwait has had an overseas investment program since the 1970s. In 1976 the government set up the Reserve Fund for Future Generations with initial capital of US$7 billion. Ten per cent of the annual oil revenues go into this fund which is invested in overseas property and industry, mostly in the United States, United Kingdom, Germany, and Japan. Investments have also been made in most of the Fortune 500 firms, such as DaimlerChrysler. By the late 1980s the returns on these investments were surpassing the earnings from the sale of oil.

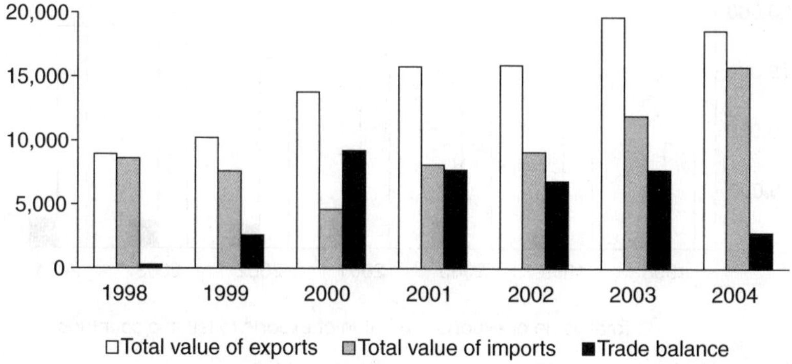

Source: Ministry of Planning and Census, Kuwait.

Figure 7.2 Exports, imports and trade balance, Kuwait, 1998–2004 (US$ million)

International marketing

Kuwait is an attractive country for international marketers as the state imports a wide variety of products from a large number of countries. Oil accounts for more than 95 per cent of the country's exports and 80–90 per cent of government income. Kuwait has enjoyed a favorable trade balance for several years (Figure 7.2). Since 2001 exports have accounted for about 42 per cent of GDP (Figure 7.3), which highlights the strong dependence of the economy on export revenue.

Since the majority of export earnings come from oil the trade balance depends on the international price of oil. The value of exports has grown since 1998, with an insignificant dip in 2002 (Figure 7.4).

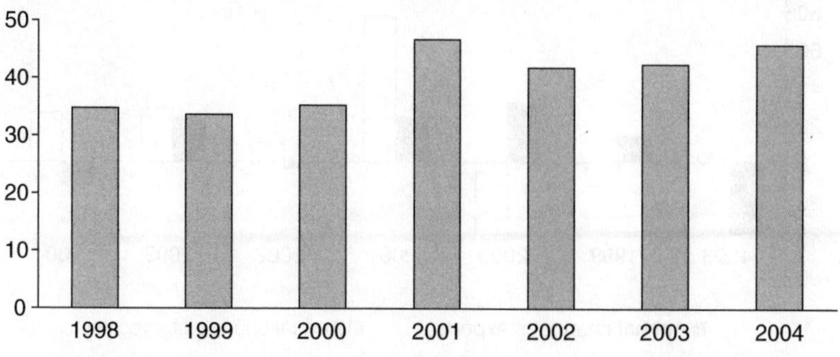

Source: Ministry of Planning and Census, Kuwait.

Figure 7.3 Contribution of exports to GDP, Kuwait, 1998–2004 (per cent)

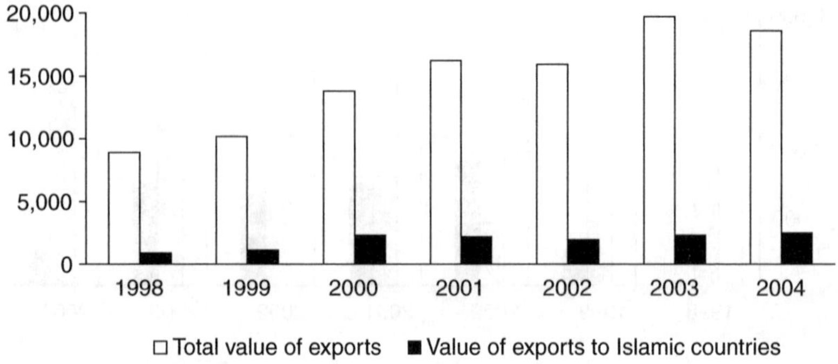

Source: Ministry of Planning and Census, Kuwait.

Figure 7.4 Value of exports, Kuwait, 1998–2004 (US$ million)

The key export destinations are the United States, Japan, and South Korea, which account for nearly 40 per cent of total exports. In 2004 the value of exports to other Islamic countries was almost three times higher than in 1998, although these exports are volatile and comparatively low in value. The annual change in exports and imports reflects the volatility of the political environment in the region, plus variations in oil prices and storage capacity (Figure 7.5).

The absence of foreign exchange controls in Kuwait attracts marketers from all over the world. The United States, Germany, Japan, Saudi Arabia and the United Kingdom are the principal suppliers of industrial and consumer imports (Tables 7.4 and 7.5).

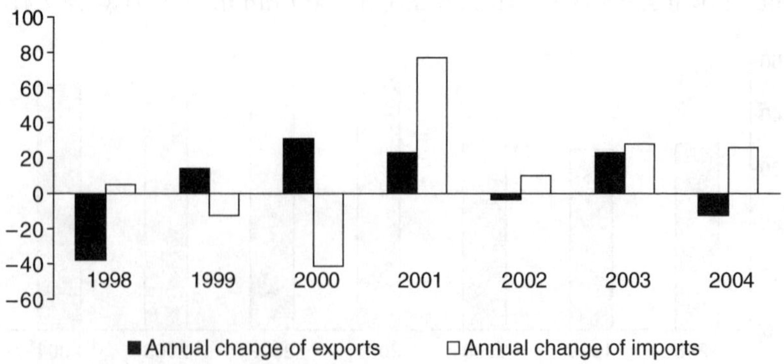

Source: Ministry of Planning and Census, Kuwait.

Figure 7.5 Annual change of exports and imports, Kuwait, 1998–2004 (per cent)

Table 7.4 Main exporters to Kuwait, 1997–2000 (per cent)

	1997	*1998*	*1999*	*2000*
United States	13.63	15.42	12.29	10.90
Japan	13.82	13.58	12.80	9.75
Germany	7.44	6.97	7.69	8.13
Saudi Arabia	6.78	6.21	6.19	7.03
United Kingdom	6.39	5.84	5.72	5.62
Italy	5.94	5.78	5.83	5.33
France	3.91	3.71	3.71	3.23
India	3.39	3.50	3.74	3.77
People's Republic of China	2.65	2.75	3.25	3.91

Source: Kuwaiti Institute of Banking Studies (2002).

Table 7.5 Composition of imports, Kuwait, 1995–2001 (million dinar)

	Capital goods	*Intermediate goods*	*Consumer goods*
1995	524.1	845.5	944.1
1996	554.6	917.8	1,011.2
1997	461.7	917.9	1,077.2
1998	528.6	924.0	1,125.8
1999	416.2	796.9	1,070.3
2000	501.6	812.8	1,123.8
2001	486.7	685.9	1,231.6

Source: Kuwaiti Institute of Banking Studies (2002).

The bulk of imports consist of intermediate (semifinished) goods and consumer goods, product categories in which there is fierce competition among a multitude of products and brands from various countries. This poses a major challenge to international marketers. Because of the country-of-origin effect, and the quality and price concerns of the targeted market segments, international marketers have to design appropriate marketing mix strategies to succeed in the Kuwaiti market. No single importing country dominates the market and market positions are highly volatile as Kuwaitis are quick to adopt the latest products and technology. While the tariff barriers are low, the natural barriers created by internationally established products and brands make it difficult for inexperienced and/or small companies to gain a foothold in these markets. Foreign companies are attracted to Kuwait by the high average purchasing power of the population and the country's dependence on imports. The rapid increase in the population and the proportion of young people with strong brand recognition and aspirational lifestyles also account for the influx of diverse global, international and regional high-quality products.

The government's globalization, privatization and liberalization policies are boosting business opportunities. Kuwait is market-oriented and has no regulations on the quantity of imports, does not impose quotas and does not require exporters to have special licenses. There are also opportunities for franchise operations. At present most franchises are fast food restaurants with Kentucky Fried Chicken, McDonald's, and Baskin-Robbins taking the lead. Automotive repair and service centers, clothing shops, cleaning services, health and recreation facilities show growth potential for franchise operations.

Consumer preferences are embedded in Islamic values but they are constantly evolving under the impact of Kuwait's overseas experiences and desire to be among the first to adopt new high-technology products. This means that companies have to change their products in line with the latest trends and innovations if they are to retain their market share, especially in the case of telecommunications, cars, household appliances, furniture, and high technology products for personal use. Female consumers are affected by the same trend in terms of cosmetics and fashion items. Hence imported cutting-edge products from countries with technological or fashion leadership, such as Japan, the United States, and France, are generally well received.

As the political situation in Iraq has slowly become more stable the importance of Kuwait as a trading post has increased. Due to the implementation of the World Trade Organization (WTO) regime it is expected that various markets, especially in the service sector, will be further liberalized and foreign participation will become possible. The planned integration of the Gulf Cooperation Council countries into a common customs union is also expected to result in greater trade among them.

Foreign exporters have to have a reliable and experienced Kuwaiti agent to handle the imports and their distribution. As noted earlier, large family-owned trading companies dominate marketing and distribution. Interested parties can find the most prominent of these companies in *Who's Who in the Arab World*. Family names are very important in Kuwait. Companies exploring international marketing opportunities should begin by contacting a number of Kuwaiti firms to verify demand and ascertain their interest in representing the company and its products. It is usual for agents to require exclusive rights of representation.[2] Agency agreements must be registered with the Ministry of Commerce's Department of Agencies within 60 days of signature in order for the agreement to be valid and enforceable. The agreement can also be registered with the Kuwait Chamber of Commerce. In most cases a Kuwaiti cannot get a license to import until the agreement with the foreign exporter has been registered.

International marketers must develop knowledge of and sensitivity to the local culture if they are to succeed in the Kuwaiti market. Islam dominates daily life and the consumption patterns and certain products, such as alcoholic drinks and pork, are illegal. All Kuwaitis are health conscious and prefer traditional, high-quality fresh food. Fresh, organic, non-genetically modified fruit and vegetables are preferred. When given a choice between locally produced and foreign sourced food, Kuwaitis are likely to remain loyal to local produce even if they have to pay a higher price for it. As the country strictly observes the requirement to fast during the daylight hours in the holy month of Ramadan, throughout that month foreign business people are advised to respect the custom and refrain from eating in public places during the daylight. Although Arabic is the official language, English is widely spoken and used for transaction purposes by business people. However for marketing communications international marketers have to use both Arabic and English to attract the attention of Arabic-speaking Kuwaitis and English-speaking non-Kuwaiti consumers.

Arab culture permeates all facets of life, including business exchanges, so international marketers must learn about this culture and the resultant management styles and adjust their behavior accordingly when conducting business in Kuwait. For example, unlike in the West, business discussions or negotiations are invariably interrupted by telephone calls and the entry and exit of other members of the company. Hence international marketers must be prepared to be patient when dealing with their Kuwaiti counterparts. Many Kuwaiti-owned firms employ expatriates as managers at various levels. International marketers may make initial contact with these managers, but they should be aware that authority and decision-making power are held by the Kuwaiti managers or owners.

Visitors are usually treated with courtesy and goodwill. A 'soft sell' as opposed to 'hard sell' approach is more effective, given the cultural norms in Kuwait. The traditional courtesy and cordiality of the Arab culture can lead international marketers to conclude that they have come to an agreement on an issue, when in fact the Kuwaiti participants may have decided that the terms being offered to them are not acceptable. International marketers must take into consideration the subtle nuances of Arab culture in order to succeed in the Kuwaiti market.

Conclusion

Kuwait is an affluent and attractive market for both domestic and international marketers. Although the country is small, its population is very heterogeneous, so consumers have to be segmented according to ethnicity as well as income (high, medium and low) and behavioral traits. With regard to ethnicity there are three principal groups: Kuwaiti nationals, non-Kuwaiti Arabs, and non-Kuwaiti, non-Arab nationals. The latter group is dominated by expatriates from the Indian subcontinent and the Philippines.

The Kuwaiti market is highly competitive as producers from all over the world are attracted by this free market economy with a stable currency and very low tariff. Therefore marketers need to design their marketing mix strategies carefully and implement them effectively. Marketers are also advised to pay considerable attention to the Arab culture and the Arab language when developing their marketing campaigns, especially in the case of marketing communications.

With Kuwait's adoption of the WTO regime many other opportunities are opening for international marketers, especially in services. Moreover legislation to facilitate foreign direct investment and protect intellectual property rights is guaranteeing more favorable business conditions. Overall, while the Kuwaiti market poses many challenges it also offers rewarding opportunities.

Notes

1. For details of the various commercial laws dealing with the establishment and operation of marketing enterprises, interested parties should contact the Kuwait Chamber of Commerce and Industry, P.O. Box 775, Safat, Kuwait 13008 (website www.kcci.org.kw).
2. One of the sources for finding prospective agents is *The Gulf Directory*. The US Department of Commerce provides lists of agents at a nominal cost and offers information about services to help companies to find an agent in Kuwait.

References

Ali, A. (1988) 'A cross-national perspective of management work value system', *Advances in International Comparative Management*, 3, pp. 151–69.

Al-Kazemi, A. and A. Ali (2002) 'Management problems in Kuwait', *Journal of Management Development*, 21 (5), pp. 366–75.

Al-Wugayan, A. (1998) 'Examining the Association between Personal and Cultural Values and Cross-National Customer Satisfaction', unpublished PhD thesis, University of Rhode Island, United States.

Chamber of Commerce of Kuwait (2003) *Introduction to the Kuwaiti Market* (Kuwait City: Chamber of Commerce).

Kuwaiti Institute of Banking Studies (2002) *Economic and Financial Data Base for Bankers* (Kuwait City: Chamber of Commerce).
Wright, C. (1992) 'Doing business in Kuwait – an update for American exporters', *Business America*, 13 July, pp. 10–12.

8
Marketing in Saudi Arabia

Marin Marinov

Source: www.geography.about.com/library/cia/blcsaudiarabia.htm.

Map of Saudi Arabia

Brief historical background

Covering most of the Arabian Penisula, the Kingdom of Saudi Arabia is one of the largest countries in the world with an area of between 1.96 and 2.25 million square kilometers (the difference here is due to undefined boundaries with some of its neighbors).

State organization of the country dates back to the mid 1700s. At that time the strong tribal ruler, Muhammad bin Saud, joined forces with the powerful Islamic reformer, Muhammad Abd Al-Wahhab, to establish an entity that gained international recognition. The period between then and the beginning of the twentieth century was volatile, with Egypt, the Ottoman Empire and numerous regional rulers and invaders challenging the existence of the Saudi state and fighting for control of the Arabian Peninsula.

Since becoming a kingdom in 1932 the country has been ruled by the Al-Saud family and since 1982 it has been governed as an absolute monarchy. The government is in control of the economy and has strong political and economic relations with the US administration. The Saudi–US alliance dates back to 1933, when Ibn Saud granted oil concessions to the US firm Standard of California. The created oil extracting company was subsequently reformed as the Arabian American Oil Company (ARAMCO) and in 1975 it came under the full ownership of the Saudi government, which now controls the world's largest oil reserves (about 25 per cent of total reserves). This has made Saudi Arabia the most important strategic country in the Islamic world.

The Holy Scriptures of the Qu'ran form the basis of the constitution and Saudi legislation is based on Shari'ah law. The national currency, the riyal, is pegged to the US dollar at the fixed exchange rate of 3.745 riyals to the dollar.

In the 1950s the capital, Riyad, was a small town of fewer than 50,000 inhabitants, but now it is the largest modern metropolis in the Middle East with 4.5 million people. Second in size and importance is Jeddah (Jiddah), a major port and trading city.

Population and custom

The peoples of Saudi Arabia comprise native Saudi Arabs, who account for more than 55 per cent of the population, plus other Arabs and nomadic Bedouins. The Saudi Arabs originate from the central and western Arabian Peninsula.

Ethnically the population is quite homogeneous, with about 90 per cent being of Arab descent and 10 per cent of Afro-Asian descent. The Saudis of non-Arab descent mainly inhabit the Hijaz region and the Red Sea coastline and come from South Asia, Iran, Malaysia, and other parts of Asia. The majority of Saudis are Sunni Muslim and a small minority are Shiite. According to the 2006 census the population numbers 27 million, including more than 5.5 million foreign nationals, mainly Arabs from neighboring countries. Other foreign workers include Indians, Pakistanis, Bangladeshis, Indonesians, and Phillipinos. Some 100 000 highly qualified US and European citizens hold well-paid jobs in the kingdom.

Prior to the 1960s the people of Saudi Arabia led a nomadic life and were spread all over the country, but due to rapid industrialization and urbanization it is estimated that about 90 per cent of Saudis have now settled permanently.

Islam governs all aspects of life in Saudi Arabia. The practice of any religion other than Islam is illegal in public places. National dress is strongly related to Islam and reflects the people's links to the land and ancient traditions. Dressing modestly is obligatory and foreigners are expected to do likewise.

The Wahabbi tradition, based on strict application of Islamic values, is used to justify the prohibition of public theatres and cinemas. In rare cases, in private compounds such as Dhahran there are theatres whose repertoires mostly consist of traditional music and plays. Cinemas that feature Arabic cartoons are planned for the near future.

Police officers are expected to enforce Islamic law. They are helped by numerous volunteers. Both policemen and volunteers are required to arrest unrelated males and females who socialize in public, and people who consume banned products, engage in prohibited games or listen to forbidden music.

Economic overview

Before the discovery of oil, the economy of Saudi Arabia relied on agriculture and trade. Most people led a nomadic tribal life and permanent settlements existed only in areas where there was water. Thus the economy was determined by the activities of independent clusters of people living near wells and oases. The nomads bred livestock and fed their animals on follage that grew during the infrequent rainfalls. In the permanent settlements craftsmen worked to meet local demands or the needs of occasional travellers. The people of the eastern province grew dates and other crops. The livelihood of people in the western province, the Hijaz, depended on agriculture, long-distance caravan trade, and providing services to pilgrims traveling to the holy cities of Mecca and Medina. The Hejaz Railway and the European colonial interests created more favorable conditions for the development of trade and bolstered the prosperity of merchant families in Jeddah and Mecca.

The centralization of power and abolition of the Bedouin tribes' exclusive rights to their tribal grazing land in 1925 accelerated the transformation of the country, while the discovery of oil brought a fundamental change to the economy. The development of the oil fields caused a boom in the construction of infrastructure, including ports, roads, water supplies, housing, and settlements. The oil industry also encouraged business growth as it required technical and logistical support. Thus the establishment of the Kingdom of Saudi Arabia and the discovery of oil in its eastern part led to a unified economy whose growth was enhanced by the US and European need for a cheap and reliable source of oil after World War Two.

Only 35 years ago Saudi Arabia held no attraction for international marketers. Just before the oil crisis of 1973 the value of imports was almost 40 times lower than at present: about US$8 billion (Tuncalp *et al.*, 1987). However the boom in oil prices during the 1970s and the establishment of Saudi Arabia as the most important world oil exporter by the mid 1980s increased the attractiveness of the Saudi market.

As a result of its dependence on oil exports the country has suffered structural imbalances and growing employment problems. The Saudi state is classified as a 'rentier state' (for detailed explanations see Looney, 2001, 2004; Ross, 2001) as the rents from oil and minerals have accrued solely to the state and businesses have mostly engaged in the distribution or utilization of these rents, with very little involvement in wealth generation. In general rentier states that are rich in natural resources have a low economic growth rate compared with resource-poor emerging markets (Sachs, 2001). Resource-rich countries have been known to experience the symptoms of the so-called 'Dutch disease' (Looney, 1992) which is characterized by the negative effects of a single flourishing export sector having negative effects on other export activities and on producers who compete with imports. In Saudi Arabia this has translated into reduced competitiveness by traditional agricultural exports and insignificant progress with industrial exports that could diversify the country's export portfolio. It has also encouraged imports of food and other products. Moreover heavy investment in the oil sector has reduced the funds available for investment in other sectors of the economy and discouraged private business growth. Another factor that has had a major effect on the development of the Saudi economy is the high expenditure on defense, which accounts for around 30 per cent of the government budget.

Thus over the years the Saudi government has invested mostly in defense, infrastructural projects, oil, and heavy subsidization of government owned businesses rather than in industrial development and diversification, knowledge creation and the encouragement of private business growth, thereby hindering technological change, production efficiency and international competitiveness.

Central economic planning was introduced in 1970 with the First Five-Year Development Plan (1970–75), the principal purpose of which was to provide guidelines and set goals for the restructuring of the economy, industrialization, and regional development.

The first two development plans (1970–79) concentrated on infrastructural development, including an extensive network of highways, power generation plants and modern harbor facilities. The third plan (1980–85) focused on education, health, social services and development of the industrial cities of Al Jubayl and Yanbu, while the fourth (1986–90) prioritized education and training. Private ownership of productive assests was also encouraged and foreign investment in the form of joint ventures was welcome. Private investment went mostly into trade, and a lesser amount into manufacturing, agriculture, finance and construction.

The major priorities of the fifth plan (1990–95) were closing the technological gap between the developed countries and Saudi Arabia and balancing technological development in various sectors of the economy, and consolidating the defense sector. The aims of the sixth plan (1996–2000) were to lower the cost of government services and to extend the eductional and training programs. It also paid attention to economic diversification with a particular focus on private manufacturing and agriculture. The effort to 'Saudiize' the workforce, initiated in the fifth plan, continued during this period. The seventh (2000–05) and eighth (2006–10) plans have concentrated on further diversifying the economy by strengthening the private sector. The latter is now expected to play a leading role in economic development. This represents a marked change from the situation that prevailed prior to 1995, when economic development was the exclusive preserve of the government and the duty of the private sector was only to ensure enterprise profitability.

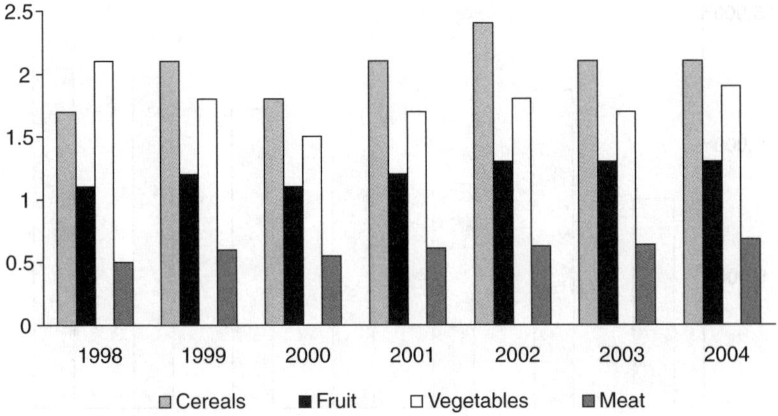

Source: Central Department of Statistics.

Figure 8.1 Agricultural production, Saudi Arabia, 1998–2004 (million metric tons)

Despite the failure to achieve all the goals of economic planning the overall development of the economy has accelerated since 1970. Manufacturing has expanded substantially. While agricultural production is limited by the climate and only 1 per cent of the Saudi territory is arable, some cereals, fruit, and vegetables are suited to the dry, hot climate, including wheat, barley, dates, tomatoes, water melons, and citrus fruit (Figure 8.1). There is also livestock farming, with more than 10 million sheep and goats and several hundred thousand camels and cattle. Fishing is a well-established tradition and more than 50 million tons of fish are caught each year, a proportion of which is exported. The development of manufacturing, transportation, construction, and agriculture have resulted in the growth of per capita GDP following a slump in 1985 (Figure 8.2).

Because of Saudi Arabia's strong reliance on oil exports it is highly vulnerable to external economic shocks. A drop in oil prices or economic crises elsewhere can have a severe impact on export earnings. The private sector is not well developed and there is insufficient domestic business growth to absorb such shocks hence the effort by the government to diversify the economy.

Foreign trade

Saudi Arabia has made efforts to encourage foreign trade by adopting liberal import and export conditions. There are no limitations on the

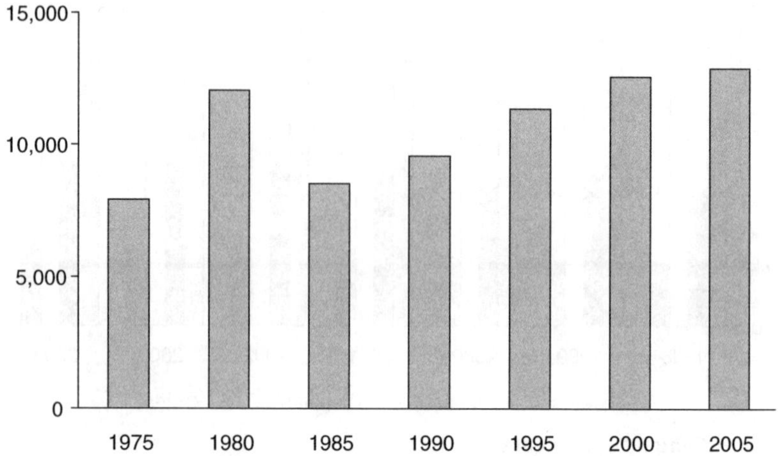

Source: Central Department of Statistics.

Figure 8.2 Per capita GDP in PPP, Saudi Arabia, 1975–2005 (US dollars)

quantity of imported goods and there are no tariff barriers or foreign exchange controls. Restrictions exist only on products that are unacceptable for reasons of religion and convention, including alcohol, firearms, proscribed drugs, second-hand clothing, pork and pork products.

The state does not interfere explicitly in the import/export transactions of private retail and wholesale companies. Government policies and the country's oil wealth have nurtured the growth of domestic companies that have a good knowledge of local market opportunities. The legal system stipulates that only Saudi nationals and companies entirely owned by them can import goods. They must possess import licenses issued by the Ministry of Commerce and secure the approval of the various branch ministries for the products to be imported. Hence local importers, wholesalers, and retailers control the distribution networks and the business–consumer interface in all consumer markets. Moreover the various distributors, wholesalers, and retailers provide different market coverage, which is an important factor in establishing export–import business relationships.

These import conditions impose limitations on international companies that wish to sell their goods in Saudi Arabia. They can only do so by finding a local agent, partner, distributor or representative who is willing to import their products. This effectively means that their products have to be approved by Saudi officials in terms of suitability,

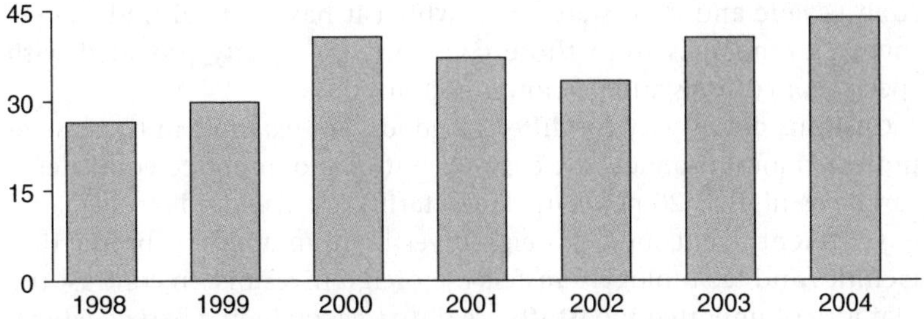

Source: Central Department of Statistics.

Figure 8.3 Contribution of exports to GDP, Saudi Arabia, 1998–2004 (per cent)

quality, price, terms of delivery, and customer service provision before they can be imported. Importers require foreign companies to abide by their agreements in respect of regular supplies, prices, support, and after-sales service. Meeting their requirements and avoiding price changes are essential for establishing and maintaining long-term business relationships. Nonetheless the highly lucrative Saudi market is highly attractive to producers all over the world.

Exports contribute about 40 per cent to the Saudi GDP (Figure 8.3). Exporting is based on industrial or agricultural licenses. The export regulations place limitations on some products that are either scarce or produced with the help of government subsidies. Items that need special government permission to be exported include subsidized food products, livestock, antiques, and Arab horses.

The export activities of Saudi Arabian companies have received some attention from academic researchers (Tuncalp *et al.*, 1987; Crick *et al.*, 1998), who have mainly focused on factors that deter companies from expanding their export operations. According to Al-Aali (1995), strong competition in foreign markets, large fluctuations in exchange rates, and high transportation costs are the principal export barriers for Saudi businesses. Crick *et al.* (1998) support these findings and add foreign market competition, lack of market information, lack of knowledge about trade agreements and foreign import regulations, and a shortage of personnel who are capable of dealing with export–import issues. The Saudi Export Development Center provides some institutional support for companies that are planning to export or to expand their export activities, but it is mostly the natural market entry barriers coupled with skill shortages that have deterred Saudi export growth. Saudi Arabia operates a special import–export regime with countries from the

Arab League and Arab states with which it has bilateral trade agreements. Companies from those countries are usually provided with special concessions and pay lower customs duties.

Customs duties vary for different goods. For example in the case of protected local products the customs duties and imported equivalents can be as high as 20 per cent. These tariffs are also used by the Saudi government to encourage foreign investment in domestic production facilities and technology transfers by foreign investors. In contrast the majority of imported foodstuffs are duty free, including barley, wheat, corn, rice, meat, and livestock. For other products the import duty is 12 per cent *ad valorem* on the cost, insurance and freight (CIF) value. The CIF value of imports is converted into Saudi riyals at the exchange rate prevailing on the date the imports are declared.

Saudi importers mostly import on the basis of an exclusive product line or regional representation and reliable service provision, including high-quality after-sales service, the supply of spare parts, maintenance services, and warranties. Agreeing a sustainable package deal rather than importing a product can form the foundations of successful long-term export–import operations and a presence in the Saudi market.

Exports were hit in 2001 and 2002 but were quick to recover, driven by a strong global demand for oil. Imports rose substantially in 2002 and have continued to increase since then (see Figure 8.4). The total value of exports in 2003 was US$87.4 billion, of which oil had a 75 per cent share. Most exports go to the United States, Japan, South Korea,

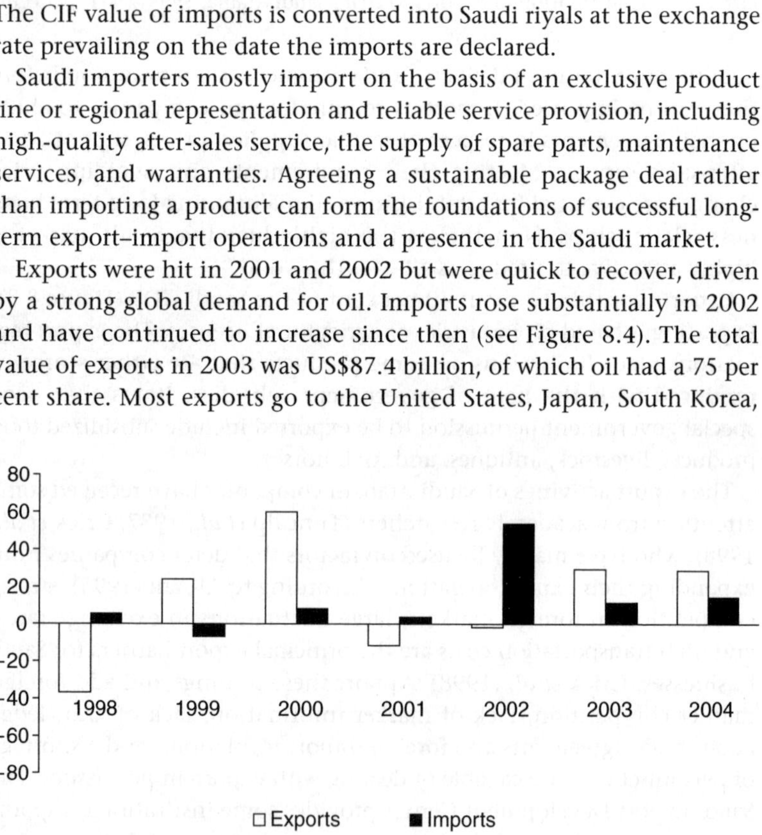

Source: Central Department of Statistics.

Figure 8.4 Annual change in exports and imports, Saudi Arabia, 1998–2004 (per cent)

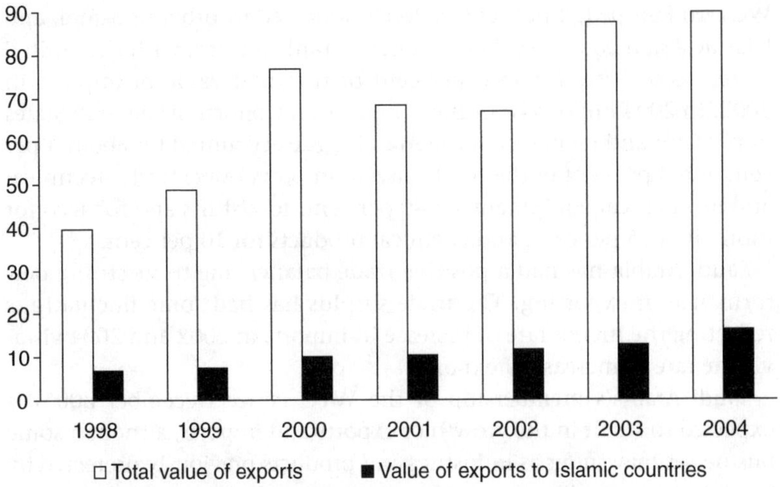

Source: Central Department of Statistics.

Figure 8.5 Value of exports, Saudi Arabia, 1998–2004 (US$ billion)

China, and Western Europe. In 2004 more than 18 per cent of all exports went to other Islamic countries (Figure 8.5). Presently China, Japan, South Korea, and India account for two thirds of the country's crude oil exports and more than half of refined petroleum products.

The gradual increase in imports since 2002 has reduced the country's trade surplus (Figure 8.6). The bulk of imported goods come from

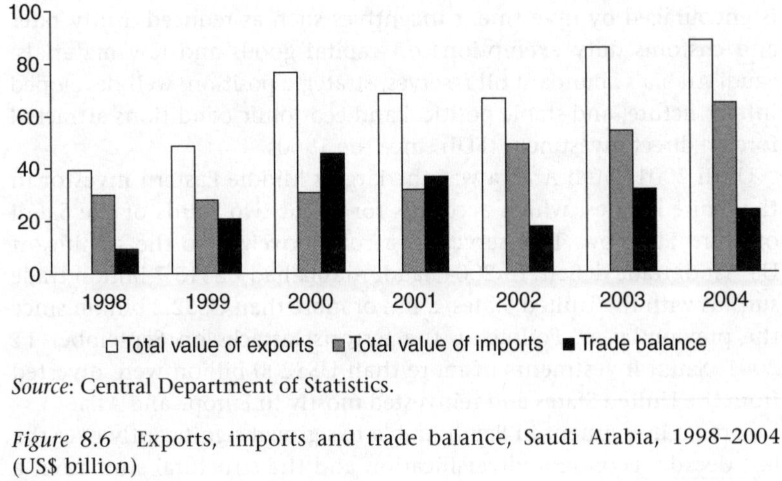

Source: Central Department of Statistics.

Figure 8.6 Exports, imports and trade balance, Saudi Arabia, 1998–2004 (US$ billion)

Western Europe (34 per cent in 2003), followed by other non-Arab and Islamic Asian countries. North America ranked third, with the United States accounting for 15.5 per cent of the total value of imports in 2003. In 2004 imports from the Cooperation Council of the Arab States of the Gulf and members of the Arab League accounted for about 4 per cent and 3 per cent of the total value of imports respectively, technical and mechanical equipment for 40 per cent, foodstuffs and tobacco for more than 15 per cent, and chemical products for 10 per cent.

Saudi Arabia has had a positive trade balance due to its strong performance in exporting. The trade surplus has had some fluctuations reflecting the higher rate of increase in imports in 2002 and 2004 vis-à-vis the rate of increase of exports.

Saudi Arabia's membership of the WTO (since December 2005) is expected to result in the growth of exports and imports, although some businesses may suffer as industries and products previously protected by Saudi legislation will be exposed to international competition.

Foreign direct investment

The Saudi government encourages foreign investment, especially in respect of the formation of joint ventures with private Saudi business partners. The state-run Saudi Arabian General Investment Authority (SAGIA) is in charge of planning investment priorities, liberalizing and improving the investment climate and approving proposed investment projects. The Investment Law of 2000 allows full foreign ownership of assets, with corporate taxes fixed at 30 per cent. Full foreign ownership is encouraged by investment incentives such as reduced utility rates and customs duty exemptions on capital goods and raw materials. Saudi Arabia's abundant oil reserves, strategic position, well-developed infrastructure, and stable political and economic conditions attracted foreign direct investment (FDI) since the 1960s.

Until 2001 Saudi Arabia was the largest Middle Eastern investor in the United States, which accounts for about two thirds of the Saudi outward FDI flow. This served as a counterweight to the significant US–Saudi trade deficit. In 2004 Saudi Arabia had US$15.7 billion trade surplus with the United States, a rise of more than US$2.2 billion since the previous year. Following the terrorist attacks on September 11 2001, Saudi investments of more than US$200 billion were divested from the United States and reinvested mostly in Europe and Asia.

Foreign investment in Saudi Arabia has grown significantly over the last decade. Economic diversification and the structural shift from a resource-based to a production-based economy has nurtured domestic business growth and encouraged the participation of foreign investors in joint business ventures. FDI is mostly in the production of value-added petrochemical and petroleum products, food processing, and industrial manufacturing. The government recognizes the importance of FDI as a major source of knowledge and technological innovation, so investment in the technological restructuring of existing production companies has been prioritized. Foreign participation is also sought by local businesses involved in import-substitution or export-oriented production. While the major motives of Saudi businesses' attracting FDI are the acquisition of managerial know-how and technological development, they readily provide foreign investors with local market support, business and government contacts, labor and production supervision. In the case of third-market access, Saudi partners often have valuable business contacts in other Arab and Islamic markets. While FDI is channeled into joint ventures and trade representative offices, some foreign investors compete for government tenders. In such cases they have to be represented by a Saudi organization and are required to subcontract at least a third of the work in question to a Saudi subcontractor.

FDI is extremely important to industrialization, which it is hoped will reduce the dependence on crude oil as the major source of national income. Moreover, with regard to the growing unemployment among younger Saudi nationals, it is hoped that FDI will support the development of small and medium-sized companies, thus creating jobs and increasing the size of the labor market.

Management practices in Saudi companies

With the rapidly changing requirements of the world market Saudi managers need marketing know-how to increase their chance of success in the domestic and international markets (Crick *et al.*, 1998; Leonidou, 1996). According to Yavas (1997), Saudi managers are well aware of the importance of efficient marketing management for business success.

Another major priority of Saudi managers is the adoption of the ISO 9000 standards. A recent survey by Magd (2006) of 175 Saudi companies has revealed that ISO 9000 certification and implementation is widespread in the country, and that this has resulted in improved quality control.

The consumer market and consumer behavior

Given the spending power of the population, Saudi Arabia is by far the largest consumer market in the Middle East and has one of the highest growth potentials in the world. Saudi consumers's purchasing power has caused them to expect innovative products and services as well as quality. The majority are highly sophisticated and well informed about the latest developments and emerging trends in fast-moving consumer goods and consumer durables. They demand world-quality products offered in consumer-friendly locations that have all facilities for an enjoyable shopping experience. Most younger consumers are early adopters of high-technology consumer durables as these are symbols of social standing and cosmopolitanism. This requires companies to provide speedy and detailed information on the attributes and specifications of new products on the market. Similarly, there should be reliable information on the features of substitutes for well-established consumer products, especially in the case of consumer durables, telecommunication products, and electronic goods.

Consumer behavior is strongly influenced and guided by religious beliefs and the restrictions imposed by Islam. This affects product choice, the timing of purchases, and the retail environment. Meat must come from animals that have been killed according to Muslim law (*halal*); alcoholic drinks, pork and pork products are illegal; daylight fasting during Ramadan is strictly observed and evening consumption is limited to religiously permitted products; and males are responsible for the family budget and therefore make the key decisions on purchases. The segregation of women limits their ability to shop where they will, but nowadays there are large exclusive shopping malls for women only, where female assistants offer diverse and sophisticated products and brands.

In ethnic terms there are two distinct consumer segments, consisting of Saudis and non-Saudis. Saudis like to shop in small traditional shops, whereas non-Saudis prefer to shop from large modern outlets. While Saudis can afford costly products they still seek value for money. The conservatism of the Saudi culture is another determinant of buyers' behavior. Saudi consumers are the strictest followers of Islamic principles in the whole Islamic world.

The eating habits prescribed by the Qu'ran are strictly observed. Staple foods that are consumed throughout the country are unleavened bread (*khobz*), lamb, chicken, deep-fried chickpea balls (*felafel*), and fava bean puree with garlic and lemon (*fuul*). Arabic coffee and tea are consumed during casual encounters and formal meetings. Traditional coffee houses are very popular, although they are gradually giving way to food-hall style cafés.

The average Saudi tends to shop at least once a day, especially in the case of fresh food. Small traditional shops are open long hours seven days a week, with five daily breaks for prayers. The busiest part of the day is the evening. Most purchases are made during the weekend, which as in all Islamic countries is on Thursday and Friday.

Saudi consumers require information on the quality, expiry date, specific features, and country of origin of the products they propose to buy. They are on a continuous quest for bargains and are keen to obtain the lowest possible price. Bargaining is aimed at concluding the best possible deal, but it is also a social ritual, particularly in respect of exchanges in small traditional retail stores.

Consumers exhibit varying degrees of receptivity to products and marketing activities from different parts of the world (Bhuian, 1997). The United States and Japan are more favored in this regard, depending on the product category in question. German marketing practices are looked on favorably. Little distinction is made between the products and marketing practices of France, Italy, and the United Kingdom, which are viewed as quite similar. A study by Bhuian (ibid.) supports the suggestion that there is a country-of-origin effect on people's perception and appreciation of goods and marketing practices.

Product issues

About 80 per cent of the diverse range of products purchased in Saudi Arabia are imported. Local products are mostly fast-moving consumer goods. Goods of foreign origin have to be suited to the climate and culture of the country, and because most Saudi households are large there is a demand for jumbo-sized packs of certain products. Consumer durables have to meet set technical standards and be able to withstand climatic extremes. All products must conform to the diktats of Islam, as discussed earlier.

There are also specific requirements for packaging. For example, as many products are stored for a long time a special protective coating is often necessary. Labelling (in Arabic) should include information about the product and reassure consumers about the credibility of the manufacturer and the reliability of the product.

There are no specific regulatory measures to deal with counterfeit products and brands. As consumers tend to personalize brands (Field,

1984; Leonidou, 1995), a variety of brands have been given generic names to increase their local appeal. While global and international brands have found their way into the market, own-brand labels are rare. This is largely due to the domination of the retail sector by small independent shops and supermarkets. The degree of consolidation of the retail sector is rather low, which poses an enormous challenge for the market expansion of branded goods.

Price

Saudi consumers have high purchasing power but are keen to get the best value for their money. According to Tuncalp (1990) and Leonidou (1995), price competition has become more intense due to pressure from more demanding and better informed consumers and the variety of product substitutes and counterfeit brands available on the market. Price competition is especially fierce for fast-moving consumer goods, and while this is good for consumers it has pushed down profit margins. Small independent shops find it difficult to match the low prices charged by bigger stores and supermarkets. Bargaining is part of the price determination process and is intrinsic to the Saudi relationship-based retail practices. Retail credit is popular with buyers of consumer durables.

Distribution

The national market can be divided into three main areas: the central region, with the capital Riyad as the major commercial center; the western region, where the city of Jeddah is located; and the eastern region, where the oil and gas production facilities and much of the labor force are concentrated.

The geographical specifics of the country, the distribution of the population, and business locations have determined the distribution practices adopted in the kingdom. As the distribution infrastructure is regionalized, it is common for companies to use different distributors to manage the distribution network in each of the regions. While no requirement for exclusive distributorships has been set by the Saudi government, it is the policy of the Saudi Ministry of Commerce for exclusive distributorships to be established in a particular region or for a specific product line. This allows distributors to develop their business without facing tough competition from other distributors of the same product or product line in their region, and it has enabled them to improve the reliability of their networks and their coverage. However, many distributors carry a variety of product lines and are not able to dedicate sufficient resources to creating an all-encompassing distribution system for all product lines. Moreover, distributors may prioritize the distribution of some product lines at the expense of others. Thus the success of a product or product line in Saudi Arabia depends heavily on the capabilities, trust, preferences, and good will of the distributor.

In the case of foreign goods it is common for distributors and agents to expect foreign suppliers to cover most of the expenses associated with market development, market growth, and sales staff costs. Hence importers can either appoint an expatriate sales person to train and support the Saudi sales representative, or visit the Saudi distributor regularly to provide the necessary services and assistance. The first option signals a long-term commitment on the part of the supplier and usually results in a more trusting business relationship. Commitment and trust are highly valued in Saudi business life, therefore a permanent presence can have a beneficial effect on the success of a product or product line. Other important aspects of the relationship are the timely delivery of goods and the on-site provision of qualified technical assistance, which makes the presence of a company representative extremely important. Service provision and prompt delivery have become key factors in gaining and retaining customer loyalty.

The national distribution system is multifold, with distribution being conducted by local manufacturers, distributors, and wholesalers. Distributors and large wholesalers have great bargaining power. Despite governmental protection of local manufacturers they still satisfy only about 20 per cent of the domestic demand for manufactured goods. Moreover they produce only a limited range of products, predominantely carpets, dairy products, soft drinks, and some fast-moving consumer goods. They are mostly located on the outskirts of large urban centers such as Jeddah and Riyadh, where the headquarters of the major distribution companies are situated. The proper functioning of the system owes much to the sophisticated market intellegence of Saudi nationals and firms (Kay, 1979) that have good relationships with the national and local governments. They are usually part of large family conglomerates.

The terrain of Saudi Arabia makes physical distribution demanding. Moreover the enormous size of the country demands an integrated warehouse system, but this is prevented by the number of private companies distributing their products by their own means. Large private warehouses exist in all the main urban areas. The rest of the country is supplied from warehouse hubs, the most important of which are located in Abha, Al Hofuf, Hail, Mecca, Medina, and Tabuk.

Wholesaling is an important part of the distribution of all product categories, but particularly for fast-moving consumer goods and some consumer durables. These intermediaries can be decisive to the market success of products, and those which earn the highest profits for the wholesalers have the best chance of success. Wholesalers often use intermediaries to supply goods to smaller retailers, but more and more they are selling direct to consumers and profiting from the rising consumption levels.

The Saudi retail sector is well developed and comprises traditional and modern outlets. There are numerous small traditional shops that sell grocery products, and *bakallas* offer a range of products to consumers at the lower end of the market. The number of large modern retail chains is on the rise, including supermarkets, hypermarkets, and department stores with a huge range of goods and serving mostly more affluent consumers. Panda is the only domestic supermarket chain and has nearly 50 stores across the country. It opened its first supermarket in 1978, merged with Azizia in 1994 and currently is the largest retail chain in the Middle East as part of the Savola Group. It has more than 5000 employees and has expanded into hypermarket retailing. Other big retailers are Carrefour Kingdom of Saudi Arabia and FARM Superstores, a food store chain owned by the Saudi Marketing Company (SAMCO), part of the Al Aswad Group.

Retailing in large urban conglomerates in the western and central parts of the country accounts for about 70 per cent of the total. *Bazaars* or *souks* are more typical in small and medium-sized towns. The small shops in the bazaars are grouped according to the type of goods they offer, mostly commodities.

Vertical and horizontal competition between distributors is fierce (Leonidou, 1995). Vertical competition takes place between the strong wholesalers and large retailers, with the latter steadily gaining more bargaining power. Horizontal competion takes place at the manufacturing and retail levels. At the manufacturing level the competion is between local and foreign producers for a larger share of the market. At the retail level large modern retailers are competing successfully with smaller and more traditional retailers (Rossiders, 1994).

Almost 85 per cent of imported goods enter Saudi Arabia via the ports of Jeddah and Ad Dammam. Another 12 per cent enter by road from Jordan. A tiny proportion of high-value, low-bulk products arrive by air. Inland transportation is mainly by road.

Promotion

About 30 years ago promotion barely existed in Saudi Arabia. Word-of-mouth recommendation was the most effective means of promotion as it fitted the tribal nature of Saudi consumers. Advertising agencies were few and only began to emerge at the end of the 1980s.

Today the largest and most powerful promotional company is Tihama, whose services encompass advertising, public relations, and marketing for large customers, most of which are foreign (Erdem and Tuncalp, 1998). Similar in terms of services offered and a direct competitor of Tihama is Marwah. Both companies have numerous branches throughout the country. Promotional companies with more specialized services include United Outdoor Advertising, Raed, and Transworld, which also have operations in other countries of the Middle East. The development of the advertising industry has been aided by the transfer of marketing knowhow via the formation of joint ventures with established foreign agencies. Promotional activities and channels in Saudi Arabia have their own specifics, some of which stem from sociocultural factors and others from the geographical concentration of the population in three regions.

Companies that are trying to increase their market share usually use more than one advertising medium. Apart from newspapers the most popular media are national fairs, festivals, promotional events, and sweepstake draws in shopping centers. There is newspaper advertising in both Arabic and locally published English language papers. The leading Arabic newspapers – *Al-Sharq Al-Awsat, Okaz, Al-Hayat, Al Jazira,* and *Al Riyadh* – have nationwide coverage and distribution. Regional newspapers such as *Al Madina, Al Bilad,* and *Al Nadwa* are used to target regional consumer segments. Magazines have become a more important advertising medium the last ten years, especially in respect of women's and children's products.

Television advertising is limited as advertisements can be only broadcast at certain times of the day. There are two Saudi channels with nation-wide coverage, one of which is in Arabic and the other in English. Many companies in Saudi Arabia opt to advertise their products on international television channels that can be accessed by Saudi viewers, including CNN, BBC World, MBC (the Middle East Broadcasting Corporation), ART (Arab Radio and Television), and Orbit. These channels offer a variety of programs that are culturally sensitive but the limitations on advertising time are not as strict as in the Saudi channels.

Direct marketing is mainly restricted to the business-to-business market but there is some limited face-to-face contact with consumers in the business-to-consumer market. Personal relationships between sellers and buyers are much more effective than any other form of direct marketing, especially in light of gender segregation and respect for personal privacy.

As most of the goods sold in Saudi Arabia are imported, promotional activities tend to be conducted by the distributors of the products in question, followed by foreign and local producers and large retail firms. Smaller retailers and wholesalers rarely engage in promotion.

The Arab–British Chamber of Commerce estimates that about 90 per cent of promotional expenditure goes on advertising. Television advertising accounts for 80 per cent of advertising budgets as this is an extremely expensive promotional vehicle. Print and radio advertising each account for about 8 per cent of expenditure. More that 95 per cent of promotional spending is on foreign goods and brands. By law the advertisements for these products must conform to the sociocultural standards of the country. The necessity for such adaptation is legally bound. Promotional spendings are skewed toward distribution related promotion, less so for sales related promotional activities. Typical forms of sales promotion particularly popular with consumers are cash discounts and speciality advertising. Consumers in Saudi Arabia are conservative and call for strict government regulation of the content and presentation of advertisements. In a study by Al-Makaty *et al.* (1996) most of the Saudi respondents stated that the government should monitor the claims made in advertisements because deceptive advertising and sensual female images were unethical and contravened Islamic principles.

Conclusion

Saudi Arabia is a country with good economic indicators and a strong performance. The market is the largest in the Middle East and has considerable potential. This is a country in transition in terms of recently created good opportunities for foreign and local businesses to participate in the economy, which is under government control.

The market is demanding not only because the average consumer has high purchasing power and the Saudis are very particular about the quality of goods and services but are always looking for the best possible bargain, and also because the functioning of the country and the market is strictly regulated by the holy scriptures of Islam. Due to these country specifics foreign companies often use Saudi Arabia as a lead market for penetrating other markets in the Middle East.

Despite the generally strict adherence to Islamic principles, consumer behavior is gradually changing. Younger generations are taking the lead but some limited Westernization and secularization can be seen among middle-aged professionals. There is a large population of non-Saudis who have different values and preferences, depending on their ethnic background.

The economy and its business base are undergoing intense changes that are providing opportunities to improve the international competitiveness of Saudi economy. It is also having a positive impact on the growth of the domestic and foreign operations of both Saudi and foreign businesses, resulting in improved living standards and increased competition in the local market.

References

Al-Aali, A. (1995) 'Obstacles facing Saudi-Arabian food and chemical exporters', *International Journal of Commerce and Management*, 5 (3), pp. 17–31.

Al-Makaty, S., G. van Tubergen, S.Whitlow and D. Boyd (1996) 'Attitudes toward advertising in Islam', *Journal of Advertising Research*, 36 (3), pp. 16–26.

Bhuian, S. (1997) 'Saudi consumers' attitudes towards European, US and Japanese products and marketing practices', *European Journal of Marketing*, 31 (7), pp. 467–86.

Crick, D., M. Al Obaidi and S. Chaudhry (1998) 'Perceived obstacles of Saudi-Arabian exporters of non-oil products', *Applied Marketing Science*, 4 (7), pp. 187–199.

Erdem, O. and S. Tuncalp (1998) 'Advertising agency scene in Saudi Arabia', *Management Research News*, 21 (1), pp. 1–8.

Field, M. (1984) *Merchants: the Big Business Families of Arabia* (London: Butler and Tanner).

Kay, E. (1979) *Legal Aspects of Business in Saudi Arabia* (London: Graham and Trotman).

Leonidou, L. (1995) 'The Saudi distribution system: structure, operation and behaviour', *Marketing Intelligence and Planning*, 13 (11), pp. 27–35.

Leonidou, L. (1996) 'Unveiling the marketing scene in Saudi Arabia: from sellers' to buyers' conditions', *Journal of International Marketing and Marketing Research*, 21 (3), pp. 123–44.

Looney, R. (1992) 'Real or illusory growth in an oil based economy: government expenditures and private sector investment in Saudi Arabia', *World Development*, 20 (9), pp. 1367–76.

Looney, R. (2001) 'Saudi Arabia: measures of transition from a rentier state', in J. Kechichian (ed.) *Iran, Iraq and the Arab Gulf States* (New York: Palgrave Macmillan), pp. 131–60.

Looney, R. (2004) 'Development strategies for Saudi Arabia: escaping the rentier state syndrome', *Strategic Insights*, 3 (3), pp. 6–18.

Magd, H. (2006) 'An investigation of ISO 9000 adoption in Saudi Arabia', *Managerial Auditing Journal*, 21 (2), pp. 132–47.
Ross, M. (2001) 'Does oil hinder democracy?', *World Politics*, 53 (April), p. 329.
Rossiders, N. (1994) 'The business climate in post Gulf War Saudi Arabia', *Marketing and Research Today*, 22 (2), pp. 118–28.
Sachs, J. (2001) 'Globalization and patterns of economic development', *Weltwirtschaftliches Archive*, 136 (4), pp. 584.
Tuncalp, S., U. Yavas and S. T. Cavusgil (1987) 'An assessment of Saudi Arabia's trade performance with selected trading partners', *Management International Review*, 27 (3), pp. 45–53.
Tuncalp, S. (1990) 'Export marketing to Saudi Arabia: the case of British exporters', *The Quarterly Review of Marketing*, 15 (2), pp. 13–8.
Yavas, U. (1997) 'Management know-how transfer to Saudi Arabia: a survey of Saudi managers', *Industrial Management & Data Systems*, 97 (7), pp. 280–6.

9
Marketing in Iran

Marin Marinov and Ali Sanayei

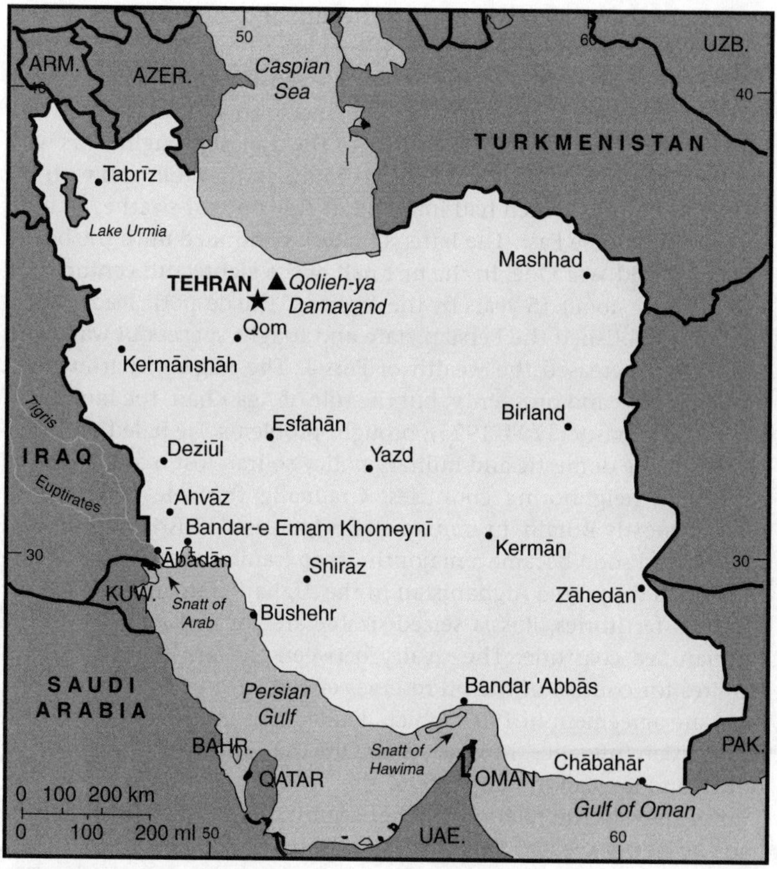

Source: www.cia.gov/cia/publications/factbook/geos/ir.html.

Map of Iran

Brief historical background

Iranian history can be traced back to the dawn of civilization. Human remains found in the area of present-day Iran have been dated as 100,000 years old. The Aryans moved to the region in 2,000 BC and one of their main groups, the Persians, formed an empire about 550 BC. In the third century AD the Persian Empire was succeeded by the Sassanid state. Continuous raids by Arabs weakened the Sassanids and in 641 AD the country came under Arab rule. In the eighth century the entire population of Persia was converted to Islam. The Ottoman Turks began to invade Persia in the tenth century and Mongol attacks took place in the thirteenth and fourteenth centuries, with devastating consequences for the region.

From the sixteenth to the mid eighteenth century the Safavid dynasty stabilized the country and the Shia branch of Islam was instituted as the state religion. The rulers of the dynasty fought wars with the Portuguese, who had established colonies in the Gulf, and with the Ottoman Empire, which had imposed its rule on vast swathes of territory in the Middle East. The latter situation continued until the beginning of World War One. In the first half of the eighteenth century Iran was ruled for about 15 years by the Afghans. The despotic leader Nadir Shah re-established the Persian state and fought successful wars with India that increased the wealth of Persia. The reign of Karim Khan brought peace and prosperity, but the rule of Aga Khan, the founder of the Qajar dynasty (1794–1925), brought problems. He failed to implement a stable domestic and military policy so Iran lost many of its territories to neighboring countries. Gradually the role of European powers, mostly Britain, in Iranian affairs increased. Russia also showed interest and soon became a major threat to Iranian sovereignty. While the British supported Afghanistan in the Afghan–Iranian struggle over disputed territories, Russia seized sizable area of Iranian land on the Caspian Sea coastline. The rivalry between the British and Russian empires for control of the oil reserves ended with in the signing of a bipartate agreement in 1907, which divided Iran into spheres of British and Russian influence. In World War One the country was occupied by British and Russian military forces.

After the war the relationship between Iran and the British Empire and the newly created Soviet Union improved somewhat. In 1921 a military coup brought the military dictator Reza Khan to power. The latter established the Pahlevi dynasty after proclaiming himself hereditary shah in 1925. He denounced the treaty with the British Empire and reorganized the economy, the education system, and the army. He also promoted the industrialization of the country.

British and Soviet military forces again occupied Iran in World War Two. They were soon joined by US troops, who were sent to ensure the safe passage of US war supplies to the Soviet Union via the Gulf. In September 1941 Reza Shah abdicated in favor of his son, Muhammad Reza Shah. In December 1943 the premier of the Soviet Union, the president of the United States, and the prime minister of the Britain signed the Tehran Declaration, which guaranteed the independence and territorial integrity of Iran when the war had ended.

As the Iranian government refused to grant oil concessions to the Soviet Union, Soviet troops seized northern Iran. In December 1945 the People's Republic of Azerbaijan and the Kurdish People's Republic were formed, both of which had Soviet backing. The Soviet troops withdrew from Iran in May 1946 after the Soviet government had been promised concessions in the Iranian oil fields. Meanwhile the unstable governments of the People's Republic of Azerbaijan and the Kurdish People's Republic were deposed by Iranian militia and subsequently the Iranian parliament withdrew the oil concessions granted to the Soviet Union.

The British government organized a total blockage of Iran, which brought the country's oil industry to the point of collapse and caused extreme economic difficulties. In 1951 the oil fields were nationalized by Prime Minister Muhammad Mussadegh and the state-owned National Iranian Oil Company was established. An uncompromising struggle between the shah and Mussadegh caused political instability in 1951–53. In August 1953 a military coup, supported by the US administration, ousted Mussadegh and strengthened the position of the shah. In return the shah promised to support the interests of foreign oil companies. Hence in 1954 Iran allowed an international consortium of American, British, Dutch and French oil companies to exploit the oil fields, with the profits to be shared equally by the Iranian state and the consortium. Aften then Iran's relation with the West improved and considerable US economic and military aid was poured into the country until the late 1960s.

In the 1960s and 1970s the government introduced measures to improve the economy and raise living standards. In the 1960s a major land reform was conducted, a compulsory education system was introduced, and a system of profit sharing in industrial enterprises was initiated. The last of these was funded by capital raised by the privatization of government-owned companies. Some democratic reforms were introduced and in 1963 Iranian women were given the right to vote in national elections.

Religious and political groups rose in opposition to the policies of the shah. There were frequent riots and the prime minister was assassinated in 1965. Iran's pro-Western policy continued in the 1970s but Islamic clergy, led by the exiled Ayatollah Rudollah Khomeini, condemned the Westernization and secularization of the country.

Westernization was accompanied by a significant improvement of Iran's relations with the Soviet bloc countries. However relations with neighboring Iraq deteriorated during the late 1960s and 1970s, with sporadic military clashes taking place along the Iran–Iraq border. Following the withdrawal of British troops from the Gulf region, Iran drastically increased its defense budget and received huge US and British military support, becoming the mightiest military power in the Gulf. Iran–Iraq tension heightened when Iran took control of three islands in the Gulf.

The wealth generated by the industrialization and privatization programs was concentrated in the hands of the shah and foreign and domestic businesses. In 1978 popular and clerical discontent with the situation culminated in rebellion, coordinated by Khomeini from France. In September that year martial law was declared and in January 1979 the shah fled the country. Khomeini returned to Iran to head the Iranian Islamic Revolution, which deposed the shah's government.

The new government put Islam and its traditions at the center of its domestic and foreign policies. All industries and banks were nationalized, all forms of Western culture were banned and women were made to wear veils. Based on a new constitution, Iran became a presidential Islamic republic, of which Khomeini was proclaimed supreme leader of the nation. Clashes between opposing religious groups resulted in numerous arrests and executions.

In 1979 US–Iranian relations became extremely tense when the Iranian military took 52 Americans hostage in the US embassy in Tehran. Diplomatic relations broke down and there was an abortive attempt by the Carter administration to rescue the hostages. The crisis was not resolved until January 20, 1981, when Ronald Reagan was inaugurated as US president.

In September 1980 Iraq went to war with Iran over the disputed Shatt al Arab waterway. The war lasted eight years, crippling the economies of the two countries and causing the loss of some 1.5 million lives. While Iraq had the support of the Soviet Union, most Arab countries and the West, Iran had few supporters, although the US administration clandestinely provided arms in the later stages of the war.

Immediately after the war the government set about revitalizing the economy, with special attention being paid to the oil industry. At the same time the tension between Iran and the Soviet Union diminished with the withdrawal of Soviet troops from Afghanistan in 1989. During the ten-year Soviet occupation of Afghanistan more than three million Afghans had sought refuge in Iran.

In 1989 Khomeini died and Sayid Ali Khamenei became president. He was soon replaced by Ali Akbar Rafsanjani, who tried to improve relations with the West in order to obtain financial help and technological transfers.

The early 1990s were marred by a devastating earthquake in Iran. After the US-led liberation of Kuwait from Iraq, the brutal suppression of the Iraqi Kurds by Saddam Hussein's forces resulted in more than a million Kurds fleeing from Iraq into Iran. In the mid 1990s Iran's international position and status deteriorated when it was accused of supporting terrorist groups and developing a nuclear weapons program.

In 1997 the moderate Islamic cleric Mohammed Khatami became president. There was a subsequent improvement in relations with the European Union (EU) member countries, but US–Iranian relations remained tense. At the end of the 1990s mass demonstrations were held by opposing groups of proreformists and hard-liners. The reformists won a landslide victory in the 2000 parliamentary elections and President Khatami was reelected in 2001. However there were still some in parliament who disproved of reforms, and changes planned by Khatami were blocked by reactionary clergy in the Guardian Council, headed by Ayatollah Khamenei.

Relations with the United States deteriorated further in 2003 after British and American troops invaded Iraq. At the end of 2003 Iran agreed to an inspection of its nuclear installations by inspectors from the EU, but in 2004 the International Atomic Energy Agency declared that Iran had failed to disclose its full nuclear program. Tension over the development of the program has continued to gather momentum.

In the parliamentary elections of 2003, conservatives won more than two thirds of the seats. On August 3, 2005 the religious conservative Mahmoud Ahmadinejad became president. Despite its radical fundamentalism, Iran is a unique case in the Islamic world in that two women, Massoumeh Ebtekar and Fatemeh Javadi, have served as vice presidents.

Demographic profile

The Islamic Republic of Iran covers 1,648,000 square kilometers, which is larger than the US state of Alaska and equivalent to the combined areas of France, Germany, Italy, and Spain. It is the most populous country in the Middle East. Official estimates put the population at more than 72 million at the end of 2005. The population consists of Persians (51 per cent), Azeris (24 per cent), Gilakis and Mazandaranis (8 per cent), Kurdish (7 per cent), Arabs (3 per cent), and others (7 per cent), mostly Baluchis, Luris, and Turkmen. More than 98 per cent of the population is Muslim (89 per cent Shia and 9 per cent Sunni). Three main languages are spoken by about 93 per cent of the population. Sixty per cent speak Persian and Persian dialects (Farsi), one quarter Azeri Turkic and Turkic dialects and one twelfth Kurdish. Since the implementation of family planning programs population growth has fallen more than three fold after an unprecedented growth of 3.3 per cent in 1976–86.

Thirty per cent of the workforce is engaged in agriculture, 25 per cent in industry and 45 per cent in services. The Islamic Revolution of 1979 and the war with Iraq changed the structure of society politically, socially, and economically. Political life in cities, towns, and villages is dominated by clerics (mullahs), who influence all aspects of life. The prominent industrialists and professionals who were favored by the political system prior to 1979 have lost their economic and social power, while bazaar traders who support the radical clerics have gained political and economic influence. Urban workers have gradually gained a higher standing and social status due to opportunities provided by the growing government bureaucracy. Despite some job creation in urban areas, unemployment remains about 15 per cent and mostly affects the younger generations. Unemployment for people aged 15–24 is in the range of 23 per cent, while that for 25–30 year-old is about 20 per cent on average. Rural areas suffer from higher unemployment. The unemployment rate for women is higher than for men in both urban and rural areas. Employment creation remains a major social concern as it has been insufficient to meet the rapid expansion of the workforce. Coupled with high annual inflation and severe impediments to private sector development, unemployment is a key deterrent of the growth of disposable income.

The economy

Since the mid 1940s the Iranian economy has been strongly dependent on oil revenues. The main oil fields are situated near the Gulf in the southwest part of the country. Oil extraction is fully controlled by the Ministry of Petroleum. If the present extraction rate is maintained

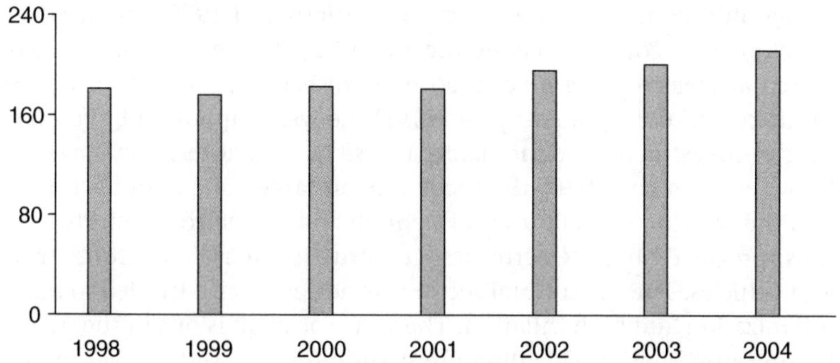

Source: Compiled from statistics issued by the Organization of the Islamic Conference.

Figure 9.1 Production of crude oil, Iran, 1998–2004 (million metric tons)

the oil reserves will last for another 80 years (Figure 9.1). Iran also has a huge reserve of natural gas. Other natural resources are coal, iron ore, copper, lead, zinc, chromites, salt, bauxite, and decorative stones. The amounts of bauxite and copper ore extracted in 1998–2004 are shown in Figure 9.2.

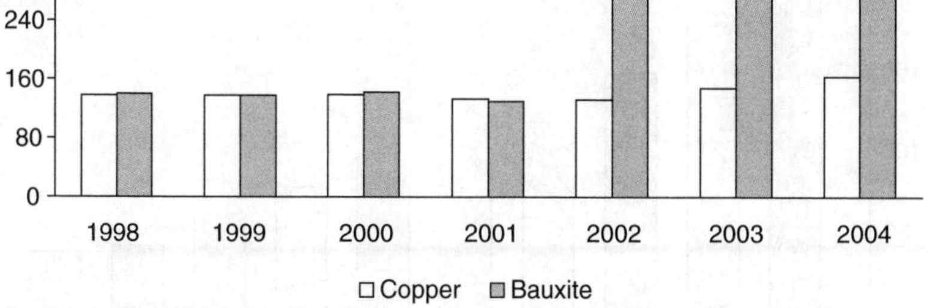

Source: Compiled from statistics issued by the Organization of the Islamic Conference.

Figure 9.2 Production of bauxite and copper ore, Iran, 1998–2004 (thousand metric tons)

The oil income generated in the late 1960s and 1970s was used to develop the economy. Economic planning during this period was aimed at creating of a diversified modern economy based on heavy industry and development projects. These were supported by foreign capital investment, technological transfers, and foreign managerial know-how. In the 1970s the focus was on large-scale manufacturing and the creation of facilities for the production of petrochemicals, textiles, processed food, electronics, construction materials, iron, steel, and vehicles. The agricultural sector was neglected and this led to mass urbanization and high inflation. The wide social divisions in the population caused nationwide discontent and protests, so the government was forced to face up to the social problems caused by its structural reforms.

Currently the Iranian economy comprises large state-owned companies, small-scale, low-intensity agriculture, and mostly privately owned services. Iran is among the 35 largest economies in the world, one of the 11 largest emerging markets and, together with Indonesia, Saudi Arabia, and Turkey, one of the four largest Islamic economies. Having the third largest oil reserves in the world (Figure 9.3) Iran is considered to be one of the most significant resource-based economies in the world. It also ranks second in natural gas deposits, with more than one seventh of the world's gas reserves (Figure 9.4).

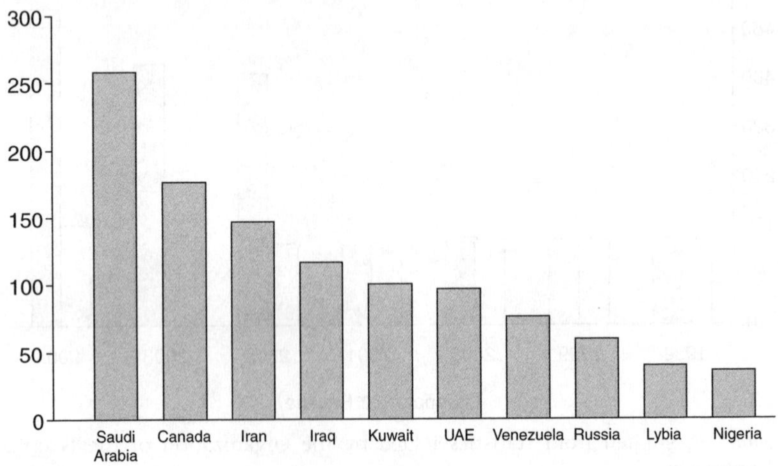

Source: *Oil & Gas Journal*, 102 (47) (2004), p. 10.

Figure 9.3 Countries with the largest oil reserves, 2004 (billion barrels)

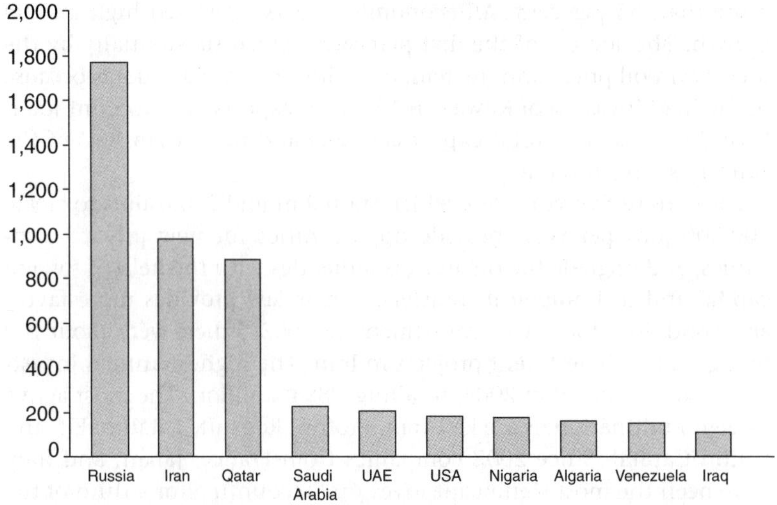

Source: *Oil & Gas Journal*, 102 (47) (2004), p. 10.

Figure 9.4 Countries with the largest natural gas deposits, 2004 (trillion cubic feet)

The eight-year war with Iraq slowed economic development, as did the Islamic Revolution and the devastating earthquake of 2004. However, the recent increase in oil prices has assisted the revival of most economic sectors, including industry, despite the instability in the region, especially in neighboring Afghanistan and Iraq.

More than 80 per cent of the economy is owned by the state and the entire economy is strictly planned and controlled by the government under the terms of the constitution. The First Five Year Plan for social, cultural and economic development was implemented in the period March 1989 to March 1994. Its primary objective was to diminish or negate the negative impact of the Iran–Iraq war on society and the economy. The plan set targets for 8 per cent annual economic growth, the creation of two million jobs and the revitalization of existing and creation of new industrial outlets, and provided some freedom for the functioning of the private sector. Specific targets were set for every economic sector and the results were mostly good. Some public sector industrial enterprises were fully or partially transferred to private ownership. There was an average annual increase in GDP of 7.3 per cent and the standard of living rose by about 25 per cent. Annual consumption increased by 7 per cent and the ratio of investment to GDP rose more than 35 per cent. All economic sectors registered high annual growth. The success of the first plan was helped substantially by the increase in oil prices and the temporary lifting of OPEC quotas because of the Iraqi invasion of Kuwait in 1990. Oil exports now account for at least 80 per cent of total export earnings and more than half of the country's gross revenue.

The current five-year plan, which started in mid 2005, aims to create 700,000 jobs per year, provide opportunities for new private companies, and upgrade the oil and gas industries with the help of foreign capital and technological transfers. A new law provides more favorable conditions for foreign investment. In 2002–5 there were about 100 foreign direct investment projects in Iran. The highest annual investment was registered in 2004, totalling US$4.3 billion. The most active foreign multinationals are ENI-Iran, Proton, Renault, TotalfinaElf, and Union Capital. Since 2002 companies from France, Japan, and Italy have been the most significant investors, accounting for a third of the FDI inflow. More than half of the capital invested went into heavy industry (31 per cent), transportation equipment (15 per cent), and business and financial services (8 per cent).

There is continuous diversification of the hugely oil-reliant economy. However as the bureaucratic and inefficient state sector controls most economic activities, structural changes are slow. While it is intended to improve efficiency by liberalizing the economy, this will certainly be resisted by the conservatives who dominate the powerful state institutions and enjoy parliamentary and presidential support.

The main economic indicators for 2003–5 are shown in Table 9.1. In 1998–2003 the economy was relatively stable. While some Islamic countries, such as Turkey, experienced a severe economic slowdown during this period, the downturn in Iran stayed in the range of 0.5 per cent (Economist Intelligence Unit, 2001). In 2000–1 there were moderate consumer price increases that leveled out at 12–13 per cent per annum. Inflation was held in control by the state money supply, which reflected large external surpluses and high foreign currency

Table 9.1 Main economic indicators, Iran, 2003–5

	2003	*2004*	*2005*
GDP (US$ billion)	125.0	145.0	165.0
Per capita GDP (US$)	1,813.0	2,112.0	2,422.0
Annual inflation rate (%)	16.0	15.5	14.7

Source: Iranian National Statistics.

Table 9.2 Economic growth rates, Iran, 1998–2003

	Gross domestic product	*Agriculture*	*Industry*	*Services*
1998	1.6	8.1	2.1	–0.9
1999	2.8	–5.6	2.3	4.5
2000	5.9	3.8	9.1	5.1
2001	5.5	5.3	5.2	7.2
2002	6.7	5.8	7.9	7.3
2003	6.2	5.3	6.3	8.2

Source: Iranian National Statistics.

reserves. The period was difficult for Iran in terms of oil export receipts because oil prices were unstable. Nonetheless it managed to achieve a 4.2 per cent average annual economic growth rate between 1998 and 2003 (Table 9.2).

During the same period savings and investments as a percentage of GDP were higher than in most emerging markets and among the highest in the Islamic world. In 2000 savings amounted to 28.5 per cent of GDP and investment to 26.6 per cent, compared with 15.2 per cent and 15.0 per cent respectively in Pakistan.

At the moment agriculture accounts for about 21 per cent of GDP, industry for about 28 per cent and services for about 51 per cent. Apart from its contribution to GDP, agriculture provides employment for almost a third of the workforce. One of the greatest impediments to agricultural expansion is the limited supply of water for irrigation. Thus dam building and subsidized irrigation projects have recently been launched. Iran is one of the world's largest importers of agricultural products, with half of the demand for some agricultural products being met by imports, although the production of staple foods such as wheat and barley is adequate. Livestock farming, although mostly primitive, is also sufficient to meet the national demand. The production of agricultural goods in 1998–2004 is shown in Figure 9.5. Iran is the world's largest producer and exporter of pistachio nuts and holds more than 50 per cent of the world pistachio market. Other exports are carpets, caviar, and saffron. The annual contribution of exports to GDP in 1998–2004 is shown in Figure 9.6.

As noted earlier all the economic sectors – state, cooperative and private – are planned, supervised, and controlled by the government under the terms laid down in the constitution. The state sector consists of all large-scale industries, institutions dealing with foreign trade, the extraction industry, banking, insurance, power generation, dams and

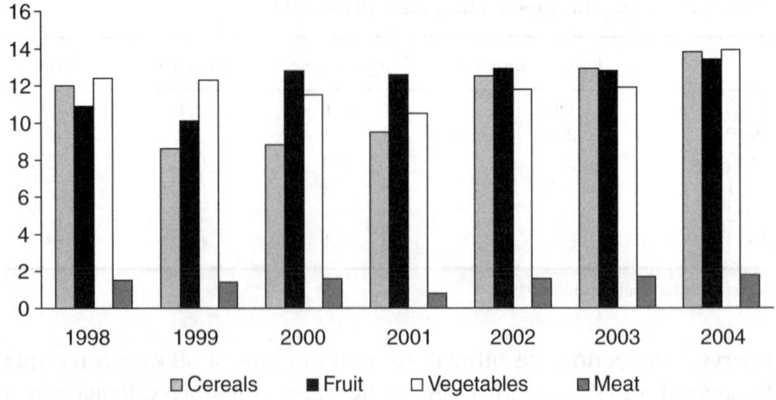

Source: Compiled from statistics issued by the Organization of the Islamic Conference.

Figure 9.5 Agricultural production, Iran, 1998–2004 (million metric tons)

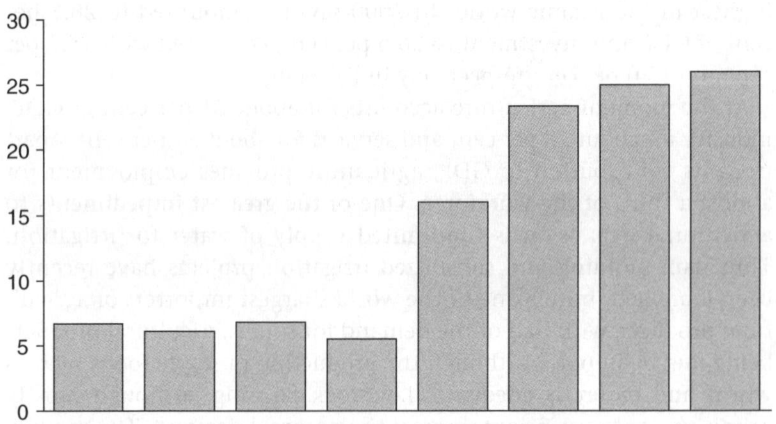

Source: Compiled from statistics issued by the Organization of the Islamic Conference.

Figure 9.6 Contribution of exports to GDP, Iran, 1998–2005 (per cent)

large-scale irrigation networks, radio and television, mail, telegraph and telephone services, aviation, shipping, roads, and railroads. The cooperative sector consists of companies and enterprises that produce or distribute goods or provide services – all of which are run in accordance with the principles of Islam. The private sector comprises small and medium-sized enterprises in the agricultural, animal husbandry, industry, trade and service sectors. With the gradual liberalization of economic activities the private sector is now playing a more significant role than the one outlined for it in the constitution.

The automotive industry contributes about 28 per cent of Iran's GDP. Passenger cars account for more than 60 per cent of the industry's revenues, followed by pick-up trucks. The growth of the industry owes much to joint ventures between foreign companies and local automotive producers. Despite this growth the supply is not meeting the demand. At the moment here are only about 50 cars per 1,000 inhabitants, while official estimates indicate a demand for at least one million vehicles for both private and business use. There are currently 19 publicly or privately owned automakers, two of which – Khodro and SAIPA – dominate the market and in 2004 accounted for 94 per cent of total production. Recently a number of foreign companies, mostly European and Asian, entered Iran to assemble cars from imported parts. In 2004, 645,389 cars and 35,816 pick-ups were produced.

A number of factors are expected to have a positive impact on the automotive sector in 2007–12. The most important of these are liberalization of the foreign investment regime, an anticipated rise in the average income, favorable reforms of the tax system and the banking sector, stable and affordable petroleum prices, and a substantial income from the Iran–India gas pipeline project.

One of the new foreign entrants to the automotive market is the German firm Volkswagen, which has set up a production plant in the special economic zone of Arg-e-Jadid near the city of Bam and plans to assemble more than 20,000 vehicles per year. At the moment all the parts and components are imported from Brazil, but if the business develops successfully Volkswagen plans to manufacture them locally.

Recently the government allowed limited car imports at tariffs of 130–300 per cent. The German firm BMW took this opportunity to reenter the Iranian market, having withdrawn in 1991. In 2004 it started to target the small affluent consumer segment with its Series 5 cars. The price of these cars in Germany is about US$55,000 but in Iran the price is more than three times higher. Nonetheless there is a continuous demand and all imports in the period 2004–5 were sold.

International trade

The annual changes in the value of exports and imports in 1998–2004 is shown in Figure 9.7. Apart from 2002 in the case of exports, both

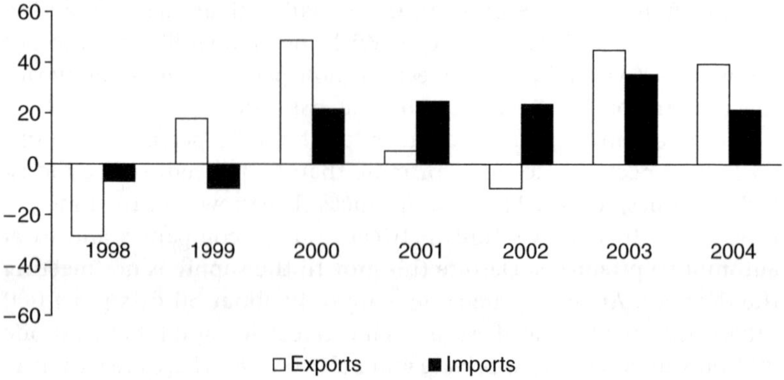

Source: Compiled from statistics issued by the Organization of the Islamic Conference.

Figure 9.7 Annual change in exports and imports, Iran, 1998–2004 (per cent)

exports and imports have been on the increase since 1999 and this trend is expected to continue during the next three to five years. In 2003 the total value of exports was US$30 billion, which allowed for a trade surplus of more than US$1.2 billion. The value of international trade and its balance are shown in Figure 9.8.

As well as oil and gas, Iran exports chemical and petrochemical products, fruit, nuts, and traditional Persian carpets. The major trading partners are Japan, China, the United Arab Emirates, Italy, and South Korea,

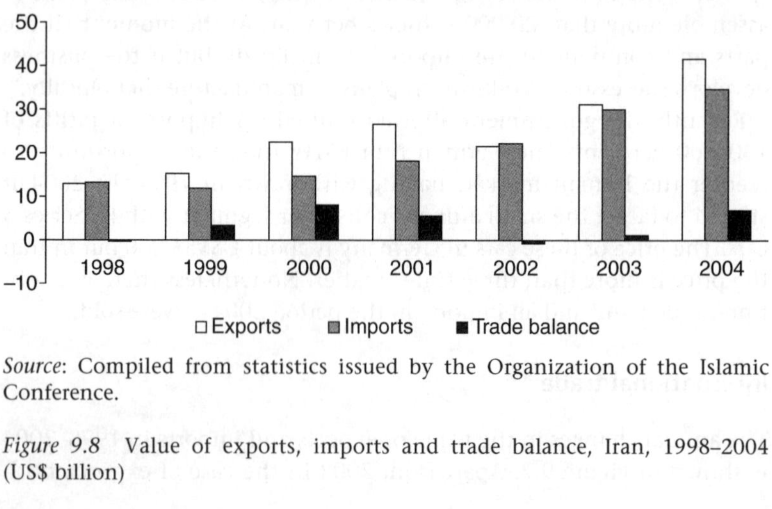

Source: Compiled from statistics issued by the Organization of the Islamic Conference.

Figure 9.8 Value of exports, imports and trade balance, Iran, 1998–2004 (US$ billion)

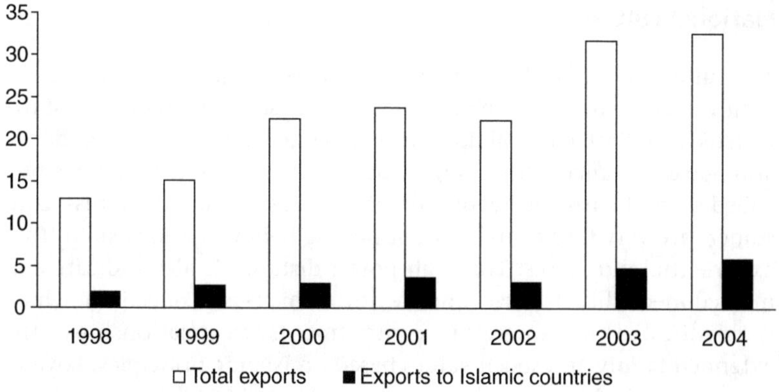

Source: Compiled from statistics issued by the Organization of the Islamic Conference.

Figure 9.9 Value of total exports and exports to Islamic countries, Iran, 1998–2004 (US$ billion)

which together account for almost half the total value of exports. Exports to other Islamic countries have increased and in 2004 they accounted for 17 per cent of the total (Figure 9.9).

In recent years imports have been dominated by capital goods (66 per cent of total imports). Other imports are raw materials, food, consumer goods, and military equipment. The five leading suppliers – Germany, Italy, France, China, and South Korea – provide about 50 per cent of imports. In terms of balanced trade the most important trading partners are Italy, China, and South Korea. The major export recipient is Japan, which in 1998–2003 took 17–22 per cent of Iranian exports. The principal supplier is Germany, which in the same period provided 11–15 per cent of imports.

Iran is a strong supporter of the idea of an Islamic Common Market and it provides support to other Islamic counties through diplomatic and financial means. It has ambitions to become the leading economy in the Middle East in order to minimize the influence of outside powers in the region. In this it has the backing of Syria but is in continuous rivalry with Saudi Arabia.

After the passage of the Free Trade Zones Act in 1993, free trade zones were established on Kish Island, Qeshm Island, and in the Port of Chabahar.

National culture

The culture of Iran is determined by national traditions, Islam and the family as the pillar of society. Iranian society scores high on two of the Hofstede's (1980) cultural dimensions, namely uncertainty avoidance and power distance. This is largely due to the conformity that has prevailed since the Islamic Revolution of 1979. Consequently Iranian consumers are very traditional in their buying behavior and abstain from experiential purchases. The high power distance is also indicative of marked inequality in power and wealth. Iranians are collectivist, which is manifested in long-term commitments to relationships, the extended family and social values based on Islamic principles. Loyalty is a matter of ethics, and all people are expected to take responsibility for their fellow members of society.

The Iranian market

Both the consumer and the industrial market have great potential, but realization of this is hampered by the government's strict control over the economy. Foreign investment and international trade are governed by Islamic law, which limits investment opportunities and forbids the importation of proscribed goods such as alcohol, pork and pork products.

Foreign companies can enter the Iranian market by establishing joint ventures with public or private Iranian partners. Many private companies are actively looking for joint-venture partners with a view to technological upgrading and the transfer of management know-how. The motives of public and cooperative companies for entering a joint venture are mainly efficiency seeking and market seeking. For their part foreign companies are able to exploit both the domestic market and the potential of the regional export markets.

The government encourages profit reinvestment and there are severe restrictions on the repatriation of profits. Because of this many foreign firms engage in joint ventures that only involve technological transfers and refrain from investing capital in production and/or marketing facilities. The government has introduced a buy-back scheme to attract foreign investment. Under this scheme the factories, machinery, production equipment, and technology supplied by foreign firms are paid for (at a pre-agreed fixed rate) with the returns from the goods produced in the factories in question.

The Iranian import regime, which is controlled by the Ministry of Commerce, is complex and constantly changing. In the past there was rigid protection of domestic agricultural products, but this has loosened lately. Since 2005 Iran has had observer status at the WTO and its application for full membership is in the final stage. However this may be postponed because of the controversial international standing of the country at the moment.

Iranian companies

As discussed earlier the functioning of the economy is in the hands of the government – via influential clergy, government institutions, and agencies – and market forces play little part. Yasin *et al.* (2002) have conducted a survey of Iranian business executives' views on the characteristics and performance of the Iranian macro- and microeconomic environment, as well as their moral values and preferences.

About two thirds of the respondents believed that the economy was functioning at less than 50 per cent of its capacity because of the governmental and religious control and the near absence of market mechanisms. Participation in foreign trade was regarded as positive in terms of increased international competitiveness. Handmade products, mostly Persian carpets, plus oil and petrochemical products, industrial products, and some agricultural goods, for example pistachio nuts, were viewed as the most promising items for export. The most preferred trading partners were developed countries that were able to provide technological and managerial transfers. The overwhelming majority of the respondents considered that the Iranian economy would grow at a rate of 1–4 per cent per annum.

At the microeconomic level the respondents thought that the performance of domestic companies was mostly successful, although only a few companies had developed a formal strategic plan that included a marketing strategy. The use of information technology in the functioning of Iranian firms was seen as very important and most of them had computerized some of their operations. Full computerization was viewed as a major priority for business success. Participation in foreign trade was considered important by 85 per cent of the respondents. Only 5 per cent thought that foreign trade was not necessary for or would be harmful to their operations.

The respondents expressed a strong belief that businesses and business people must abide by moral principles, that moral principles should be universal and that morality is rooted in God's law. They were also of the opinion that business should be conducted for the good of the society and profits should not be the primary goal.

The consumer market

About 50 per cent of Iranians are below 20 years of age and almost 75 per cent are younger than 30. Most unemployed people belong to the latter age group. In general the income of the members of this group is relatively low and their purchasing power is limited, so although the group is large, consumption is restricted by income. Those who are in employment aspire to the improved quality of life that is associated with better jobs and increased income.

Another feature of present-day Iran is rapid urbanization. Currently about 66 per cent of Iranians live in large urban areas, and about 50 per cent of the remainder live in small towns and rural villages. Few people still live in tribal settings. Rural people usually satisfy their basic needs with local products or are self-sufficient. Incomes tend to be low so purchasing power is limited. These demographic and income specifics affect the regional demand for products and services. There are two market segments, one of which is characterized by growing demand while the other is largely stagnant with restricted purchasing potential.

A third of Iranians live in the five largest cities, each with at least a million inhabitants. The enormous metropolis of Tehran is home to around 12 million. Job opportunities in these cities are perceived to be the most important driver of urbanization. The consumption patterns of urban consumers are shown in Figure 9.10.

Many urban consumers like Western products and the demand for them is on the increase. However the lack of reliable market information and the underdeveloped distribution system are major impediments to foreign companies that wish to access the Iranian consumer market. Moreover promoting products is problematic as many of the types of promotion used in developed markets are banned. The import of goods is strictly controlled and regulated by the government. Apart from all this, Iran is a promising consumer market with great potential. Affluent Iranian consumers are brand and quality conscious with a liking for home entertainment systems, cars, real estate, jewelry, household appliances, clothing, cosmetics and fragrances, but the market is mostly undersupplied with such goods.

Recently efforts have been made to upgrade the retail network by creating modern retail outlets. However the traditional urban bazaar is still the dominant form of outlet. Bazaars are generally centrally located and consist of small shops grouped according to the type of products or services they offer.

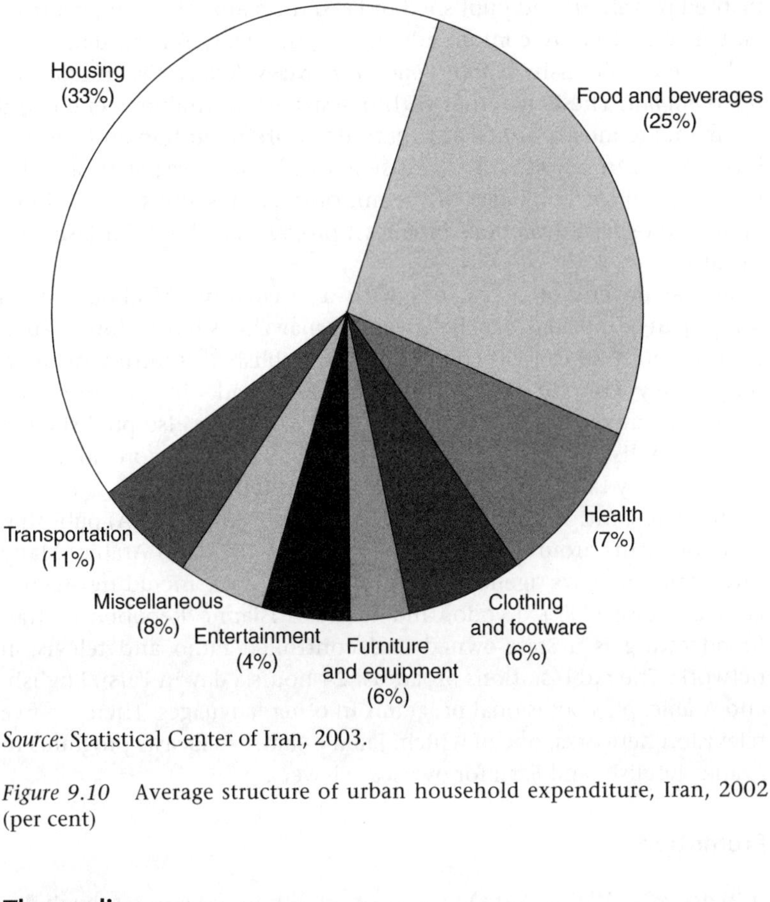

Source: Statistical Center of Iran, 2003.

Figure 9.10 Average structure of urban household expenditure, Iran, 2002 (per cent)

The media

The Iranian constitution allows freedom of the press provided that the published materials are in accordance with the rules of Islam. Censors scrutinize all the media.

Since the Islamic Revolution the number of newspaper has been on the rise. In 1978 there were only 86, of which six were dailies, whereas now there are is more than 1000. There are several dozens of daily papers with nationwide circulation. Those with the largest circulation are *Jomhouri Islami* (Islamic Republic), *Salaam* (Peace), *Hamshahri* (Fellow Citizen), *Iran*, and *Abrar* (Free People), which are printed in the morning, and *Etelaan* (Information), *Kayhan* (Universe), and *Resalat* (Mission), which are printed in the afternoon. All these newspapers are printed in Tehran and published in Farsi (Persian). They target a mass audience and rarely contain advertisements. Four Tehran dailies are published in English: *Tehran Times*, *Iran News*, *Iran Daily*, and *Kayhan International*. These, together with newspapers in Arabic, French, and German, are mostly aimed at expatriates working in Iran and contain business information and advertisements. Local newspapers are also published in the languages of the minority groups and some regional radio and television stations broadcast programs in Azeri, Turkish, and Kurdish.

Several dozens of magazines with a circulation of about half a million are published weekly. Specialist magazines have a low circulation of about 20–30,000 copies and are published monthly or quarterly. They contain limited business and trade information and occasional advertisements. Quarterly magazines are also published in Arabic, English, French, and German. These contain more advertisements as they target expatriates and Western tourists.

The state-controlled Islamic Republic News Agency (IRNA) publishes news bulletins around the clock in Farsi, English, and Arabic. Many international news agencies have offices in Iran, including Agence France Presse (AFP), Kyodo, and Reuters. Islamic Republic of Iran Broadcasting is a state-owned and controlled radio and television network. The radio stations broadcast 24 hours a day in Farsi, English, and Arabic, plus occasional programs in other languages. There are five television networks, one of which, Jaam-e-Jam, broadcasts programs in Arabic, English, and Farsi for overseas viewers.

Promotion

Initiated after World War One promotion in Iran has gone through different stages that reflect the unique national context. Between the late 1940s and the the Islamic Revolution in 1979, promotional activities were very similar to those in the developed countries and used similar tools and techniques. The most used and effective media were print, outdoor advertising, television, and radio. Between the Islamic Revolution and the beginning of the Iran–Iraq war in 1980 promotion underwent a radical change. The government took full control of the economy and run it according to religious principles and with a strong anticapitalist, anti-US bent. Promotion was officially condemned as a negative manifestation of commercialization and consumerism and a sin associated with the Western secular way of life. As a result advertisements rarely appeared, apart from occasional strictly censored advertisements in print media. Informative advertising was also banned. Thus the functioning of the market was restricted and distorted.

With the end of the Iran–Iraq war there was a new era of gradual political and economic change. From the 1990s the government loosened its control over the economy by privatizing some productive assets and allowing some play of market forces. Promotional activities gradually returned. Foreign companies operating in the Iranian market have had a considerable impact on promotion and the number and of advertising agencies has grown. There is increasing use of promotional media, mainly television and radio.

After the revolution television advertising was restricted to sound and still pictures. Later these restrictions were eased to allow live characters. The few women who appear in television advertisements are dressed in full Islamic attire, but in general only men and children are used. Advertisements have a strong family focus and there is little or no music.

Outdoor advertising is also gaining popularity. With the enlargement of the overall market in Iran the need for promotion has increased. It is a must for local and foreign companies and is a crucial element of their marketing strategies.

Conclusion

Iran is a large country with abundant natural resources. The organization and functioning of the country are strictly in accordance with Islamic principles, with a decisive role being played by the clergy and the state. This, in combination with anti-Americanism, anti-Semitism and the country's nuclear program, have to an extent isolated Iran from the global political scene and international business developments. Trade with the United States is non-existent and the foreign investment and technology transfers needed for the development of the economy are limited.

Iran is striving to diversify its economic structure, which is somewhat obsolete but relatively well balanced. Both the business-to-business and business-to-consumer markets are growing. Whilst the population is increasing the country's market potential is limited by the relatively low average purchasing power of Iranian consumers. Since the Islamic Revolution consumer behavior has been governed by Islamic principles but the tight restrictions are being loosened in some regards. The consumer base is ethnically and culturally diverse and there are significant variations in the purchasing behavior of urban and rural consumers.

Iran has recognized the need for business cooperation with the Western world and is providing some opportunities for foreign businesses to enter the country. Thus supplies are becoming more plentiful and there are opportunities to improve the international competitiveness of the Iranian economy.

References

Asian Development Outlook (2001) (Oxford: Oxford University Press).

Economist Intelligence Unit (2001) *Country Reports and Country Forecasts*, (London: EIU).

Hofstede, G. (1980) Culture's Consequences: International Differences in Work-Related Values. (Newbury Park, CA: Sage).

Statistical Center of Iran (2003) *Iran Statistical Yearbook* (Tehran: Statistical Center of Iran).

Yasin, M., J. Alavi and T. Zimmerer (2002) 'An examination of the impact of economic variables and cultural values on Iranian business organisations', *Cross Cultural Management*, 9 (1), pp. 3–18.

10

Marketing in the Islamic Countries of Southeast Asia

Marin Marinov

Source: www.cia.gov/cia/publications/factbook/reference_maps/pdf/southeast_asia.

Map of Southeast Asia

Brief historical background

Southeast Asia covers more than four million square kilometers, which is almost the size of Europe. At the end of 2005 the population amounted to 570 million. The region comprises 11 countries, namely Brunei, Burma (Myanmar), Cambodia, East Timor, Indonesia, Laos, Malaysia, the Philippines, Singapore, Thailand, and Vietnam. Three of them – Brunei, Indonesia, and Malaysia – are predominantly Muslim. Indonesia is the largest and most populous state. It occupies half of Southeast Asia and is home to about 40 per cent of its inhabitants. It is also the fourth largest and most populous Islamic country in the world.

It is believed that Southeast Asia was inhabited more than 60,000 years ago and that the early inhabitants lived on hunting. Primitive metalworking began at the dawn of human civilization. A wave of migration around 3,000 BC brought farming to the region. Trade among the settlements started at around 700 BC, and 600 years later merchants from Southeast Asia were trading all over Asia. This also had an effect on the social, cultural and scientific development of the region. Hinduism was adopted from India and for many centuries India's influence on the region was crucial. Ports, cities and other urban settlements were established. The first kingdoms were Langkasuka and Fu-nan. From the sixth century AD powerful kingdoms emerged, the most significant of which were the Khmer Empire and the Srivijaya state. The Thai Kingdom gradually gained strength and by the beginning of the fourteenth century it had displaced the Khmer Empire and gained control over most of Southeast Asia, where it ruled for four centuries. In the fifteenth century small sultanates such as Brunei were founded. By the sixteenth century the Malacca sultanate had become the most important trading country and the major disseminator of the Islamic faith in the region.

From the end of the thirteenth century there were huge migration waves. Millions of Chinese migrated to the region, especially during the colonial period. Nearly 80 per cent of the present day inhabitants of Singapore are Chinese, and there are sizable Chinese populations in Malaysia and Thailand. The majority of the rich upper class in Indonesia are of Chinese origin. European colonization began in the sixteenth century. The Portuguese were the first to come, followed by the Dutch, the Spanish, and the British, and for more than three centuries the region was divided among them. Their purpose was to exploit the region's resources and benefit from extended trade. Over time they consolidated their business and commercial interests.

The appearance of the French in the eighteenth century heralded a new era of development, with the interests of French industrialists clashing with those of the British. By serving as a buffer between the British and French, Thailand – then named Siam – was the only country that managed to preserve its political independence but it lost territory to the two colonial powers and remained economically dependent on trade with its colonized neighbors.

Colonization boosted the economic development of the region. The British established huge rubber plantations in Malaya (now West Malaysia) with seeds smuggled from Brazil. Tin mining also underwent expansion with the aid of new mining technology. Elsewhere advancements were made in agriculture by the British and the French, mostly in Burma and French Indochina. At the end of the nineteenth century the United States entered the colonial scene, having gained control over the Philippines after its victory of the Spanish-American War. The US industrial colonization spread quickly throughout Southeast Asia.

During the colonial period Southeast Asia was mostly treated as a source of wealth and the region remained largely undeveloped. Although important harbors and trading posts such as Singapore became rich and advanced, most of Southeast Asia remained predominantly rural with some primitive manufacturing.

The Japanese invasion in World War Two changed the political landscape. Powerful movements for independence were born from the fight against the Japanese and local peoples sought national freedom. The Philippines and Burma were granted independence by the crumbling colonial powers, but Indonesia, which became independent in 1949, had to struggle to win its freedom, at the cost of many lives. Brunei remained a British protectorate until 1983 as it had lucrative oil reserves.

Meanwhile the lives of the peoples of French Indochina were buffeted by the colonial forces, the aspirations of the communists and the conflicting ideals of the Cold War era. The communist advance in Vietnam, Laos, and Cambodia, supported by the Soviet Union and China, triggered a massive counteraction by the capitalist Western powers and domestic political forces. The armed conflicts culminated in communist victory of the wars in Vietnam and Cambodia.

This regional instability caused a massive outflow of people. From the mid 1970s millions of Vietnamese sought refuge far away, mostly in North America, Australia, and Western Europe. Since the early 1980s high unemployment has prompted millions of workers to migrate to the Middle East, Japan, and Hong Kong.

Population

There is considerable ethnic and cultural diversity in the region. There are more than 550 ethnic groups and Indonesia alone has 312, each with its own traditions and language. Regional communication is complicated by the lack of a common language. The most widely used are the dialects of Malay that are spoken in Malaysia, Indonesia, and Brunei, mainly by the Muslim population. English is used in business transactions but is mostly spoken only by well-educated members of society.

Apart from the indigenous cultural traditions and those developed by the colonial powers, India and China have also had a strong impact on Southeast Asian culture. Religion reflects the complexities of historical development and the various influences absorbed over the ages. Buddhism and Islam are the majority religions, the former mainly on the mainland and the latter principally on the islands. Although the principles of Islam have been embraced, the approach to it is more liberal than in the Middle East and Southeast Asian Muslim countries have reconciled Islamic principles with industrialization and rapid business growth. Hence Malaysia has developed the image of a progressive Muslim country.

The role of women in the region is significant even in the Muslim areas. Recent studies in Indonesia and Malaysia show that, similar to the situation in Japan, the women of the household usually manage the family budget and have a strong position in the household. Moreover newly wed couples from all social strata traditionally live with the parents of the bride. Nonetheless gender inequality exists in terms of better educational provision for males, employers' preference for male employees, and the payment of higher salaries to the males. In addition millions of women and young girls have been forced to work in the sex industry in order to make a living for themselves or their families. The modernization of life has diminished the importance of the extended family throughout the region and nuclear families are becoming far more commonplace. These changes have resulted in patterns of consumer behavior.

Economic development

After World War Two, military conflicts, and instability in the region hampered economic development and technological advancement. There was poverty and considerable dependence on natural resources.

In the 1970s and 1980s Malaysia, Singapore, and Thailand introduced import-substitution policies that were supplemented by export-oriented manufacturing. However import substitution did not produce the desired results so it was replaced by low-cost export-oriented production capitalizing on country competitive advantages and growing international competitiveness (Iwami, 2001).

In the early 1970s Malaysia made a radical shift towards high value-added products for export. The benefits from the success of this policy were distributed among the ethnic Malays, thus discriminating against the Chinese citizens of the country. Foreign investors were lured by means of tax holidays and free trade zones, with the result that the share of manufactured goods in exports tripled in ten years. Many Japanese firms relocated to Malaysia and large sums were poured into automotive, chemical and electronics plants.

By the 1980s, Malaysia together with Hong Kong, Singapore, South Korea, Taiwan, and Thailand, was enjoying high economic growth and constant export growth. Indonesia also had an export-oriented industrialization policy, focusing on the clothing and electronics industries.

Overheated economic growth and a gradual reduction of international competitiveness combined to cause the Asian economic crisis of 1997. All the regional economies suffered a sharp fall in exports, an enormous divestment of foreign capital, large inflation in the value of stocks, and a huge slump in the national markets. For example by the end of 1999 the Malaysian market had lost more than 80 per cent of its 1996 value. Help was provided by international financial organizations such as the International Monetary Fund but many countries had no choice but to introduce austerity measures, including cutting government spending and sharply increasing the price of basic goods.

Foreign investors gradually returned and by the end of 2004 the stock of foreign direct investment exceeded its pre-crisis level. In 2003 Malaysian exports were valued at 114.3 per cent of GDP; in Brunei the figure was 87 per cent and in Indonesia 43 per cent. Since 2000 the GDPs of Brunei, Indonesia, and Malaysia have fluctuated but growth has been consistent (Figure 10.1). This reflects the rise in the world prices of oil, gas, palm oil and metals as well as the determination of the national governments to overcome the consequences of the crisis.

Per capita GDP has also increased in these three countries (Figure 10.2). Its high level in Brunei is linked to the size and structure of the economy (based on oil and gas exports) and the small size of the population. Brunei is among the richest countries in the world and provides a high living standard for its citizens. The steady growth of per capita

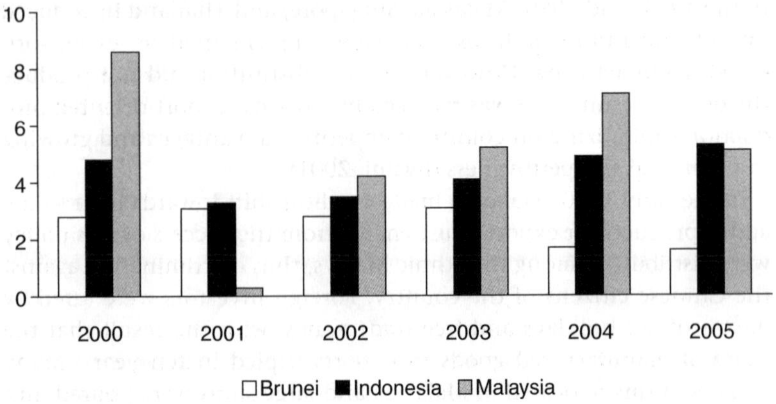

Sources: National statistics.

Figure 10.1 Annual change in GDP, Brunei, Indonesia and Malaysia, 2000–5 (per cent)

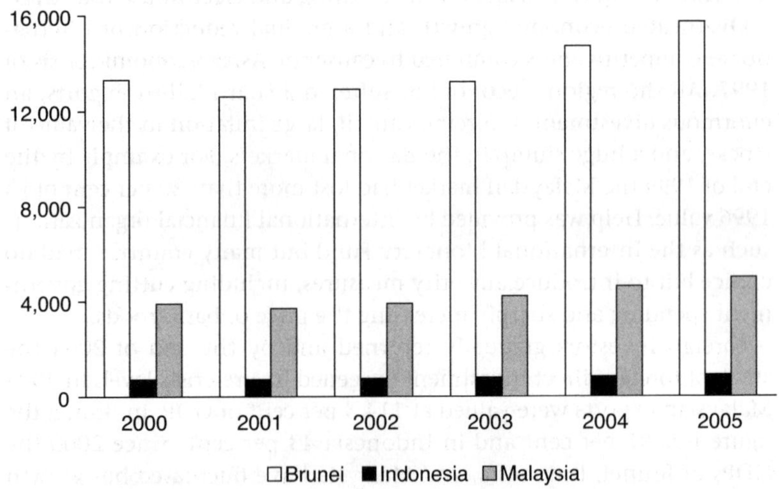

Sources: National statistics.

Figure 10.2 Per capita GDP, Brunei, Indonesia and Malaysia, 2000–5 (US dollars)

GDP in Malaysia is due to the well-developed manufacturing industry, which makes a strong contribution to exports and GDP. The high proportion of the Indonesian population engaged in primitive agriculture and the slow pace of increasing the production of high value-added products for export are hampering the government's ambition to invigorate the economy and raise its living standards.

Since the intensification of industrialization in the 1960s the countries of Southeast Asia have urbanized at differing rates. The process has been rapid in Malaysia and Thailand but relatively slow in Cambodia and Vietnam. Agriculture has diminished in economic importance but 35 per cent of the regional workforce is engaged in it. In Indonesia 50 million people or more than 40 per cent of economically active people work in agriculture. The major products and export items are rice, spices, fresh and dried fruit, rubber, tea, coffee, and sugar.

On average the value of exports has been rising since 1998, with a dip in 2001 (due to the September 11 terrorist attack) driven by the high price of oil, metals, and palm oil (Figure 10.3). The increase has been particularly large in Malaysia.

Indonesia mainly exports oil and gas, electrical appliances, plywood, textiles, palm oil, and rubber. In 2005 the value of non-oil and gas exports was US$59.9 billion, or more than 75 per cent of Indonesia's export earnings. China's booming electronics industry has prompted a greater demand for metals such as copper, nickel, and tin and caused a steady increase in their price. The growing demand for palm oil and rubber has also boosted export revenues. Indonesia's main export part-

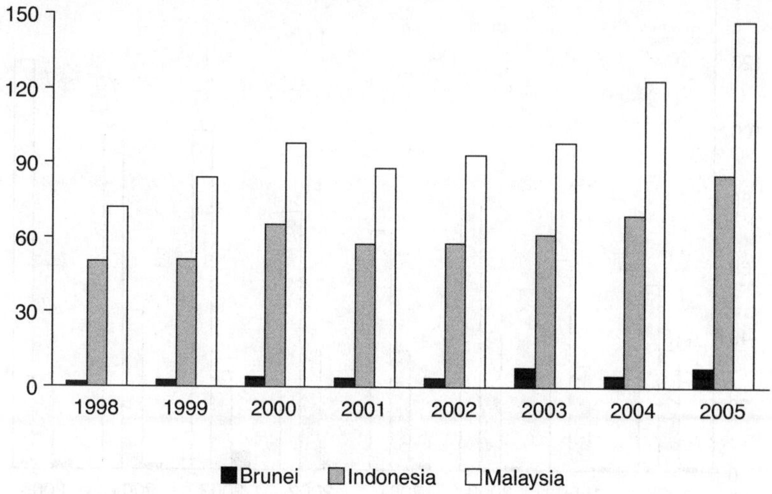

Sources: ASEAN Surveillance Coordinating Unit; CIA World Factbook.

Figure 10.3 Exports from Brunei, Indonesia and Malaysia, 1998–2005 (US$ billion)

ners are Japan, the United States, Singapore, South Korea, and China. The main exports of Brunei are crude oil, liquefied gas, and petroleum products, the bulk of which go to Japan, South Korea, Australia, the United States, and Thailand. As well as its traditional natural resource exports Malaysia has gained expertise in the production of high value-added electronic products. Its exports are sold to the United States, Singapore, China, Japan, Australia, and Western Europe.

Imports include materials, equipment, and inputs that are scarce in the region and are required for the processing and extraction sectors, as well as to meet the growing consumer demand for more varied products and services. In 1998–2005 Malaysian imports grew at a faster rate than those for Indonesia, whereas in Brunei they stayed comparatively flat (Figure 10.4). The composition of imports varies as the three states have different approaches to promoting economic growth. The most important exporters to Indonesia are Japan, Singapore, China, the United States, Thailand, Australia, South Korea, and Saudi Arabia. Indonesian imports mostly consist of machinery and equipment, chemicals, fuels, and foodstuff. Brunei imports manufactured goods, chemicals, food, and machinery and equipment from Japan, Malaysia, Singapore, the United Kingdom, Thailand, and Australia.

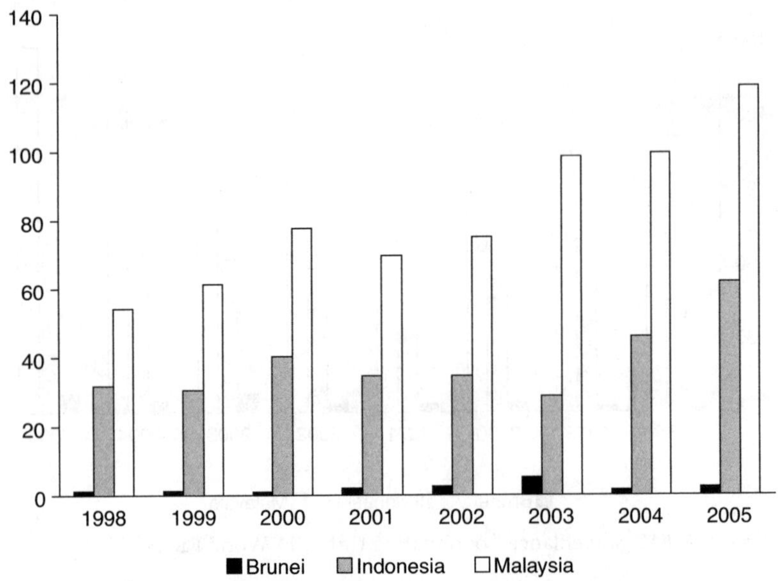

Sources: ASEAN Surveillance Coordinating Unit; CIA World Factbook.

Figure 10.4 Imports to Brunei, Indonesia and Malaysia, 1998–2005 (US$ billion)

Regional integration

The Association of Southeast Asian Nations (ASEAN) was created on August 8, 1967 in Bangkok. The founding members were Indonesia, Malaysia, the Philippines, Singapore, and Thailand. Brunei joined in 1984, Vietnam in 1995, Laos and Burma in 1997, and Cambodia in 1999. Home to more than 8 per cent of the world's population, in 2004 this regional bloc had a combined GDP of US$737 billion with an annual growth rate of 4.6 per cent, and its total trade amounted to US$720 billion, a rise of about 5 per cent since the previous year.

The ethnic and cultural structure of the ASEAN countries is diverse. There are in excess of 250 million Muslims, more than in any other geopolitical entity in the world, plus 180 million Buddhists and 140 million people of other religions mostly Catholic. The governments of the member countries have different political doctrines and range in governing style from democracy to authoritarianism.

The main objectives of ASEAN are to accelerate regional economic growth and facilitate social progress, cultural development and integration. It also promotes regional peace and stability by respecting justice and the rule of law in the relationships among the countries and adherence to the principles of the United Nations charter.

Before the creation of ASEAN interregional trade was insignificant. During the fourth ASEAN summit in Singapore in 1992 the ASEAN Free Trade Area (AFTA) was introduced. The strategic goal of AFTA is to increase ASEAN's competitive advantage and its participation in world trade as a regional bloc. In 1997, the leaders of the member countries established ASEAN Vision 2020, whose purpose is to reinforce the bloc to ensure its prosperity and competitiveness with a free flow of goods, services, and capital. ASEAN also intends to create regional transportation, energy and resource networks. It has boosted exports and investments among its member states and established closer trading and investment relations with China, Japan, and South Korea. Participation in international trade has made ASEAN one of the most active developing-country economic blocs in the world. Moreover most of the member countries have managed to accrue a sizable trade surplus including Brunei, Indonesia, and Malaysia (see Figure 10.5).

Marketing in Brunei, Indonesia and Malaysia

Brunei

Brunei is a small country in terms of both area and population, which numbers just 373 000 people mainly Malays. It is a hereditary Islamic

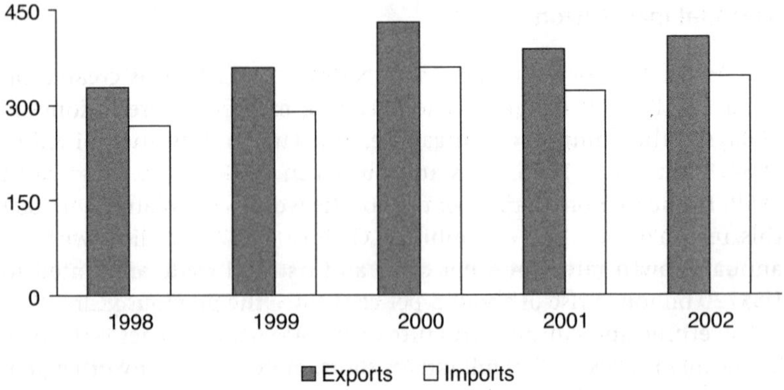

Source: ASEAN Surveillance Coordinating Unit.

Figure 10.5 Exports and imports, ASEAN, 1998–2002 (US$ billion)

monarchy and the sultan is the absolute monarch and patriarch of the people as well as the highest religious authority in the country. The workforce consists of about 160 000 people about half of whom are non-Brunei.

Being the third largest oil producer in Southeast Asia (after Indonesia and Malaysia) and the world's fourth largest exporter of liquefied natural gas, Brunei is one of the most prosperous countries in the region. Moreover due to its strategic geographical position it is able to promote itself as a regional hub and trans-shipment point for the trade of goods and services within ASEAN. The government encourages entrepreneurship and the creation of service and IT enterprises.

The non-extraction sectors – mainly garment manufacturing, production of construction materials, and financial services – account for about two thirds of the country's economic activities. The financial sector has the strongest potential for development. In 2003 its share of GDP was about 6 per cent, but it is expected that this will rise to more than 20 per cent by 2008.

Brunei is one of the few states in the world that does not tax personal income. Nor are there any export, sales, payroll and manufacturing taxes. New foreign businesses are exempt from profit tax or pay only a small tax for the first five years. Whether they are taxed or not depends on the amount of capital invested. The business tax on profits for all established businesses is 30 per cent.

The national language is Malay but English is used for business communications and high school and university education (Hallinger,

1998). Free education is provided to all citizens, thus the literacy level among the adult population is 98 per cent and 11 per cent of people have university degrees.

Product restrictions are based on Islamic principles. It is illegal to sell alcohol and its consumption in public places is banned. However foreigners and non-Muslim citizens are allowed to bring a limited amount of alcohol into the country from abroad for private consumption in the home.

Most households in Brunei own the latest and most sophisticated home appliances, vehicles, and electronic entertainment systems. Outside the home, concerts of modern music are popular. These are generally organized or sponsored by Western embassies or foreign private businesses to promote Western culture, values and lifestyles. No restrictions are imposed on cinema and theatre programs. These are mostly US, European and Japanese movies and plays and are popular with teenagers and expatriates. There are four privately owned cinemas and eight government-owned mobile cinemas that cater to the differing tastes of audiences.

Imports are diverse, but about 55 per cent of the value of imports is accounted for by machinery and transportation equipment, semi-finished products, food, beverages, and live animals. Imports come mainly from Singapore, Malaysia, Japan, Australia, and Europe. Customs duties are not levied on most imported goods, including foodstuffs, but product categories such as household appliances are subject to a 20 per cent import duty and luxury items such as perfumes to 30 per cent. The food and beverage market is limited by the small size of the population. About 95 per cent of the food and beverages are imported from neighboring countries, with Malaysia, Singapore, and Australia accounting for about 80 per cent of the value of imported food and beverages. There are few restaurants and those which are available cater to very affluent, mainly non-Brunei, citizens and tourists.

Food retailing is well developed. Outlets consist of numerous traditional shops and modern retail complexes. The Yayasan complex has a large number of shops that sell a huge variety of imported branded goods. There are also department stores such as Hua Ho, Tiong Hin, Liang Toon, and Supa Save, which offer a wide range of consumer goods. However, affluent consumers (about three quarters of the population) often do their shopping in Singapore or Kuala Lumpur and combine this with entertainment and other leisure pursuits.

The Brunei government owns most of the media, including the television and radio stations and print media. Broadcasts are in Malay but one of the television stations has some programs in English, Hindustani, and Mandarin. There are also a radio station and a cable television channel privately owned by Kristal Astro, and the British Forces Broadcasting Service has a radio station that broadcasts BBC programs. There are very few newspapers. The daily *Borneo Bulletin*, printed in English, carries advertisements that mainly target expatriates working in the oil and gas industry. There is also a Malay language daily newspaper, *Media Permata*, which provides news and articles and carries a limited number of advertisements.

Technology transfer is taking place in tandem with foreign direct investment in joint ventures. Japan is one of the most active countries in this regard (Hussain, 1998).

Indonesia

Indonesia covers 1 826 440 square kilometers of land and has an ocean territory of 93 000 square kilometers. There are three large islands – Java, Sumatra, and Kalimantan (Indonesian Borneo) – and over 13 500 smaller ones. The total coastline stretches for more than 50 000 kilometers. The capital Jakarta is home to more than 13 million people from all Indonesian ethnic groups. In all, Indonesia had a population of 242 million in 2005. The growth rate is positive and there is a large proportion of younger people – only 5 per cent of Indonesians are over the age of 65. Eighty eight per cent of the population is Muslim, which makes Indonesia the most populous Islamic country in the world, and it is also home to Christians (8 per cent), Hindus (3 per cent), Buddhists (1 per cent), and some follower of Judaism. Before the adoption of Islam the most widespread religions were Hinduism and Buddhism, and some Muslims still practice a Hindu-influenced version of Islam called Abangan. There are also adherents of the animist traditions that were commonplace in the past.

Ethnic relations in Indonesia are tense due to the tendency to divide the population into 'native Indonesians', including the Pribumi peoples, and non-native people, mostly of Chinese descent. The economic hardship that followed the Asian financial crisis led to violent attacks on Chinese Indonesians, who have traditionally been perceived as holding a disproportionate share of business power and wealth (Ang *et al.*, 2004). At the time of Dutch rule the Chinese were involved in commerce and banking and enjoyed a higher status than Pribumi workers and peasants, which caused considerable resentment. The integrative role of the government is expressed in providing equal opportunities for higher education for every Indonesian citizen regardless of their ethnicity (Idrus, 1999).

Politically Indonesia has been unstable since the fall of President Suharto in 1998. Multibillion dollar investments in infrastructure, mining, and petroleum are on hold because of concerns about terrorism and political instability, and that is stifling the creation of new jobs. Moreover labor-intensive factories are shutting down because of growing competition from China. Most of Indonesia's wealth is concentrated in Jakarta, and even resource-rich provinces such as Aceh have a much lower living standard than the average in the capital. The island structure of the country has resulted in the formation of numerous homogeneous ethnic communities who are tightly knit and exhibit a high degree of ethnocentrism. This has often triggered conflicts, such as those between the Javanese and Madurese and between the Dayak and Madurese peoples.

A strong feature of Indonesian society is its rigidly stratified and hierarchical structures. In business only managers in top positions are allowed to make decisions and their opinions and decisions may never be questioned by subordinates. This is in line with the high power distance and risk aversion dimensions of the national culture. Being collectivist in nature Indonesians, irrespective of their ethnic and religious backgrounds, place utmost importance on the extended family, especially in rural areas. After the family, ethnic (*suku*) and religious community associations are of major importance.

Indonesians have high regard for foreign products and perceive them as superior to locally produced equivalents, except in the case of fresh fruit and vegetables, traditional foodstuffs, clothing, and footwear. Nonetheless brand recognition is low, apart from among affluent consumers in urban areas (Kamath and Codin, 2001).

Indonesians have a relaxed approach to time. They consider that hurrying people is impolite and do not like the strict scheduling of appointments and meetings. Thus any marketing efforts that are based on speed, time-governed business arrangements, and formal appointments are frowned upon. Instead, relationship building, politeness, and relaxed conversations are expected and form the basis of loyalty and commitment in business relations, and are therefore crucial to marketing success. Consumer loyalty depends on personal attention and care. Many Indonesians shop for groceries on a daily basis and prefer to go to local open-air or indoor markets where they can socialize with sellers and friends. The importance of shopping as a form of socializing is reflected in promotional messages.

While prices in up-market stores, hypermarkets and supermarkets are set, bargaining is typical in traditional markets. As already noted,

Indonesians are mostly brand indifferent, apart from affluent consumers living in the capital and large urban centers. The leading brands in Indonesia are either foreign or owned by foreign companies. Unilever has a leading market position in soy sauce with its brand Bangso, and it owns the best-selling tea brand, Sariwangi. Danone owns the top-selling bottled water brand, Aqua. Aqua, Evian, and Volvic hold almost 90 per cent of the bottled water market in Indonesia. Helios Nyam-Nyam cookies dominate the market; they are produced by Helios Arnott Indonesia, which is owned by the Campbell Soup Company. The local Sari Husada brand, bought by Dutch Royal Numico in 1998, is presently the market leader in baby formula products.

Multinational corporations in Indonesia implement pricing strategies that are aimed at keeping profits high, despite the slump in demand. Since making their acquisitions they have streamlined production and started peddling their products aggressively in small and medium-sized towns. Unilever has recently signed agreements with 12,000 wholesalers that supply 800,000 traditional vendors, and bottled Lipton iced tea is carried in motorcycle saddlebags to villages where the lanes are too narrow for cars. Unilever also produces advertizements that exhort Indonesians to brush their teeth twice daily with Pepsodent toothpaste, rather than the once-daily brushing that is standard in the country.

The low production costs in Indonesia – at least 50 per cent lower than in other Southeast Asian countries – make it a good production and export base. For example after buying the condiment maker ABC Central Food in 1999, Heinz produced and exported Heinz ketchup to Malaysia and the Philippines meeting more than half of the demand for ketchup in both countries. Because of the huge market potential in Indonesia and adjacent ASEAN countries, foreign multinationals operating in Indonesia have reinvested profits in expanding their operations. For instance Unilever has invested US$500 million in expanding the seven local brands it owns; Coca-Cola has invested US$70 million in Ades bottled water since 1999; and after acquiring a majority stake in the baby formula Sari Husada, Royal Numico invested US$35 million in building a new plant in Central Java, thereby becoming the largest milk processor in Southeast Asia.

New market entrants should not only strive to build up the trust of those with whom they do business, as discussed above, but it is also essential not to conduct promotional campaigns that might offend ethnic and religious beliefs and behavioral norms. Indonesians of Malay origin prefer to do business over meals, while those of Chinese origin tend to prefer formal meetings and apply common sense to business matters. Malay business people tend to be more impulsive and emotional than their Chinese counterparts and rely on their intuition.

Information gathered in the process of market entry and penetration should be treated with caution as local data on market potential, size, and growth rate can be unreliable. Hence, companies should do extensive market research and test the markets beforehand. Most arrangements between foreign and local companies are cooperative agreements or joint ventures as a local partner is needed to obtain information and market intelligence, as well as to provide advice on the best marketing mix strategies for particular markets.

Malaysia

The Federation of Malaysia consists of two demographic and economic regions: West Malaysia, which is located on the southern part of the Malay Peninsula, and East Malaysia, which comprises Sabah and Sarawak on the island of Borneo. The country is divided into 13 states and federal territories. At the end of 2004, Malaysia had a population of 25.6 million. There is evidence that the earliest settlers on the Malay Peninsula came from China. These early inhabitants were the ancestors of the Orang Asli, the indigenous minority inhabitants of peninsular Malaysia.

The Malaysian economy is in the process of restructuring. Until 1960s the country was totally dependent on agriculture and primary commodities, but since then it has gradually transformed its economy into one based on the exporting of high value-added, high-technology products and the development of knowledge-based and capital-intensive industries. One of the notable achievements is the so-called multimedia super corridor, which brings together a legislative framework and an advance telecommunications infrastructure in eco-friendly surroundings to offer the best environment for the development of multimedia industries.

During the last decade, the economy has achieved an average annual growth rate of 7 per cent. The growth of GDP has been even more significant, reaching RM219.4 billion (US$57.7 billion) in 2002. These account for Malaysia's stable macroeconomic indicators (Table 10.1). The country also has been running a trade surplus. In 2002 exports reached RM349.6 billion (US$92.0 billion) and imports RM298.5 billion (US$78.6 billion). Thus Malaysia is among the world's top 20 trading nations and is one of the five major emerging markets. Its main trading partners are shown in Table 10.2.

In 2002 manufacturing accounted for 30.6 per cent of nominal GDP, services for 50.7 per cent, and agriculture for 18.7 per cent.

Table 10.1 Main macroeconomic indicators, Malaysia, 2000–5

	2000	*2001*	*2002*	*2003*	*2004*	*2005*
GDP (US$ billion)	90.3	88.0	95.2	103.7	117.8	129.4
Per capita GDP (US$)	3,876.0	3,665.0	3,880.0	4,150.0	4,626.0	4,989.0
Value of exports (% of GDP)	124.4	116.4	114.8	114.3	121.8	131.8
Annual inflation rate (%)	1.5	1.4	1.7	1.1	1.5	2.3
Unemployment rate (% of workforce)	3.1	3.7	3.5	3.6	3.5	3.7

Source: Malaysian national statistics.

Table 10.2 Main trading partners, Malaysia, 2004

Exports	*Percentage of total exports*	*Imports*	*percentage of total imports*
United States	18.7	Japan	15.9
Singapore	15.1	United States	14.5
China and Hong Kong	12.6	Singapore	11.1
Japan	10.1	China and Hong Kong	10.9

Source: International Monetary Fund statistics.

Manufactured goods account for 86.5 per cent of export revenue. In the past Malaysia was the world largest producer of rubber and tin. Nowadays it is among the world's leading exporters of semiconductors, computer hard disk drives, audio and video products, and air-conditioners. Industrialization has been boosted by a huge inflow of foreign direct investment.

Despite adverse external events in the early 2000s, including the terrorist attacks in the United States, the SARS epidemic, the Iraq War and the overall global uncertainty, the Malaysian economy has continued to grow and this has had a positive effect on disposable income and consumer confidence. Malaysian consumers have mixed feelings towards foreign goods, including Japanese products. This is a consequence of the Japanese occupation during World War Two, plus the perception that the Japanese sometimes treat Malaysia and its workforce as subordinate and are not prepared to transfer know-how and up-to-date technology. On the other hand Japan has provided huge investments and created numerous jobs thus facilitating industrialization and improved living standards. Japan is not only Malaysia's major source of foreign direct investment but also its principal trading partner. Moreover the knowledge and efficiency of Japanese managers and engineers are highly appreciated and aspired to. Thus young Malaysians who are open-minded and more cosmopolitan admire Japanese products such as toys and electronics, while older Malaysians especially of Chinese origin strongly resist Japanese products as they have negative associations with the past.

Trade relations between the United States and Malaysia are also a matter of controversy. The Asian financial crisis, which some associated with rogue trading by US funds, had a rather negative effect on consumers' attitudes towards products from the United States, and this was further aggravated by opposing US and Malaysian political statements following the September 11 terrorist attacks. Nevertheless there is a positive attitude towards the United States in respect of US investments, job creation, and the provision of technological innovations, which are associated with better living standards.

Global companies and brands occupy a major place in the food sector. For example the dairy sector is dominated by Nestlé and Kraft Foods International; Kellogg is market leader in breakfast cereals; McDonald's, KFC, and Pizza Hut lead in the fast-food sector; and Cadbury-Schweppes, Mars, and Van Houten dominate the chocolate, sweets and snack market. Brand recognition and brand association are far higher among urban than among rural consumers.

Domestic food production is fragmented and includes small companies that cater to local tastes. There are more than 3,000 small, family-owned cottage industries that produce local favorites such as noodles and cakes, among many other products. Most of the rural and about half of the urban consumers prefer these products, which are mostly sold in the numerous traditional stores. The majority of consumers shop daily in small quantities and look for high quality at low prices. Urban consumers who shop in large department stores, hypermarkets, and supermarkets tend to be more affluent and buy their supplies once or twice a week. Because of consumers' preference for traditional local products or foreign products produced locally, distributors, wholesalers, and retailers mainly use local suppliers.

Relationships are a very important part of the purchasing experience. Shoppers in traditional stores enjoy chatting and inquiring about the goods stocked and the availability and features of future supplies. That is why successful foreign chain retailers such as Giant try to make the shopping experience enjoyable by providing facilities for eating, drinking, and socializing.

The ethnic diversity in Malaysia, with Malays living side by side with Chinese and Indians, the religious heterogeneity (Islam, Buddhism,

Taoism, Christianity, and Hinduism), the variety of spoken languages (the official language, Malay, plus English and Chinese dialects such as Hakka, Mandarin, Cantonese, and Hokkien) create a challenging environment for those involved in promotion and advertising. They need to consider not only language, religion, and ethnicity but also legal restrictions aimed at safeguarding cultural values. Regulations affect not only imagery but also the types of media, product promotion and promotional messages used. Moreover the heterogeneous cultural context has enormous implications for the scope and cost of promotion in terms of standardization and adaptation.

Products that are illegal to advertise are mostly associated with the maintenance of social order and norms and encompass gambling, religious groups, political parties, and funeral services. There are also products, such as those forbidden by the Qur'an that are viewed as offensive by Muslims but not by the Chinese. Such products are difficult to promote as not all media are tailored to particular segments. Goods such as alcohol, female hygiene products and underwear, to name just a few, can be promoted but within strict government-defined limitations. The images used for advertising cosmetics must also follow strict guidelines and there can be no nudity or sexually suggestive images.

While control over Internet advertising is difficult to impose, there are stringent restrictions on television, newspaper, radio and outdoor advertising content and presentation. In 1990 the Ministry of Information issued the Advertising Code for Television and Radio with a view to preserving the Malaysian identity and culture within the values of Islam (Deng *et al.*, 1994). This code forbids the adaptation or projection of any foreign cultural traits that go against the cultural beliefs and norms of all groups in Malaysian society in terms of actions, behavior, words, slogans, and clothing. For example intimate, suggestive or sexually arousing images and adult kissing cannot be shown. Any promotional messages that could threaten the ethnic and social peace in this delicately balanced multicultural society are also forbidden. In addition there are severe restrictions on imported advertisements. Under the 'Made-in-Malaysia' rule advertisements must be produced locally with Malaysian creative teams, artists and support staff, although the Ministry of Information may approve the use of foreign scenes that it deems appropriate or for which no Malaysian substitute can be found. According to the code no other form of English but 'Malaysian English' (Parker, 1982) can be used in advertisements that are broadcast or published in English.

Religion has a huge impact on advertising content, with the result that personal aspirations and desires are usually downplayed, social responsibility is emphasized, group and community rather than individual benefits are promoted, hard work is encouraged and modesty and generosity are praised. The portrayal of women must conform to a strict dress code – skirts must be long enough to cover the knees and armpits cannot be shown – and it should reflect Islamic values such as modesty and hospitality. Despite these rigid requirements some leeway is allowed when targeting individual consumer groups via specialist media, for example alcohol can be advertised in publications printed in Chinese.

The retail sector has been mainly controlled by the Chinese since the early years of the British colonial era (Mohd Roslin and Melewar, 2000). The sector is dominated by small traditional convenience and neighborhood stores, but recently the rapid rise in consumer spending has encouraged local and international retailers to establish supermarkets, department stores, hypermarkets, and warehouse clubs.

According to AC Nielsen (2003), in 2002 the retail sector in peninsular Malaysia consisted of 29,656 outlets, more than 95 per cent of which were grocery stores. There has since been a small decrease in their number but they still account for more than two thirds of consumer retail expenditure. Meanwhile the number and turnover of hypermarkets, supermarkets, and department and convenience stores are constantly on the rise. Nevertheless the importance of seller–purchaser relationships based on Asian cultural values remains strong in Malaysian retailing.

There has been a continuous rise in consumer expenditure and retail sales since 2000. In 2003 total retail sales increased by 2.3 per cent to RM48 billion (US$12.65 billion) and accounted for about one third of overall consumer expenditure, which in the same year amounted to RM161.7 billion (US$43.79 billion). Average per capita consumer expenditure was RM7170 (US$1,898) and household expenditure was RM32107 (US$8,453). Based on the current 5–6 per cent consumer expenditure growth it is predicted that by 2008 consumers will be spending more than RM212 billion (US$56.6 billion). In 2004 the retail sector contributed 11.8 per cent to GDP and employed 6.8 per cent of the workforce.

International retailers such as Carrefour and Tesco jointly account for about half of the hypermarkets in Malaysia. These have grown in popularity and in 2005 about a third of urban consumers used them as their main shopping venue. The operations of Tesco are based on a joint venture arrangement with Sime Darby. Over the last three years the Hong Kong Giant Group has invested US$100 million in the development of a chain of hypermarkets in the Klang Valley and supermarkets all over the country, thus presenting fierce competition to Carrefour and Tesco. Giant is part of Dairy Farm, a leading Pan-Asian food and drugstore retailer, with a majority ownership by the Jardine Matheson Group. It sources 95 per cent of its products locally. The small proportion of imported goods consists mainly of consumer durables from elsewhere in Southeast Asia. It aims to become a market leader by offering an extensive range of fresh food and consumer products, low prices, personalized service and a variety of family entertainments.

Conclusion

The Islamic countries of Southeast Asia occupy more than half of the territory of the region and are home to about half of the population. While the practice of Islam is more liberal that in other parts of the world, recent events have caused tension between the various religious groups. Ethnic differences are exacerbated by differences in social status and income distribution, and this has sometimes resulted in violence. The region was badly hit by the Asian crisis of 1997 and its consequences are still being felt in Indonesia. Natural disasters such as the tsunami in December 2004 and the earthquake in May 2006 have exacerbated the situation.

Economically, Brunei is largely dependent on oil and gas but is attempting to diversify its economy, whereas Indonesia and particularly Malaysia have managed to create more balanced economies that include high-technology production. As is the case with traditional retailing, the functioning of the economies is relationship-based. The market structure and the sophistication of the consumer market are most developed in Brunei and least developed in Indonesia, with the exception of the capital and several other large urban conglomerates. Indonesia's value as a low-cost production base has attracted many multinationals that use it as an export base for ASEAN and other foreign markets.

There is regional trade and economic cooperation but the most important trading partners are developed economies such as Japan, the United States, European countries, Singapore, and Australia. China's importance as a trading partner is growing.

References

AC Nielsen (2003) *Retail Management Services: Kuala Lumpur* (New York, NY: AC Nielsen).

Ang, J., A.Tourani-Rad, and J. Yu (2004) 'Some lessons from price bubbles and market crashes in Southeast Asia', *Managerial Finance*, 30 (7), pp. 1–18.

Deng, S., S. Jivan and M.-L. Hassan (1994) 'Advertising in Malaysia: a cultural perspective', *International Journal of Advertising*, 13 (2), pp. 153–66.

Hallinger, P. (1998) 'Educational change in Southeast Asia: The challenge of creating learning systems', *Journal of Educational Administration*, 36 (5), pp. 492–509.

Hussain, S. (1998) 'Technology transfer models across cultures: Brunei–Japan joint ventures', *International Journal of Social Economics*, 25 (6–7-8), pp. 1189–98.

Idrus, N. (1999) 'Towards quality higher education in Indonesia', *Quality Assurance in Education*, 7 (3), pp. 134–41.

Iwami, T. (2001) 'Economic development and environment in Southeast Asia: an introductory note', *International Journal of Social Economics*, 28 (8), pp. 605–22.

Kamath, P. and C. Codin (2001) 'French Carrefour in South-East Asia', *British Food Journal*, 103 (7), pp. 479–94.

Mohd Roslin, R. and T. Melewar (2000) 'Discovering relationship bonds in channel relationships: a case study of Malaysia', *Journal of Global Marketing*, 14 (3), pp. 49–76.

Parker, E. (1982) 'Malaysia', in G. Kurian (ed.), *World Press Encyclopaedia* (New York: Facts on File).

Singhapakdi, A., M. Rawwas, J. Marta and M. Ahmed (1999) 'A cross-cultural study of consumer perceptions about marketing ethics', *Journal of Consumer Marketing*, 16 (3), pp. 257–72.

Index